UNFINISHED
BUSINESS

UNFINISHED BUSINESS

Paul Ferris

Stuart Wheatman
Steve Wraith

Mojo Risin'
Publishing Ltd

First published in 2018 by Mojo Risin' Publishing
Copyright © 2018 Paul Ferris & Stuart Wheatman
All rights reserved

British Library Cataloguing in Publication Data:
A catalogue record for this book is available from
the British Library

Several people got shot, stabbed, slashed, knocked
over, blown up and robbed over the course of this book

ISBN-13:
9781911482031

Cover photograph
© Brian Anderson

Including additional court documents supplied by
HRH Queen Elizabeth II

Cover design
DS Creative

Printed & bound by CPI Group (UK) Ltd

Proudly published up North

TO REG

Paying tribute and turning up to pay my respects,
I knew that Reg's funeral was different.
He had planned it all beforehand – just as in life
Reg focused on the here and now.
He would die when he chose to let go.
Brave man? Legend? Absolutely.

That's what it's all about in the end – tributes;
about how people remember you and how you are
missed. Sometimes words are hard to find.
That was never a problem for Reg though.

He often reminded me about words and to
choose them carefully. This is my tribute to my
friend, my mentor and partner in crime-writing.

Reg McKay – the king of crime writers
July 15, 1953 to October 19, 2009
Rest in peace

CONTENTS

COURT DOCUMENTS

ROTHESAY

December 12, 1984
24 Argyle Street
Isle of Bute

There are not many times in your life when you think you're going to get murdered. Most people, anyway. This was my time. Many career criminals will tell you that they fear no man – and that's true. To an extent. There's always going to be a moment when the toughest, most fearless bastard in the world stares death in the face and realises it could be over in a split-second. Most just won't admit to feeling fear as an emotion – it comes from having something to lose. No man can beat a bullet.

I could hear their heavy breathing, the panic in the atmosphere, there was uncertainty; a different uncertainty than just a raid. There was one who was in 'control'. A big bloke; a mountain of a man with snowy white hair. It was a show of strength for the wee man. He ordered them around like he'd ordered me on my knees and my hands to my head. The same one who had a look of pure hate in his eyes when they burst in. I felt his whole weight grinding down into my spine through his knee. He dug his forearm into the back of my neck, squashing my face into the floor as hard as he could. Forcing me to turn my head, gasping for air.

He leaned in. I felt his breath on my ear. The adrenaline had kicked in, his voice was unsteady.

'You're getting it now, son,' he said. 'You're getting it, you little *bastard*!'

With that, he pushed himself up off me to cause more pain, and composed himself. He said something to the others – something to the effect of hold him down. Then there was the unmistakable silence, the fumbling in the pocket. I could see bits, glimpses of legs, snapshots, white-faced expressions, shock and disbelief like they were about to witness a public hanging. And that's what it was – an execution, but a private one. I was kept face down on the floor as I heard another unmistakable sound of him cocking his gun. I struggled, but it was useless. I hated that feeling of powerlessness. That exact point when you know you're finished is something I've only experienced this one time. He leant in again to hiss something through gritted teeth. Whatever it was, he wanted me to know it was over. He jammed the gun between the top of my neck and the base of my skull. I took a second to... to almost relax and accept my fate. He had me and he knew it. It was his moment. There was a surreal silence as the realisation descended on everyone – no going back now...

At this point, I was untouchable, 21 years old and working for the main man in Glasgow. So, how the fuck was I lying face down on the floor with a knee in my back and a gun to my head?

The click as the trigger was pulled back that last time; the deadly silence.

And then it happened...

PAUL FERRIS

Here we go with another true crime book... Ferris cashing in on his crimes again. I don't blame anyone for thinking that at all. Writers make a living out of having a book published and people buying it. That's the job. It's slightly different to having a proper job (no offence intended, writer friends) in that you put in a year's graft and then see if you get paid after it. The publisher chucks in a load of money with the same idea. If the book's good, it may shift a few copies. If it's not much cop (pardon the pun), no one gets paid. That's how it goes. It's a bit like being a criminal. I'm not suggesting all writers are criminals here, but a bohemian lifestyle is great as long as you can get away with it and so is being a criminal: a good run, rise to the top, hit a rough spot, climb back up, wonder why you do it and why you keep on going, but you don't know what else to do, and you look for that big break that you can retire on. See – who was I describing, a writer or a criminal?

To those cynics out there amongst you; I have never put pen to paper to make money. I'm not interested in that side of it. I'm interested in people knowing my story. I love that people would want to read a book or watch a film about me and hear what I have to say. That you've invested time and money to know more about me is a great honour and nothing to be flippant about.

The publishing world, just like any other industry, has its trends. We've had misery memoirs, celebrity cookbooks, celebrity comedians, journalists and TV stars all part of the oversaturated market trend of *celebrity*.

Our fascination with true crime kicked off with a masterpiece about everyone's favourite criminal brothers; the Krays. John Pearson's book is the original and best you'll ever get and it spawned countless others and created a new genre. It was only later when the others followed that we realised it *was* a genre. The twins commissioned Pearson to write *The Profession of Violence* in 1967, when he was hot property from publishing Ian Fleming's biography. It created a thirst for readers to find out about what gangsters get up to and it was ground-breaking stuff: the intrigue of a dark side of society no one knew anything about other than what they read in the newspapers, the confessionary side to the tales, the unbelievable nature of committing such crimes and us lapping it up as bystanders; voyeurs in this brave new world of the celebrity gangster. There they were in their clubs, in flash cars, Savile Row suits, mixing with A-listers of the day, mingling with politicians – no one knew stuff like this could be real. And then that cover shot by David Bailey... they say don't judge a book by its cover, but they are totally wrong with that one. It's got to be the best image ever captured of Ron and Reg. If there's anyone who doesn't know who David Bailey is – he's the photographer who could have been the next Brian Anderson! The twins though, they were the first to be known criminals and, in terms of 'celebrity,' they were the first. It was of its time. It was massive. Post-war Britain had never experienced the likes. If social media was around then it would have been mental:

Here's me with Lord Boothby. WTF?

LOL, Here's Princess Margaret downing some champers in one go ☺

And then years later, Dave Courtney got in on it and the genre exploded! The celebrity gangster was well and truly here to stay and he had an over-the-top suit to confirm it. Lenny, Roy Shaw, Nosher... they were all over the best-seller lists in that zeitgeist moment. John Blake Publishing was banging them out every few minutes and we were lapping them up. And he published Jordan's (as she was known back then) first biography and we couldn't get enough of these tell-all books that would create not only celebrities, but helped to create brands for these people. We're celebrity mad. It's big business. Every publisher was looking for the next trailblazer. And the way we're consuming celebrity, each form of media is creating the other: *Big Brother*, *Celebrity Big Brother*, *I'm a Celebrity...*, *Gogglebox*, *Britain's Got Talent*, *X Factor* and whatever the next thing is or will be. Spin-off books, spin-off TV shows, YouTube stars – there's no real distinction now.

3

Paddy Doherty went from being on *Danny Dyer's Deadliest Men* TV show to that Gypsy Wedding thing, got on *Celebrity Big Brother* and got a book deal as a result of it all. Good on him – it just proves that the lines are blurred between how you actually become famous these days. People were rubbing shoulders with him in the house and most likely didn't know the kinds of things he'd gotten up to in his life. But by then, he'd reached celebrity status. *Famous for being famous* has been around for years and is more relevant now than ever.

Where do I fit in amongst all this? Well, hopefully, I don't. Even without my books, I was pretty notorious. My story became known from being in newspapers for crimes and my ongoing trials. Scottish media seems different to anywhere else. There's a real fascination with my trade. There was the ice-cream wars, and old man Thompson, McGraw and me. Up in Scotland, it made us the equivalent of the Krays. Or so I'm told. In Scottish Gangland, there are many more players than that now. There were many before us as well. There wasn't a rulebook – you just got into it and worked as you saw fit. If you knew what you were doing, you survived. And then the books followed. Savvy writers team up with us lot to publish stuff because they know stories like this are interesting. And it could result in getting that elusive paycheque after working flat out for a year, surviving on bread and water. In fairness, regardless of the trust an ex-criminal has in a ghost-writer, the writer also has to trust what the ex-criminal tells them is the truth. This is the difficult part. Yes, biographies are confessions. You can get a lot off your chest and tell your version of what happened in known situations. And that's the point – it's *your* version of *known* situations. You're not going to let slip about those 12 murders no one knew about... unless you're dumb or just get caught up in the whole thing, like Dave Courtney ended up doing. So, yeah, we'll always present an edited version of the truth – just like anyone else would – and tell you the stuff we want to tell you about.

I became infamous. And that suits me much more than being famous. Think about it...

'Hey, are you famous?'

'Nah, mate. I'm fucking *infamous*.'

It seems to me that fame is something that people crave and chase. I don't. I'll answer to interest, rather than trying to attract it. Going back to my writer analogy – my situation is like preferring to be critically acclaimed, rather than seeking the fame and fortune. But, hey. I realise I can come across as a hypocrite as well. How can I claim to not want fame and fortune if I've done documentaries and a film? Fair point. More people watch films than read books – who wouldn't want their life story turned into a film? It's a no-brainer. And if you haven't seen *The Wee Man*, get it watched. Martin Compston is brilliant in it!

I can't think of any gangster, criminal, call them what you may, that have written a tell-all book and said at the end of it 'crime pays.' Who'd give more money to a fat cat gangster with more money than sense, who was bragging about beating the system? And if you were a good successful criminal, then surely you don't want to draw attention to yourself and brag about crimes you got away with. You'd just get nicked and lose everything. As we know, 99.9 per cent of these books discuss crimes that they've been done for and can discuss openly. Same goes for me – I can discuss stuff that I've been up in court for or imprisoned for because it's a fact and I have an opinion on it.

Some of us have moved on to bigger and better things *legitimately*. That's the thing – not many do because crime is all they know. If you can be smart enough to get out of that life, you can be smart enough to apply your street knowledge to other enterprises. Transferable skills.

Should I encourage crime and tell you that it's brilliant and you should go out and rob banks, tax drug dealers and enforce protection rackets? Hmmm... morally, no one is going to publish a book like that. And there'd be some legal implications, I dare say. Like most things, the life of a career criminal has its ups and downs. And as a career criminal, there aren't pension schemes. So, if you didn't make the big time, a book can be a last-ditch attempt at making some legitimate money to live off in your old age.

6

In writing this, it's around 10 years since my last book was out. I've been asked so many times, why didn't I write another, why wait until now? The reply is always easy: out of respect to Reg McKay, my good friend and co-writer, ghost-writer, confidant and brother in arms. Working with someone on a book goes a lot deeper than a job description. If you find a good writer, who you can trust and work with over time, then you've found the perfect partner. It doesn't happen often. Treat them well, cos they're your voice. Reg knew me. He *got* me. We had a great understanding and rapport and our journey as a writing partnership worked.

Steve Wraith asked me what I thought about writing another book and, because it was pitched as a tribute to Reg, I had little hesitation. I knew what I was getting into and I knew that my story, at that point, was unfinished. I was without a storyteller. To work with anyone else on my story, I'd need to know we'd have the same trust and mutual respect as Reg and I built up over the years. You can't just turn that on. You can't just sit down with a journalist and have them immediately understand what you're about and interpret your story correctly. It's a process. It wasn't about the speed – it was about recapturing the soul that Reg would bring to the table. We didn't have a timeframe or a deadline; we worked organically to see where it went. We knew it could go either way, but I was certainly intrigued.

I've had to confront a lot in my life. By working with new writers, I saw this process as an opportunity to not only put the unfinished business to rest, but to learn something new about myself while also paying tribute to Reg. I hope you learn a bit more about me as well. We learn more about ourselves every day we live and breathe. A favourite book of mine, which was turned into a brilliant film, is *Fight Club* by Chuck Palahniuk. In it, there's an exchange between the protagonist Tyler Durden and his alter-ego: 'How much can you know about yourself if you've never been in a fight?'

I'm not suggesting you go out and have one; I'm just letting you know about a powerful quote. I grew up in a place where that's what you had to do. I didn't for a long time. I was bullied every day until I fought back. Every day I'd hide my cuts and bruises, but they were just the physical scars. Each night after the beatings, I'd take another – I'd beat myself up. Metaphorically, internally, psychologically... being bullied on a daily basis conditions you to become what the bullies are making you. Moulding you into a different person. And this is true of all forms of bullying whether one-on-one, a gang, an organisation or a country. And that's why you need to stand up to them.

You know who I am; you know most of what I've done. Books of this nature are tricky because of the criticism you get for your actions. There isn't much middle ground with my story. I'm not setting out to make thousands of friends from writing about my life – just presenting you with my account of it. You get accused of over-exaggerating or under-exaggerating the truth to your own advantage. It's standard and, as I've mentioned, of course it happens. That's just human nature. Even if you're a non-combatant straight-goer, you'll never tell the complete truth about your life because one day you'll come across as a total fucking arsehole and the next day you'll redeem yourself. We're a paradox; we're as inconsistent as we are consistent.

Is that disclaimer enough?

Whether you're pro or anti-Ferris, at least you've picked this up to read the rest of my story. I'm not asking for anyone to agree with me, not looking for forgiveness on anything or glamorising the world of crime, but cheers for your interest. I'm a bloke making his way in life. I was a young man who'd started to make his way. I was a teenager who set out to make his way. All of them by any means necessary.

STEVE WRAITH

I got interested in crime after seeing the Krays attend their mother's funeral on TV in 1982. I picked up the book *Profession of Violence* in 1986 and read it from cover to cover in two days. I was allowed to study it for my GCSE exam and passed with flying colours. From there I decided to write to the twins and tell them of my success off the back of their life of crime. That's where my fascination with Gangland began: I read a book, walked inside the book and met all the major characters.

Working in the crime world means keeping everybody happy. You have to navigate murky waters and keep up to date with current affairs. If you don't, then you can find yourself saying something which can be misinterpreted and cause you some serious problems.

The biggest challenge for me was the NME football hooligan book. A lot of the firm wanted the book written but there were a few objections. I have faced confrontation on the street about the book on a few occasions. It's the risk you take.

It can be scary, it can be bizarre. Over the course of the last 25 years, I have met them all. The Krays, the Richardsons, the Nashes, the Great Train Robbers, Shaw and McLean, the Sayers, Paul Ferris – you name them and I've had some dealings with them. I have attended both of Charlie Bronson's weddings and both I suppose were bizarre because the groom was not in attendance. Instead, on both occasions he sent along a tape of him singing for the gathered wedding guests to listen to. I respect them all because they have reached the top of their chosen profession, despite the risks to their liberty. Do I condone what they do or what they have done? Of course not. At the end of the day, as Paul would say, I'm a straight-goer. It just happens that I know people on both sides of the fence.

People are always very inquisitive about the people I have met, but loose lips sink ships and I play my cards close to my chest. When you are meeting former criminals they are entrusting you with a lot of sensitive information and you cannot abuse that trust. Some feel it is odd, but on the whole, people can understand my interest. I have met a lot of serving police officers who do not like the fact that I promote criminals and their exploits. They see it as former villains making money from other people's misery, but if I wasn't doing it then someone else would be.

My friendship with the Krays has been well documented in *The Krays; the Geordie Connection* (another Wheatman and Wraith classic), but while my mam encouraged it, my dad hated it. My wife Dawn understands it, but has concerns at times about the people I have written about. She trusts my judgement though and has been a good sounding board when I have had issues to deal with. She tends to be the voice of reason – you need that otherwise you can easily get caught up in the politics of it all as well.

I had read Paul's books, seen the documentaries and watched the film before meeting him, so I had a preconceived idea going into this project. I knew a lot of people who knew him or who had met him and they all spoke very highly of him. I take people how I find them, and I was expecting Paul to be sussing me out at the first meeting. We spoke on the phone and Paul was not thinking of writing another book at the time. It was something I kept in mind, though.

There is no doubt Paul Ferris is one of the most respected men in UK crime. He is spoken about in the same way as Freddie Foreman is in London, Paul Massey in Manchester, the Sayers brothers in Newcastle and Curtis Warren in Liverpool. He is a very quiet and respectful man, but do not mistake his politeness as a weakness. What surprised me quite a lot about him was his love of football! It caught me off guard... but then, why should it? He's as down to earth as you could imagine and has an amazing knowledge of his beloved team, Celtic.

STUART WHEATMAN

I started writing true crime around 20 years ago. My first book was *The Machine* (later published as *Cage Fighter* with John Blake). Charlie Kray had just died and Steve had become friends with Ian Freeman, the cage fighter I was writing about. Steve took Ian down to London to go to the funeral and meet up with some contacts.

I originally got in touch with Ian to make a documentary about cage fighting, which was in its infancy in the UK at the time, but he was a pioneer. I pitched it to Channel 4 and our local ITV channel, Tyne Tees, and both rejected it. They added that they were considering other similar projects – TV-speak for *we're going to steal yours*. Back then, MMA had next to no rules and was outlawed in many US states. From there, and bearing in mind I'd read Roy Shaw's book, I did more research on Ian and knew it had to be a biographical story... it was the same type of thing. The book was first published by a bloke with a penchant for large cigars and not paying writers, who name-dropped everyone from Charles Bronson to Freddie Foreman and Dave Courtney. He put me in touch with Steve and a guy called Kenny 'Panda' Anderson, a face from Newcastle's Geordie Mafia. Hindsight is a wonderful thing. At that time, it seemed like finding a trustworthy publisher was like finding marriage material on Plenty of Fish. Luckily, when it was republished with John Blake, some decent sales came in.

Being part of this genre is as mad as it can get. All those people I'd first read about in early Kray books, or seen portrayed in films or saw interviewed in crime documentaries were soon in my contact list. I had to know who was in favour, who was pissing 'the chaps' off (the chaps?), who was the new kid on the block that people were wary of... and that's what it was like.

I'm a bit of a cynic; I write with my tongue firmly in my cheek, I laugh up my sleeve. I live a different life to the people I've written about. I know most of them probably couldn't give a rat's about me or my life. That's not me being bitter, it's just how the job works. They don't know what I've been up to and have little interest. For all they know, I could have been locked up ten times, got into dozens of fights, been homeless and dabbled in crime, a junkie or whatever, but in the grand scheme, I'm irrelevant; I'm a ghost-writer, it's a job and it's not about me. I'm the one who asks the questions. All they need to know about me is that I can stick words on a page and make it sound like they said it. Of course, it helps the whole process if I write about someone who is as affable and accepting as me. I'm laid back enough with a decent sense of humour to keep me sane, but sometimes this job can really test your resolve. It all requires an elephant's skin and a duck's back.

14

I've probably spent more time on projects that haven't gone into publication than I have actually writing them – and they too have some mad adventures attached to them, like being asked to keep hold of a stolen Shakespeare first folio worth millions, asked to keep a bag of guns safe for someone, running over 30 miles a day across America, offered into a multi-million pound drug deal, propositioned by a porn star (I know!) and foiling a kidnap plot on Zippy from *Rainbow*. The list goes on and I love it.

There is a reason for my back-story. Regardless of how brilliant or utterly shit it can be, that first book started me off as a writer and then a publisher and got me hooked. It got me in touch with Steve. He approached me to write his book about the Krays at *The Machine* book launch. I wasn't really sure what direction I was heading at the time. I was a college lecturer and doing freelance work in film. I always feel that writing chose me – if you're a writer, you'll know what I mean. It's not a decision; you either are a writer or you aren't. You're probably lucky if you aren't!

From those early days, I'd always been aware of Paul Ferris. I didn't know his story as such. I'd heard of Arthur Thompson, the ice cream wars and, like everyone, I knew Glasgow's reputation. I read a book about Glasgow gangs when I was doing A level English. It resonated; an ethnographic study of gang violence between teenagers in 1960s Glasgow. I love that side of life – it's always attracted me: the questions it poses... anything a bit different and I'm there. I got into writing non-fiction because I love telling interesting stories about the darker side of life. Surviving in that world is enough to secure a reputation and Paul Ferris lived it. It's like he's been around forever. I don't consciously recall a first time I heard his name or anything about him, he was just omniscient, like the Krays; up there as an almost mythical figure. I didn't think our paths would ever cross, but writing this, it was as though it was mapped out.

And that's where Steve comes back in. We always seemed to drift together to work on something. One thing that bound us was our love of this genre. And so we started writing together. After we finished the Krays book, I wanted to get my teeth stuck into a Newcastle hooligan book or one about the Sayers mob in Newcastle. After some donkey work, I put the hooli book on the back-burner. I'd met up with some undercover cops over in Sunderland and dug up a lot, but other projects took priority and I revisited the idea with Steve in 2013. He got in with some of the older and new breed of Newcastle hooligans and we went from there. We worked with some genuinely nice blokes who we're still in touch with. Importantly for us, it rekindled that working relationship.

Having a few books under my belt, I know how laborious the interview process can be. Add that to the writing process and it is very time-consuming. It's difficult to fit around a working life when you've got bills to pay. That's why I used to do temp jobs that I could just leave when I wanted, and use them to support my writing because massive advances are scarce. So, combining our two strengths, Steve can gather the information together around his day job and I make sense of interviews and piece it together to tell that person's story. There are always more sit-downs required, but that's part of the job. I couldn't do it without knowing the people I write about. Sharing the work means we (in theory) cut the time down and can confer with each other along the way. It's probably a unique way of writing – I don't know of many others who work like this. Unfortunately, sharing the work and sharing the credit means sharing the royalties... but let's not get bitter about the state of author royalties and comparing them to the National Minimum Wage. You definitely have to write for the love of it because those Harry Potter advances or sales figures don't really happen that often.

Our last project was *The Sayers: tried and tested at the highest level*. As we were writing it, the name Paul Ferris came up. And there was our link. He gave us a foreword for the book, so we were all well and truly on each other's radar from there. Of course, there are many people out there who'd break out in a cold sweat if they knew they were on Paul's radar. As a true crime writer, this is the kind of thing you want. You always want to be stepping up your game. A long shot that might just work is always shortened when Steve's networking comes into play. You're reading this – it worked. We signed the project up and here we are. Now the most daunting task is that Paul wants to pay tribute to Reg. This is two of us trying to fill a role that one man used to cover. I have tremendous respect for Reg and I also want this project to work for him.

IT AIN'T WHERE YOU'RE FROM

I don't think this is going to be a book begging for forgiveness or glamorising crime and then saying I learnt from it and it doesn't pay. Like any line of work, there can be ups and downs, but it's obviously one of the riskiest things you can do. The stakes are high, the rewards are high.

Did I set out into a life of crime? Of course not, but like most others with a story to tell, I was born into it. In a way. I'll add that to my disclaimer. I say I was born into it because I saw my dad doing 'certain things' and your dad is your role model, superhero and teacher in one. Of course, observing their behaviour is going to influence you. In the environment that I was brought up in, if you never had somebody in prison or you never had somebody who was up to no good, you were looked upon with suspicion! That was just how it was. My dad's dad came from a broken family from the Gorbals and lived like a large clan with extended family from the Pirrie, Chalmers and Paker families. Most of the family had been in prison for one thing or the other since the turn of the century and Barlinnie was the end destination. When you know stuff like that it makes you wish you'd broken the cycle. No one wants to be a fucking case study, do they?

And bearing in mind that I was from Blackhill, the criminal profilers would have been licking their lips at wee Paul's beginnings and subsequent journey, high-fiving each other and saying, 'I told you so.' You see, Blackhill was quite a place. It didn't spawn too many Oxbridge graduates, but that's not to say that it was a scheme full of thickos. Intelligence comes in so many forms and Blackhill lads had street intelligence. That's how they survived and it's what makes the difference between winning and losing. And you'll find this is the case in most crime areas and tough estates. Not many attended school on a regular basis, but they could tell you what a third of £2,560 was without thinking. It was different situations that we got our education from: timing, planning, cunning, care, attention to detail, stealth, keeping a low profile and sharing the profits was what made a successful blag at a jewellers and being around to learn and hone your skills, rather than an unplanned smash and grab to either get caught legging it or a day later when you're flashing the cash.

Blackhill was commissioned and redeveloped from wasteland to a new housing scheme, and was built as a council estate in the 1930s. It was basically all about rehousing and getting rid of the slums from the 19th century to form newer ones. For example, in 1935, nearly half the population of Blackhill was made up of rehoused tenants from the overcrowded Garngad district to the west. Constraints in funding meant that there was no real opportunity for aesthetic refinement in architectural design (Grenfell, anyone?) and things like shops and public transport were lacking. In short, it was a bit of a hole. It was built without much thought to how it looked because, in *their* eyes, it was just to house the slum-dwellers and they'd not give a fuck about where they live. The notion was that Blackhillians were lacking in qualities of responsible citizenship. It stigmatised the community. The message that was projected was that we weren't worth spending money on because we wouldn't know what decent housing and quality of life was. The place was always gonna be stigmatised from the word go. It always happens though – the state of the living conditions portrayed in *Our Friends in the North* was no different to any other brutalist shite that was thrown together under the guise of progress. And what has all that concrete been pulled down to make way for? Newbuild shite with paper-thin walls and rooms you can't fit beds in and garages you can't fit a car in. Blackhill was named as such because that's apparently where they buried people from the city who died from the Black Flu in 1918. So they took them away from the city to bury them up there in a mass grave and then they built a fucking estate on top of it. That *Poltergeist* revelation and the poor conditions just made residents – or tenants, as they'd refer to us – know they were always gonna be on the shitty end of the stick.

It was in the late-1920s and 30s that razor gangs appeared amongst the youth of Glasgow. If you thought it was confined to the 1960s, then think again. The Glasgow gangs in those more recent years were probably more violent than the first wave, but it still must have been a fucking tricky time to be a kid back then. I mean, I'm trying to sound shocked just to give some sort of moral balance. If you know me, you know I'd have fit in well back then and would probably have been leading the charge. The *Glasgow Evening Citizen* listed 24 gangs operating in the city during the 1920s and 30s and I've heard the media (*the fucking media*) say there were six times more gangs in Glasgow at one point than there were in London. And London is 10 times bigger than Glasgow. So, you do the math and all that – what it all means is that there's been a fuck-load of NEDs (Non-Educated Delinquents) slicing people up for near enough 100 years. Alexander McArthur and H. Kingsley Long wrote all about the razor gangs in their novel *No Mean City*, published in 1935. So we were nothing new; gangs will always exist in certain areas and we were all just part of the life cycle. It's no different now than it was all the way back then, it's just that the clothes are a bit different.

After the war, before I was born, there were improvements to the area, but this was still an estate of around 1,500 houses in a small area. So, it was overcrowded and experienced all the social problems we now know emerge from such places. The negative image continued to dog Blackhill until the late 20th century. I mean, think of an area near you that's been done up. Even if parts have been flattened and new builds are up. It's still the same place; it still has the same reputation. Memories are long. It takes a while for somewhere to re-establish itself.

I asked The Googles about Blackhill not too long ago, just to check when it had been built – you know, so my facts were correct and all that. There isn't much on the Wiki page to retell other than:

There was (and is) a strong sense of neighbourliness, partly encouraged by the enclosed nature of the site, due to industry, railways and main roads cutting it off from other districts. It was, however, built close to a gasworks and a distillery, which did not add to the health of the area and, perhaps for this reason, it gained a reputation for being 'difficult to let'. Nearby is a prison, HM Prison Barlinnie, which may also have encouraged negative evaluations of the area. The area has been comprehensively redeveloped in recent years, with much of its housing stock having been demolished and replaced with improved stock.

It goes without saying, really. There is generally a sense of community in such places. The older folk seemed to enforce that more and the younger generation never seemed to see it that way. Wiki then goes on to say that a recent community survey reported residents' concerns were similar to those in other urban areas:

In the last issue we reported the findings of a local survey that helped to pinpoint the top 10 priority issues for your neighbourhood – things like road safety, litter and vandalism, dog fouling, dumping and youth disorder all featured strongly.

And – hilariously – on the same page:

pinpoint the top 10 priority issues for your neighbourhood – thing safety, litter and vandalism, dog fouling, dumping and youth diso featured strongly."

See also [edit]

- Paul John Ferris

It seems there's more to write about me than there is about all of Blackhill. I take that as an honour. So it didn't sound like there was ever that much change in Blackhill from when it was built to when I arrived in the world. 'Youth disorder' as they call it – I just think will always exist in areas that are less well-off than others. Criminals don't usually come from well-off areas because there's no reason to. You don't join a gang in a posh area because there's nothing to rebel against – it's all good, what's to go radge for? But the kids, it's not like they'd smash Blackhill up all the time. It's just they'd get together and do whatever it was that gang mentality suggested. There was no science or master plan behind any of it. It was about territory. It was recreational violence; not for profit. Stuff didn't go on for any other gain than to better a team who were on your patch – not to nick a watch or a wallet. That's probably what the police could not understand. In their eyes, there had to be a higher reason behind it all.

In a way, yeah, kids were raging against the machine, but in fairness, it was just groups of kids defending their own streets, seeing off their rivals. If you weren't from that street, why the fuck were you walking through it? There were instances where you'd have one gang at one end of a street and a gang based down the other end. You'd have a no man's land in the middle.

In digging around, I found this piece from the *Glasgow Herald* in January, 1968:

Within the present confines of Glasgow there are the remains of the villages engulfed by the city in its extremely rapid expansion since 1830. Some villages remain in name only, such as Gorbals, Anderston, Partick and Maryhill. The trouble is that the growth of Glasgow has dehumanised many of these villages. The spread of the tenements swallowed up street after street, regardless of whether this was the main street of the village, and equally regardless of the buildings, the church, the castle or the prison which had to be destroyed to make space for them. In Glasgow at present there are many ordinary tenemented streets, no different from the countless others, which at one time were the main streets of villages.

The beautiful and romantic Kelvin is now overgrown with weeds and surrounded by rubbish. The neat village has a trunk road running through its centre. The old houses overlooking the main street are blacked, bricked up and ruinous. The canal is concealed behind walls and hoardings, and the view over the hills is obscured by dingy street lights and disfigured by waste and derelict ground.

Up to a point, I never really saw myself or our family as a typical Blackhill one. We weren't. We lived at the top end and had a pretty stable set up. We weren't 'well off' as such, we didn't have a butler, but weren't on the bones of our arse either. I dare say if it wasn't for the pull of Blackhill, I'd have lived a pretty average and unassuming life. But we know that was not the case! Blackhill was of its time. Of course, the press slowly caught on to the gang culture. Stories on youth disorder first started appearing in the papers in the 50s and 60s, but it was probably the mid-60s when it seemed that's all that was going on. There was one headline from 1965 that proclaimed *The Gangs are Back!* when the slashings, group disorders, vandalism and lawlessness appeared rife. It got so bad in Glasgow that vigilante groups formed in Easterhouse in the East End in 1966. It all died an early death when the senior magistrate for the city declared that anyone taking the law into their own hands would be treated like any other transgressor of the law. After a rethink, a group of dozens of shopkeepers got together and roped their local MP in to tackle the problem and an anti-teenage gang committee was formed by the Lord Provost and the Chief Constable. It gathered momentum and got recognised in the national news where phrases like 'stabbings are no longer news in Glasgow' were bandied about. Crime figures at the time revealed that 850 people had been arrested for carrying an offensive weapon and over 1,500 had been done for breach of the peace, with around the same done for disorderly behaviour. There were well-known gang names I remember from growing up. They had names like the Blackhill Toi, the Provy Young Team and the Provy Rebels. Thing is with Glasgow, it's a fucking tough city. It always will be.

I grew up with two older sisters Cath and Carol and an older brother, Billy. I was the bairn until my youngest sister, Maureen was born. When I said earlier that I was born into this darker world... I actually was fucking *born* there! Right in the bedroom at 19 Hogganfield Street on 10 November, 1963.

My dad, Willie, worked as a bus driver and Jenny, my mother, was a housewife. These days, you'd say she was a stay-at-home-mum, but neither of those tags are accurate or sum up the extent of the job description. To Mum, I was her blue-eyed boy. Even if I did something wrong, my mum always, you know... she didn't bury her head in the sand, but she'd always take the idea that it wasn't me first. She did that all her fucking life! Even if I was wrong, I don't think she would have said anything against me, but I never put her in that position. She was an honest woman and if you did anything in front of people like that, then you deserved everything you fucking got. She was brought up in a devout Catholic household, she would never tell lies to anybody including the police, much to my dad's amusement (which he found out the hard way as well). She just didn't know how to lie. Anything at all to do with me, she always complied with the cops. If you know somebody is liable to give you up for whatever you've done, then don't talk about it in front of them – you were asking for it.

Like everyone else, Mum and Dad moved to Blackhill from the Garngad, which was like a dumping ground for Irish migrants. My mum came from the McGinty clan but she met my dad at the ballroom. For my dad to go somewhere like that and to where my mum was from, it was just like fucking two polarised positions... almost impossible to imagine it happening. They must have really loved each other, eh?

My peers probably thought of me as leaning more towards middle-class. Or as middle-class as you could be in that area. This is where we were less typical: my dad had work as well as morals and was a self-starter with his own legitimate business. He had a work ethic. Most of my mates lived in the middle of Blackhill and didn't have that kind of influence on their life. I don't mean that anyone from a broken home was never gonna amount to anything; that old stigma is well past its sell-by-date. I mean when you see someone getting up on a morning to do some honest graft to put food on the table, you see from an early age what it is to be responsible and look after a family. And I'm not being a hypocrite here either.

I'm not about to say that it put me in good stead to go straight into regular work and knuckle down to that way of life. Whichever path I would take, or whichever path chose me, having my dad there gave me someone to look up to. The family still lived by Blackhill codes though: don't let anyone get away with anything, look after your own, and never involve the police. Having the police at your door was bad for a family reputation on so many levels.

With my mates living in the middle of Blackhill, that's where I'd spend a lot of my time. The middle of Blackhill meant you were right in the thick of it. We'd knock around there on a night and at weekends. It wasn't salubrious at all. This was the rougher part, where the lawlessness was. This was where you had to be tough to survive. Gangs of teenagers didn't just sit around on a wall smoking and sharing a bottle of blue WKD. If you walked past, you were on their turf and you'd get a severe kicking, maybe hospitalised, sliced up, whipped with a bicycle chain, stabbed – anything. And this wouldn't be a robbery or mugging (there was nothing to nick off anyone), it would be a vicious attack because you were there. That's how it was. If you didn't belong, weren't streetwise or tough – you were fucked. Everyone carried a knife and everyone was looking for an excuse to use it. So, I had the regular life on one side and the more criminal or violent life on the other side of the estate. There was a balance, but if you're inclined to it, the bad

29

stuff could drag you down and upset that balance. For a youngster, it was like being on an adventure in a forest, but going too far into the thick woods where the environment soon changed for the worse and before you knew it, you were lost in the darkness. It was all black streets dimly lit by pale orange lighting. The ubiquitous broken glass, empty beer cans, bottles and bits of house brick lain around that were either left behind after a battle or could be used in one. Any wooden fences that remained round gardens were just dirty sticks. Fences were either used in warfare or knocked down so you could run freely from one end of a street to the other. The gardens they were supposed to protect and keep as part of a property were trodden into mud. Most shopfronts and walls were grafittied to fuck... standard.

Going back to crimes committed, this is probably where we have this opinion of community. People didn't steal from each other. It was one of those unwritten rules. The phrase 'you don't steal from your own' should be suffixed with something like 'because they've got nothing to steal'. You do hear this being said a lot when the good old days are discussed: you could leave your door open and all that. Anyone stealing from neighbours would soon be found out and community punishment would be dished out. I only really heard of snowdroppers doing it – lowlife scum who'd steal clothes from washing lines. In a place like Blackhill, clothes were hard to come by as it was difficult enough to keep your head above water. It was a personal thing to do to a family and it was the mums who got to dish the punishment out if a snowdropper was caught. It was the mums' jobs to deal with washing and hanging clothes out, so anything like that was a personal slight on them and they were not to be fucked with. That was a big reason for never bringing the police in on anything. Firstly, there were no secrets in Blackhill. Everything that happened was known about. This was another reason for not committing crime against thy neighbour; if you stole from someone, there'd be a lynch mob at your door before you got home. We could deal with trouble ourselves; the police added an extra level of complication to a situation. They were never liked in areas such as ours and they were never wanted or needed. It was almost like they were offended by that. They were certainly imposing on us any time they were there. A friendly (yeah, right) copper saying hello to you on the street could get you done over for being on their side. If anyone did go out on the rob, it would be out of the area. Hitting a shop on the estate was just counter-productive to the community's needs. Doing a blag away from home meant you could return as a hero and spread the wealth.

IT'S WHERE YOU'RE AT

Where was I at? Growing up is confusing as fuck to begin with. You've got school, you've got hormones, finding out who you are, finding your path in life... all the regular shit, but on top of that, there's Blackhill.

We lived in a four-in-a-block and I had the luxury of growing up in a mixed household of Protestant father and Catholic mother. I don't think Dad was ever involved in any politics or anything that went with it, though. Mum was only slightly involved cos we only went to Mass and to Holy Communion. I wasn't really bombarded with religion as some may assume in that situation. My brother's actually named after King Billy and so was my dad, so my mum kind of evened things up and called me after Pope John Paul VI. Honest, man! I don't think I even knew my dad was a Protestant until many years later, not that it mattered or anything. My mum made sure that we went to chapel and I ducked out on some occasions and spent the donation money that she gave us on cigarettes. Shit – I smoked the money that was going to God! I told mum lies as well. Am I going to hell?

People say I look more like my mum. But since I've started losing my hair I look more like my dad now. You can't get a better compliment than looking like both sets of your parents, but because I was the youngest at the time before my younger sister appeared, I was definitely Mum's blue-eyed boy, so any naughtiness my dad wanted to cuff me for, she was on side to say she'd do it and conveniently forget. And we'd hear my dad would shout in the background, *That'll teach you a lesson*! He never knew, bless him. My mum was just a normal woman, not tall, not small. My dad used to get called The Tank. Because he was a delivery driver, he used to have like 20 kilo bags of maize, grain, potatoes and what have you and was strong as an ox.

My older sisters, I can't remember too much, but the tales that they used to tell me, we'd have a laugh when we were sitting round the table. They'd come out with stuff like, 'I used to change your nappy,' and, 'I was like your second mum and she was like your third mum,' and they loved it. Sadly they've all moved on, but they've got kids of their own and grandkids. Growing up, my sisters left, my brother left, my young sister was staying with my gran and I was the only person in the household. What I liked about it was that there was a flight of stairs to get up to the main door and then another flight of stairs to get up the stairs! That was a good point for me for security but a bad point for anybody that was trying to come up... especially if half cut like my dad, sliding down the stairs. And it was a long fucking way down the stairs. Happy memories!

I witnessed the religion of football from an early age. With Dad running Hogganfield Coaches, it meant that there'd be a coach trip every Saturday, without fail. There'd be an away game, either Celtic or Rangers, and I'd get to go along for the ride. There was always a kind of gentlemanly thing where there was a whip-round – a cap got passed around between passengers and coins or whatever were put in to show their appreciation for the driver. My dad would do weddings and stuff but his bread and butter was the football. Sometimes he had to do Glasgow-Aberdeen, Glasgow-Inverness and he had his bus windows put in a few times. I was never into football at that time; I was too busy being a kid. A great thing about being on the buses was that I got to dig around, lifting the seats and checking the floors for extra money. I earned a bit more pocket money by cleaning the buses at the end of the awayday, but I probably found more under the seats than I actually earned. Sometimes, if I was feeling cheeky enough, I'd nab an extra 50p out of my dad's whip-round cap for underpaying me. When I say I cleaned the buses, what happened was I'd sweep them before my dad mopped the floors down. He probably let me sweep up first cos he knew I'd find money. He'd usually turn away, so I didn't feel so bad pocketing it, or go out of his way to congratulate me on my find. Daft bugger! It was pretty cool having a dad with such a job. The perks were decent for a kid.

I'd go to school some Mondays with more money on my hip than the teachers. Some lads I went to school with probably hadn't even had a fucking breakfast. It was a bit of a stark contrast. I wasn't flash or anything like that, I suppose it was just me wanting to have fun. At dinnertime we'd go to the shops, and I'd be like,

'You get this, and that... and get bonbons, cola cubes, crisps, juice,' and whatever else we could carry. They probably thought I was a fucking shoplifter.

'Who's paying for all this, Paul?' they'd ask.

'I am. I had a good weekend on the buses.'

I know people made money over the weekend *on the horses*, but *on the buses* would have thrown them if they didn't know my dad's job. I loved being able to treat my mates. I remember another time when we were playing football and one of the lads kicked the ball so fucking hard. It was one of those penny floaters, so it just whooshed all over the place, bounced off a roof and landed on a spike of a fence. You could see it happening a mile off, but there was nothing anyone could do.

Everyone was like, 'Fuck, what we gonna do now?' and I said, 'We'll just go and buy a new one.' I've always had a view that when you've got money you can maybe change somebody's life and put a smile on their face, and know you've done it for the right reason. You don't need to walk about with placards about how good you think you are. It should stay in your heart and in your head for you to remember.

One of my earliest memories is Mum going out and leaving Cathy, who is 10 years older than me, in charge. Mum used to leave coins for Cathy to put in the meter so that we'd come back from school and the cooker, the heating and the water would be on. The thing is, being too used to having coins when I was with my dad on the buses; I kept nicking the ones my mum left. I'd been doing it from before my dad was away, so it had been quite a while. Nobody knew I'd been taking them and my sister was getting the blame for it. Over the years, it was still something that got brought up as one of those family things you could have a laugh about, but the story always ended up with Cathy as the culprit. I told my mum years and years later.

'Remember those coins? Well... it was me,' I said.

Get away! And we gave Cathy such a hard time!'

It was after Mum had passed away that I told Cathy. I'd been carrying the burden of guilt for too long. But she let me tell the whole thing and get to my apology before telling me that she'd tidied up one time and found all the coins behind an old chest of drawers! After we laughed about it again, I asked if she gave them back to Mum.

'Did I fuck...? I kept them!'

But, soon after that, Cath became pregnant and moved away. My youngest sister was moved in with my gran after my granddad passed away. Thinking back now, there were visits where I'd hang around as he worked in his allotment. We made a bow and arrow one time and others, if the weather was good, we'd lie back, listening to the birds and enjoying the warmth of the sun on our backs as we lay there. He'd always point stuff out, vegetables, what was in season, what bird we could hear chirping... it was the best. When my granddad passed away and because he was a McGinty, there was a full Catholic funeral where the body lies in the house. I know the rituals now, but as a kid, it was all a bit overwhelming. Everyone was all lined up to go and kiss my granddad goodbye and I didn't want to do it – I was terrified, because he was dead and it was one of those things where you were taken over and lifted up and basically forced into doing it. Remember when you used to go on a family visit and when it was time to leave, you were forced into that awkward moment of having to hug and kiss everyone? Well... now imagine it when one of them's fucking dead. It was an awful situation to be in; getting lifted face-first towards a man I wanted to remember as having good times with. To me, the man wasn't my granddad, not anymore. And then thinking all the way through that day, all that night and even when I woke early the next morning... the first thing on my mind was, *I'm gonna die, I'm gonna die.* Having those kind of thoughts in my head as a young kid made me aware that nobody lives forever; it's what you do in the here and now that counts, not what you say that you're gonna do. You do what you said you were gonna do in the first place – just do it, man, you might not even be around in five minutes to finish doing it.

Messing around by the canal was always a good one. Without wanting to sound ancient, back then you played out next to power stations, on building sites, in rivers, up trees and no one died. Well, in fairness, some probably did. That's what all those infomercials were about, eh? All we did in the 70s (it seems) was risk our young lives doing stupid shit. Fucking quarries – people still go swimming in quarries. What's that all about? Anyway – the canal. We used to take the old doors off the houses that were gonna be knocked down and make rafts by tying two of them together with loads of string, using my mum's washing line prop as a quant pole like we were punting our way around Oxford. Thing is, if you fell in you were dead. No one would have survived the canal and none of us were capable of saving the other, but we didn't know that at the time! Luckily it got turned into a motorway, allowing us to play human Frogger from time to time. And then there was the loch. And to get to that you had to go through the graveyard. As if that wasn't bad enough, you had to scale a six foot wall that was around three times as high on the other side cos the grass verge dropped down. You had to follow the gang and you'd quickly learn how to do commando rolls or learn how to get home with broken legs. The good old days! But going through the graveyard, after the experience with my granddad, I don't think death fazed me at all.

I was sent to a residential school. I think I was probably around eightish, going into the summer holidays. It was a total culture shock being plucked from my concrete jungle to that place – fresh air, greenery, big blue skies and the sounds of the great outdoors. I never knew I was going. There was no warning and next to no packing. I was just told I was going to this school for six weeks so that was any plans I had out the window in an instant. Not that you have many social events as an eight year old. There were a few other kids from Blackhill and Provanmill, gathered in the city centre with our parents, then we were put on a bus and taken to this big, stunning countryside retreat in Kilmarnock called Whitecraigs Residential School. Some people have vivid memories of it, purely because it was a way for families to give the parents a bit of ease. Respite, they call it; a place for the kids to enjoy a change of lifestyle while the parents have a break. Everyone's a winner, eh? I wasn't sure what I was having a break from. I was quite lonely at first, feeling a bit like I'd been abandoned while the rest of my family fucked off on a cool holiday somewhere. The new place was still a school with discipline, but it gave the impression of something else. You didn't mind it being a school when you were in the middle of the country. It was where I learnt to play chess, and where, for the first time, I actually sat down and watched a TV series: *Skippy the Bush Kangaroo* – I was totally bamboozled by it! How did they always know to follow the thing to the mine shaft to rescue the kids? I had a go at Backgammon as well – I was totally going all highbrow with these boardgames. Chess and Backgammon were unheard of in Blackhill and you'd probably get your throat cut if you suggested a game at real school. Chess was fascinating for me. It's all about strategy – the long game, sacrificing the minions and getting to the kingpin. No, I'm not going to relate it to a life of crime... get your mind out of the cliché gutter – you're better than that, man! It's just a cool game that doesn't get enough credit cos people assume it's for the geeks. It is, but give it a go before you judge.

I learnt quite a lot of other things in there as well. I took a keen interest in gardening. I was familiar with it from being around my granddad and his allotment. He had his potatoes, his carrots and whatnot. It was a bit of a dying art, but growing veg is definitely on the up. You can't beat the feeling of growing and eating your own stuff. And not to be a 'these dayser', but kids can't even differentiate a carrot from a piece of broccoli – and they don't even know they grow in the ground. All they know is you get them in a shop. Stupid bastards, eh? I was gifted with a plant pot with a little plant in to take home and I remember thinking, *I'm gonna give that to my mum*. I've got brilliant memories from it, great flashbacks. Kids need stuff like that in their lives... you know, Cubs, Scouts, Brownies, Girl Guides – all this stuff is invaluable learning experience. When Carolyn showed me the property that we currently live in, it took me back to that place straight away.

And then years later I went to see a friend of mine, an ex-crime reporter for the *News of The World*, *The Sun* and *Daily Record* – the guy who took the 1992 trial. As coincidence would have it, he actually lives at Whitecraigs. It's been converted into luxury flats now – nice job. But, going in through the front door again was absolutely amazing. When I first met him, I had no idea where he lived until that visit. I never realised that it was even still there – it was just a fond memory. Apparently, it had been burnt down and rebuilt with all the infrastructure still intact. As soon as I walked in, I knew exactly where to go but it really did take me right back in time to the dormitory… the milky tea and biscuit before you went to bed at night; waiting for my letters to come through during the week with a postal order in it and some comics, magazines – reminding me that although this place was the ultimate getaway, there was still an outside world waiting for me. Fucking hell – the amount of time I've wasted sat on a bed waiting for letters to arrive – it's criminal! I was so chuffed to visit the place again – so unexpected. The fucking difficult part was the other memory that it triggered.

The reason why I'd been packed off to the summer school in the first place became apparent when my dad wasn't there to pick me up. They both knew that he was going away and that was it – neither of them wanted any fuss or to upset me with it all. It was so sad. It wasn't until much later that I appreciated the way they handled it. I think. In the longrun maybe, but not at the time.

He'd got 18 months for not paying his taxes and ended up in Barlinnie. That was wrong on so many levels – it changed our family and it changed my dad – and none of it for the better. Barlinnie, Bar-L, is a total fucking hellhole. It's no place for a family man whose only crime was that he'd dodged his taxes to bring a bit more money in. This was white-collar crime that didn't deserve the punishment.

Being 'at' Blackhill wasn't something you could escape. It was part of everyone who was in it. There was the escapism mentioned above, if that makes sense, the little things like time with your mates and your family, but you could never quite push it from your mind completely. Although I felt our family was different, in many respects, we were as much Blackhill as the rest of them. It consumed anyone who lived there. In whatever way, it did something to you; it was like a cancer that ate away at something you loved and cared for.

WILLIE FERRIS

My dad was on a mission.

'Is that him?'

'What do you mean?'

'You know fucking who, the lad that's bullying you.'

I'm sure he had the best intentions, but it was never going to solve my problem. Even if we saw any of them, there's no way I'd have said anything for a number of reasons. I mean, firstly, I'd be declaring myself a grass and there'd be repercussions just for that. And then, of course, I didn't want to see my dad caught up in my feud and have to endure what I was going through. No one wants to see their dad rounded up on by a family armed with knives and fuck knows what else. Each youngster we passed in the bus, I just said they were pals of mine.

'If you're fucking telling me lies, I'll leather you if you don't fucking leather them.'

I was around 10 when he got out of Barlinnie. I remember because I eventually told him about all the bullying. He took me to school in the bus and stopped at every street corner with me in the front with him, pointing kids out. On the plus side, I didn't take a beating on the way to school and I got my own private, chauffeur-driven bus to the gates. No one else had that and it put such a smile on my face as we pulled up, pistons hissing as the doors opened and other kids looked on. For the first time in fuck knows how long, I arrived at school happy. But as soon as I was through those gates it was snatched away from me, even though I could turn round and still see my dad, I was in a different territory and this was a place where he couldn't protect me.

Typically, Dad met people while he had been inside and, as one thing led to another; they got together and plotted a bit of work. I mean, come on... you can imagine how it would go down:

'Hi, mate. What do you do on the outside?'

'Me? I'm a driver.'

'A *driver*, you say...'

And this is where I can 'blame' Blackhill again. Dad was as straight as they come. He'd been in the merchant navy in his earlier days before starting his own business. He had the bus company and was a hard worker. He was very much the provider for the family and was different to many dads in that he was actually there and that he had a proper job. When he got sent down, that was it: he became an absent father and it changed him. He didn't know anything about prison or anything like that. He had been 100 per cent straight up until then. He did his minor crime, did his time and, like many, he came out to commit more crime because the stigma of his prison record preceded him and his reputation was tarnished. He couldn't maintain the company or hold down another job after doing bird. Blackhill, man.

Dad still had the contract for the local school and used to take the kids swimming. It was a perfect front – no team of bank robbers would be so bold as to use a busload of schoolkids as a getaway car, would they? Well, they fucking well would in Blackhill! And they'd have got away with it if one of them hadn't broken one of the rules. He got stopped at Heathrow airport because of an IRA security scare. The police heard his accent, you know sometimes people mistake Scottish accents for Irish? Well, police stupidity meant that they searched him, found a bundle of money, traced it back to the bank, found out who he was... and rounded everyone up – my dad included. He'd hardly even been back five minutes and then he was given five years. Five fucking years!

The thing was, the bank was in Riddrie, not too far from Barlinnie and handled all the wages for the prison officers. So, because of my dad, the screws didn't get paid that week. Not the best fact to have them know as you walk through the gates.

Over time, when I followed in his footsteps (shit – spoiler alert – sorry!) and progressed through the juvenile system to Bar-L, a few screws would come up to me like, 'I know you... you're Willie's son! He nicked all our wages!' It was a good bit of banter and a nice ice-breaker to have.

The first change I noticed when Dad was away was the difference between having money and

45

having nothing. Dad was the one who brought in the money. Going to my gran's and having beans on toast and then having the same when my mum came back wasn't the best culinary experience in the world. People always cite it as something you have when you're skint – *quick, we have to live off beans on toast now* – but it's certainly not the worst meal you can have. But going from 'normal food' to that was quite a jump. I remember thinking, *Where's the bus, where's my dad?*

There were other things I notice now, looking back. Some things that'll come out within these pages and other bits that will be kept to myself. It was a fucking huge thing to happen in my life, like it put me on par with all the kids from broken homes that I knew. I didn't feel I'd been better than them at all – it was just one of those things that had made us quite unique in Blackhill and now it was gone. My dad not being there made me more of a loner, I think. Maybe a bit withdrawn. It didn't stop me knocking around with my mates, but it made me – I don't know, I suppose it made me want to fit in somewhere as much as it gave me that sense of loneliness. I felt more inclined to rebel. Knowing that my dad was locked up, there couldn't be any parental high ground. I could relate more to my mates; hang around the streets for longer, give less of a fuck about rules.

It ain't where you're from, it's where you're at is a throwaway line, but could be profound at the same time. Maybe I've laboured where I'm from and the disadvantages I feel it caused. Is that me just finding excuses in it, though? I mean, I was actually *born* there – so in the literal sense, I was born into that way of life as well as having close family locked up for committing crime. Where you're at... I take that as being anywhere you want. It's a metaphor. You're at where your family is, where your love lies. Maybe as our family dispersed, I had to find my own way. I can look back and blame the area, the weird pull, the things that Blackhill did to people as much as I can blame us all for doing it and becoming that case study I never wanted us to be; a living, breathing nature/nurture debate. If I was starting to give less of a fuck about the rules, where would it take me?

VISITING TIME

I went to see my dad in Barlinnie in 1970 – the first time I set foot in a prison. It was certainly scary as fuck for a seven year old. It leaves a mark on your mind... one of those things that a kid shouldn't experience.

Barlinnie dates back to 1882. It was always one of those things around Blackhill where it was referred to as *the big hoose*. And it was. It was a big imposing place, especially knowing there were hangings there before capital punishment was outlawed. I suppose it was one of those almost-mythical places that could be used as a threat to kids: *be a good boy, or you'll end up in the big hoose*, and that's unfortunately what happened to a *lot* of people from Blackhill. It was well situated, let's say. It was a tough place to visit and even tougher to live. I checked out their Wiki page as standard. Notable former inmates: there I am at number one. Duncan Bannatyne is in there as well, two places above Stephen Gough, a naked rambler repeatedly imprisoned for public nudity.

As a child, I wanted my dad to come home. Yeah, it was never gonna happen, but how the fuck was I supposed to know and deal with that kind of shit? Seeing your dad locked up is bad enough, but then having to make those minutes count before being told to leave him there was unbearable. I don't know what was worse; seeing him and having to leave him there or just not seeing him until he got out. It wasn't a totally conscious decision for me to visit my dad, it was that my mum couldn't just leave me in the house alone.

In some respects, it would've been better not to have seen my dad in there. I don't know – it's a difficult call. But then I knew how horrible the place was as well, so that was upsetting. And you know, it's really fucking horrible being ordered around. Getting there and being looked up and down as though I was a fucking drugs mule or whatever. The coldness of it all: *Stand there. Wait. Go through that door. Stop! Wait there, I said. No hugging allowed. Do not hold his hand. Time's up. Time's up – out. Now*!

All I know is that not having a dad for those years was unbearable. I kept telling myself that he'd be back. I knew he'd be back, but five years is a long time for a child. We were just like the other Blackhill families now; we were Blackhill as fuck. My brother was gone and my dad was gone. I felt alone; I was the man of the house when I was still a child.

THE WELSHES

I think there is a big misconception about this family from *The Wee Man* because I've been asked about them so many times. I don't expect that you're reading this cos you know everything about me – I'm not that fucking arrogant. So, as usual, everything that happens in the film couldn't have happened in real life, and vice versa. I don't mean it's all made up, I mean it's based on my real life story. I know you're not daft. I just think it's harder to make that leap when you've seen it play out in a film; you can't unsee the association and perception it creates.

They were serious as fuck. They were an established family like any of the others. They were probably more serious contenders because there were so many of them. When you've got that much backup from family, it makes a huge difference. There's the loyalty that you just cannot get from anywhere else. Who'd wade into a knife fight to help you out first, your elder brother or someone you knock around with on a night? Their age ranged from something like 40 years all the way down to babies. A lot of you will know about me and them; it had a huge impact on my life. I've written about this before, it's well documented. It wasn't just bullying and it wasn't just one of them – it was all of them and this lot were fucking insane.

When my dad found out I was being bullied by them, I'm surprised he didn't know. If he did know, he'd have kept as quiet as me about it. His was none of your namby-pamby snowflake approach to parenting. Let's face it – you stop bullies by beating the shit out of them. That's how they learn their lesson, not by talking to them about their feelings. So, by telling me to deal with it, I think it eased his conscience a bit. He knew that I *knew* what to do; maybe he felt I was letting him down by not sorting it out. He wasn't long out of prison and even doing 18 months toughens you. He'd have seen and done things in there that made him more protective of his family and he just wanted to see me sort it out the Blackhill way. I could have, if I had an army behind me. And I certainly would have. But I didn't have that luxury. I was one. A child against a family. A notorious family, for fuck's sake.

School was right across from where that mad fucking family lived. My first encounter with them was probably when I was aged about nine. We were playing a game of marbles and somebody had a green flash through this marble and I thought, *I like that and I want to win it*! So imagine this scenario: A crowd gathered to watch. One of the family of brothers came up and grabbed the marbles while we were heids doon and oblivious to it. Fucking sly bastard! I was up in a second.

'Give me my fucking thing back!'

'No,' he replied.

'Fucking give it back. *Now*!'

'No.'

So I grabbed the handful of marbles back off him, and we went back to setting a new game up. It wasn't like it had to be an issue – it was just a kid doing what kids do and that was the end of it. What I didn't know was he went away and got his brother. His older fucking brother. Who was bigger. I remember being in the kneeling position when he kicked me square in the face. He'd had all the time in the world to measure it up. I was oblivious to it and it nearly took my head clean off. It was a cowardly thing to do to a young lad, but that's just the law of the playground: I'd 'said something' to his younger brother and he came for revenge. I was totally rocked by it, my head had snapped back with the force and I got that horrible fucking taste, like a chemical taste. Blood.

Somebody asked if I ever tried boxing. I did, and I got the same taste. Nobody told me how to fucking hold my arms, so when I put them up, the other guy hit my gloves and I hit myself in the fucking nose! If you've seen the brilliant *T2Trainspotting*: Spud's foray in the ring isn't a million miles off. I thought, *Boxing is not for me, running's for me*. I was not one to get into any fighting or violence, nothing at all like that because I just didn't like it. It might come as a surprise to a lot of people that I don't like violence. I never have – you get pushed into it and you've got to deal with it. That's just the way it is – a situation brought your way that you never asked for and then you have to react to it.

After that performance, it just kept going on and on and on with this family. What I really remember was the fear. People talk about fear but unless you've really experienced it, you can never totally understand it.

You wouldn't think it to look at them, and I knew nothing of it at the time as a youngster, but this lot could easily have given the Thompson clan a run for their money. It was only their sheer ugliness that made you think they were just a bunch of uneducated toe rags. They were evil, vicious fuckers who were good at violence and could pretty much do what they wanted on the streets cos there weren't that many who could stop them.

There are two ways to deal with it; you run away and hide or you face it by taking it on the chin. *Literally* – I ran away, got caught, got beaten up and I never ran after that. I just had to stand and take it, which in turn makes you very bitter, resentful, angry and vengeful later in life. When there's no closure to it all, it's always there, always festering, breeding, and the slightest thing can trigger the explosion. My friends, they would fuck off as soon as they saw these people. Afterwards, I'd walk away and as soon as I got around the first corner, there'd be tears streaming down my face. I'd never do it in front of them and that wasn't me being big or tough or anything, I just wouldn't give them the satisfaction. I'd be slapped about, let them punch me, kick me or whatever they had to do.

My dad hadn't been out long enough to do anything before he was back inside and Billy was doing time as well, but this wasn't for them. It was my problem. I was always getting told to stop telling tales on my sister at home. So, all this family stuff that you learn in the house does help you when you need it. My mum did find out about it, though. Friends at school went back and told their mums who were friends with my mum. So, back in school, it was like, *You fucking grass*. But I wasn't.

And this was another Blackhill thing: for all the goodness and happiness I had, it was always short-lived because of the impending kicking I'd get from any of them at any time. It could be while out playing football, on my way to the shops or coming back from school. They were Blackhill.

If my dad had insisted that we were brought up as Protestants then we would have gone to Smithycroft School rather than St Philomena's, which would have been closer. And the irony of total fucking irony is that if I'd gone to Smithycroft, what would have happened to me at school? Possibly nothing. And everything with them may never have happened. Hindsight's a wonderful thing... if only, *if only*. But look at the facts: I went to St Philomena's and had a couple of good years there. Shit happens, life rolls on. You can't dwell forever. I only am now because

I'm writing about stuff that I've been through. In a weird way, I think it helped me and my dad bond that brief time when he was back home and gave us that common ground thing. It didn't just fizzle out, as people like to hope. I was more of a realist and knew it would all have to be sorted out properly at some point.

THE ELEPHANT IN THE ROOM

'Stu, for anyone who's only seen the film, it doesn't show the level of bullying I went through. Even though it shows them killing my dog.'

Bullying had a massive impact on Paul's life. And to say *had a massive impact on* is just a line we use without giving much thought to it. It doesn't mean anything – its impact is lost, in that sense.

As we write this book, I want to do it without giving any of these fuckers a mention. I had an idea about a story device to use. I've worked closely with Paul on this, discussed it with Steve so many times and it's at this point where I feel Paul should be moving on from giving them any air time. I've always felt that, for the people I've worked with, writing books is a therapeutic process – it gets rid of the demons. I feel that the family who hounded Paul for years and made his young life a living hell... they're gone now. As Paul's friend, I feel it's time for him to let go of that part of his past. I know he has let go of it, and I wonder if it's counterproductive to dwell on it all over again. For me it's like; *that was a part of your life, but your story has moved on from there. They don't have to be mentioned in the same sentence as Paul Ferris all the time.*

I know this is a bold move within a true crime book. This isn't how they go. It's all about bravado and not having any emotion. I can accept that. You don't want to pick up a book about the mafia to listen to someone tell you that their transition from Italy to New York was terrible and they couldn't make many friends in the neighbourhood. Likewise, you don't want to pick up a gangland Britain book and hear someone saying they were gonna bump a load of people off, but felt sorry for them and took them for a cup of tea instead. But emotion and empathy are what make us human and there's a misconception that being beaten shows a weakness.

A danger is that I don't want Paul justifying any actions because of this family's bullying and I don't want the book to be an analysis of their impact on his life. It's an easy trap to fall into. You know, with the reader nodding along at how bad Paul was and it could have been predicted early on: *bullied kid turns bad shocker. Read all about it in Unfinished Business*. Paul was barely 10 years old when he was systematically kicked to shit every day. My heart and my writer's mind is telling me that they *didn't* make him who he is. Fuck them. They don't define him as a person. Bullies only exist through fear, and he isn't scared anymore. We talk about Blackhill and the kind of place it was... is this family of bullies not just a product of that, and a product of what their parents and their parents were before them?

Sure, we're defined by our actions; how we act and how we react and by what we say. We don't understand ourselves as humans, we don't understand ourselves as characters in a book. To be a proper victim of bullying, do you lose your identity and become one yourself? If that's the case, I know Paul rose above all that to become who he is today.

In this case, I've felt that by bringing them to the forefront of his story each time, he isn't exorcising them, he's keeping them there. He's keeping them inside and he's letting them define who he is or who he was. I didn't mean *don't mention them just to wind them up*. I get that there have been a lot of players in Paul's story and they're all going to be scanning this book for the juicy stuff – and most likely, surviving members of this family will read it.

As a writer, am I doing the right thing by going over it all again? I remember talking to Steve a while ago and asking if he discussed the family in his interviews. Steve couldn't recall exactly. I couldn't find a mention of them. I was getting a sweat on wondering how I could write Paul's story without mentioning them. I said something like, *They're the ones that caused it all. Where the fuck are they? They are what made him who he is!* And now that feels totally wrong.

I'm trying to convince Paul of this idea. I feel like I've spotted a revelation. I know the way he acted back in the day was very clinical and he saw everything 'as business'. That family beating him up – battering him, bruising him, cutting him, making him cry and live in fear was the most personal thing anyone could have done. It was robbing him of his personality because everything was replaced by anxiety. For the family, was it

58

personal or did they just see it as business? I don't know. It became as much a part of their lives as it was for Paul's.

He used to run away from them. It made it worse the next day. They hit him with hammers one day. This is grown men attacking a child with hammers – what the fuck's that about? He could easily have died then or any other time. He got to the point when he stopped running. It was pointless doing so. He started to accept his beating and go about the rest of his day. It would mean that they weren't out looking for him for a bit. And the important word here is that he accepted it. He was a kid and he had to accept that as part of his life and that's so fucking wrong and so fucking tragic. As a kid, the psychological aspect comes into it. It's not really worse than the physical pain because it hurts like hell. But it does go away. Psychologically, the pain increases by the day. It breeds, it consumes you.

'I'd really enjoyed school until I became a victim of those Welsh brothers. It was at that stage in my life that my mind was opening up to a different world to what I'd been taught about – rapidly leaving my infancy and entering an altogether differing state of reality. I was truly frightened because I was only 10 and had another two years of primary school in the sullied hands of them. I wasn't very physically well-built and I could only withstand so much of the beatings. I knew they only wanted to make me cry and I wouldn't do it.

They didn't like it that I would always try to defend myself. Pure and simple, they were just a bad bunch of vicious, evil bastards.'

I wasn't precious about it; I think I wanted to get Paul to buy into an idea. He got what I meant. He totally got it. Then the idea seemed less and less relevant the more we talked it over. I put it down to being just one of those writer things. I felt I'd put the bullies to bed, so to speak, by having the idea to remove them.

'I can remember the swollen testicles, the cuts, the bruises, the beatings and the hatred. I stopped running. I stayed to take the beatings and tried not to cry in front of my pals. But I did cry when I got home. The hatred and desperation built up inside me and I still get upset even recalling those early days. Bullying is incredibly powerful; far more powerful than adults really understand.

We need to listen to children. They don't often have the words to truly express the depths of their anguish, we don't realise what they're feeling or indeed have empathy with their continuing black turbulent emotions.'

We shared some difficult conversations. Paul was ok with me wanting to remove the family from his story, but left it up to me to decide. We could have gone with different drafts of the book, put them out to readers and got feedback. If you know Paul's story, you may realise they're not in and then nod along with us because you could see why they were left out. Sure, we'd hint at stuff. But – if you're new to Paul's story, you'd have no idea. We'd have erased them. In that sense, the technique would only have a chance of working if you already know his story and if you get that we've done it deliberately. When we got to the end of the book, it felt totally wrong to remove the opportunity of discussing an emotive subject.

'I really feel for anyone else in or that has been in that situation. It's fucking terrifying at any age to get bullied. How do you sit down with somebody whose kids are bullied at school? What do you tell them? Do you tell them to do what you've done, or do you tell them a crock of patronising shit that you don't even believe in yourself? Do you give them good advice, or what? And then it's back to that you stop bullies by beating the shit out of them. That's how they learn their lesson, not by talking to them about their feelings. We're all amateur psychologists though, aren't we? Everyone's got their own answer or their own method that worked. I've seen a lot of attempted rehabilitation in prison and I have to say, a lot of it is not that effective. But you know, it works for some and that's good. But in the playground is where the education is lacking. Most bullies do it because they know they can get away with it. Kids in schools don't pick on bigger ones – they lean on someone they're bigger than. It's been around for years and it will never stop. If there's one

*thing I can shove down a reader's throat here it's
– if you see that your kid is bullying another,
fucking well put a stop to it. Don't be soft. If
you've been bullied, you'll know the physical and
mental torture. That's the one way of stopping it.
Lead by proper example and be proud of them for
following your lead – don't be proud of them
because they can raise their fists. It's not fucking
cool.'*

So, what became of the Welshes? You may well
wonder...

BILLY FERRIS

Billy moved to Corby in Northamptonshire. I was left without my older brother and my dad was away. It was a lonely time for me. Billy had got out of Blackhill though – actually got out and created a new life and a new beginning, and then threw it all away by robbing a post office and getting nicked. You can take the man out of Blackhill...

While he was in doing his sentence, his wife was fucking around behind his back. Word got back to him. It's bad enough being banged up without having to worry about what your wife's up to; you need to know your relationship is safe.

Once he'd served his time, he was out drinking with a friend in the local social club one night:

'There he is. That guy over there.'

It's easy to turn the other cheek in a song or in a film, but not on the street. Or in this case, in a club. Billy couldn't sit there and not say anything. He went over and words were exchanged before they went out to the car park to sort it out. It was never going to end well. They were both carrying. Billy was in a bad way. Well, it was more than a bad way – he was as close to dying as he could get. He was an inch away from death. The other bloke came off an inch worse. It was a fight to the death and Billy came out on top.

Next day, he's nicked for murder. He's still lying there barely able to breathe. In court he didn't say a thing, offered nothing and was lifedoff to the big house. He could have told his side of it and the emotional stress he was under in that situation and it may have helped a bit. As a youngster, I wanted him to fight in his corner. But in time, I'd learn: he was just doing what you do. You don't grass, you don't point the finger. But... *really*? I was thinking it wasn't like he was giving someone in to the police, and the bloke was dead anyway. By saying he had no other choice but to fight and he had a knife pulled on him, as closer to self-defence than the mindless and motiveless killing of a random bloke. But what do I know?

He got out around 1990, after escaping while on a home visit. It was a comedy of many errors. He ended up in Blackpool, where I've got some good friends. And he got a room in this big hotel on the seafront. All good so far. But what he didn't know at the time was that an annual conference for chief constables was taking place. In the same fucking hotel! He must have thought the thousand or so coppers rocking up at the front door of the hotel were coming for him! Imagine the panic!

I got a phone call and booked a room under a snide name and had a look around the place. It was swarming with coppers. There was a notice board in the lobby about it being a conference and details of the night's speech. My first thought was to get Billy out of there before he became the topic of it. I caught up with him; he'd grown a moustache as part of a disguise. I think. It's the only reason why you'd want one, eh? Billy's got sallow skin and dark hair – it must be from the

McGinty side of the family. It was good to see him. But not good to see him in such a stressful situation. And with a moustache. I tried to calm him down; he was pacing the room and looking out the window every time he got to it. It just became a nervous tic – he wasn't even focusing on anything, really. And then he'd go to the little spy hole in the door and back to the window. The corridors were buzzing with police as well. Even when you're in a hotel room with the door locked and someone approaches, weirdly, you still think they're gonna try your door. Now imagine you're on the run and there's dozens of police toing and froing outside. I couldn't help but think he'd draw attention to himself just by being in the room if he wasn't careful. I was trying to tell him that he couldn't have been in a better place – there's no way on earth they'd expect a jail-breaker to be in the same hotel as a police conference. He'd have had a heart attack if I didn't get him out, though. It was time to act.

Blackpool is a bit of a home from home for me. There are always plenty of friends to call on in times of need. I gave my mate Paul Jonas a shout – he used to babysit Charlie Kray's boy, Gary. Gary had psychological problems, though. I wasn't convinced I was putting Billy in the best environment, but what can you do? He couldn't stay there and anywhere else seemed like it would be better for him. I used to give him money and he was always giving it away or going out to the arcades, but Paul was an absolute star and kept an eye on him the best he could.

All the family ended up down there one weekend. It was the first time we'd all been together since Billy had been away. And, as it happens, I couldn't make it down to see everyone so when I went down on the Monday to see Paul Jonas he said, 'Look, mate. Fuck the bill for the rooms. It's fine. Just sort the bar bill out.'

'That's very decent of you. How much is the bill?' I asked.

'Two grand,' said Paul. Straight-faced.

'Two *fucking* grand? For a bar bill?!' I thought he was joking, but...

'It's your Billy. He's nuts, man! Fucking *nuts*!'

What the fuck had he been drinking, *gold*? It wasn't just what he he'd been drinking – he was also dishing it out; rounds of drinks here and there – *here you go mate, it's on me*. Working the room like the captain of a cruise ship, talking to everyone. And that's cool – but *take* drinks, rather than give them away. It didn't register with him – it was all free, on the tab, and he just had no grasp of finances. He'd been locked away for 18-odd years, so you know, he was just cutting loose a bit. The bar itself was nothing special. If you've been to a typical Blackpool guesthouse, you'll know what I mean: untouched for years and I bet it's still the same now. So, there's the guy behind the bar, usually the only one in there, wiping the dust off the optics and glasses every so often and wondering where it all went wrong. And then there's Gary Kray in his white Japanese Imperial Commander's jacket with gold tassels. Did I not mention that earlier? Fuck me, it was a sight to behold. All it was missing was a few fucking medals and it wouldn't have looked out of place on the QE2. What with him in that and Billy meeting and greeting like the cruise ship captain, well, what more can I say? It was the most bonkers scene I'd ever witnessed.

As much as I could have died laughing if I'd let myself, I was disappointed. Billy had the jacket on at one point and I felt unappreciated. I was pulling strings to look after him – the young brother looking after big brother – and I couldn't tell if he was just taking the piss. He apologised for spending too much. We had a talk and I said a few things to him; a few home truths to clear the air. It worked and we were ok.

'You've lost your shit about finances, Billy. You enjoyed yourself, Mum enjoyed herself, Dad enjoyed himself. Everybody enjoyed themselves, but I'm gonna get you back for this. Big time. I'm paying for all this, man. Think about me for a bit, will ya?'

It would have been a much better speech if we were sat in a five-star hotel and I could've gestured to grand surroundings for effect. It loses its impact when it's in a virtually empty bar that's on its last legs with a would-be Japanese Imperial Commander sat at the bar ordering afternoon tea and deliberating on fruit scones or cheese – even though they never served afternoon tea. It wasn't a fallout or anything, just that he needed to know that he wasn't there for a long holiday – he was supposed to be 'under the radar'. In fairness, I was probably asking a bit much – who could really lay low in a place like that? You'd go insane within days if you didn't have a few distractions.

In the end, he turned himself in and got an extra two years for his trouble. Was it worth it? Probably. Considering the amount of time he's done since, there are not that many tastes of freedom and fresh air for him to remember.

DO ME A FAVOUR

I was a bit older when I went to visit Billy on my own. I'd just turned 15. Because of his predicament, I learned very early on that no matter what hurts your heart – don't go to prison because of it. Keep your cool, think before you react. Harsh as this may be, it is what it is. I didn't know then that I'd end up threatening the life of a copper who had a gun to my head and that my life story would be made into a film, though. Funny old world, eh? Fair enough, I'd threaten a copper in years to come, but with Billy it was like – *fucking well think before you do anything. Ever*. He killed a man for sleeping with his wife – it was the wife that was doing it, so she essentially fucked him over good and proper. Although... her lover was now dead. Swings and roundabouts.

Prison in the 1970s and '80s was fucking grim. I mean, as I was there as a visitor, I could see how bad the conditions were, but it still didn't seem to put me off a life of crime. What the fuck was that about? They take school kids into prisons now to show them what a shitty existence it is to stop them offending. Maybe I didn't see it that way. Don't worry, you don't have to yawn your way through me banging on about how harsh it was back then and how all prisons are like holiday camps now and blahhhh-blahhhh-*blaaahhhhhh*...

So, prison is a punishment, you lose your liberty, you hopefully get rehabilitated and you see the error of your ways. Society recognises that even prisoners have human rights now, and cells are (again hopefully) a bit more comfortable. Yes – comfortable. Outcry. *Daily Mail*. Shock, horror. Political correctness gone mad.

He was in Maidstone prison in Kent. He told me to follow this big lump of a man out of the visiting area when we were done.

So, once our visit ended, I did as I was asked and walked behind the big chap who turned round and said something in a thick Cockney accent. I had no chance of deciphering it. He probably thought the same when I replied. I did catch his name though: Bill. Cockney Bill, no less. What else could he be called?! We got out to the prison car park, where we shook hands and he beckoned me over to his car. I noticed that he was driving a red E-Type Jag with a soft top and he looked well minted; dressed as sharp as a razor. Was I impressed? I would like to find anyone who wasn't.

While sitting in the car, it became obvious that there was a communication problem and I started to talk slowly. I tried to soften my Glaswegian accent a bit, talking a bit more neutral to Cockney Bill. It seemed to work – he was nodding his head and smiling, but really – fuck only knows what he thought I was saying. Not only was he nodding away when I was talking, but he was writing things down on a pad with a pen. It was the equivalent to when you're talking to someone these days and they've got their beak in their phone and you know they're not listening. Cockney Bill seemed to be listening though... when I finished talking, he handed me the note and said I was to take a butcher's at it. A butcher's? In time to come my butchery skills would improve, but what the fuck he meant, I had no idea. A butcher's hook is widely accepted as cockney rhyming slang *now* – back then it was a foreign language. I looked down and the note got my head spinning:

2 x hot-water bottles – 1 red and 1 blue
1 btl whisky
1 btl vodka
2 oz hash
1 strip LSD

A shopping list! A prison fucking shopping list! Once I read it, Cockney Bill took out a wad of notes and counted out £300. He told me to give the list to someone who was gonna visit my mum in Glasgow. Or that's what it sounded like he said. He gave me a lift to the train station in Kent, then I headed back to Euston on the tube and then back up to Glasgow.

It was a big adventure of sorts for me and I didn't want to let my brother down. I wasn't in when the guy eventually visited my mum's house in Hogganfield Street. Our downstairs neighbours were Mr and Mrs Wilson and they also had a big family. They were nice and they let us use their phone to talk with Billy and my dad in prison. I have very fond memories of them and hope they are all doing well. They were brilliant – very kind of them to let us do that and I can't thank them enough for the decency and support that they had shown my mum during that turbulent time in her life. And, of course, they were nice enough to take in the package that arrived via Cockney Bill. God, if only they knew.

This surprise package was just that – a big surprise. It was several pairs of trousers that had a dozen or so buttons just on the waistband. And there were loads of jackets and shirts. I scanned through them all and realised they'd all once belonged to Billy – just a pity that they were a decade old and well out of fashion. You could make a mint from stuff like that these days – they'd be retro cool. There was a note inside with a phone number and another £300. I went straight downstairs to ask Mr and Mrs Wilson if I could use their phone. They agreed. I went through the farce of trying to communicate with Cockney Bill again. I had no idea what I was talking about either. It was worse on the phone cos there was no body language or lip-reading to make note of. The upshot, what bits I could make out; I was to buy the items listed and then I'd get instructions as to what to do next when I visit Billy.

I made contact with an older guy called Davie Moran, aka Davie McAuley, who I'd got to know through selling wheels, car stereos and custom speakers – basically stuff that the lads nicked from the stolen cars –and I got a few quid selling them on to him. He was a Blue Angel biker with a knack of fixing anything mechanical and I looked upon him as a big brother figure at the time. He was a sound bloke and someone who spoke his mind. I asked to speak to him and showed him the shopping list. He looked right back at me and smiled. He said he could sort it out and asked if I wanted to buy a car I'd shown an interest in some days before: an old two-litre Wolseley with all leather seats and, believe it or not, a fucking cocktail cabinet in mahogany finish in the rear. I'll say that again – the coolest car I'd ever seen… *with a fucking mahogany cocktail cabinet in the back.* Even if you kept it SORN you could open it up as a nightclub. We shook hands on £300 and off I went like I'd won the pools! In many ways it felt like I had. We were both happy to seal the deal and I went back to planning my next visit to Billy.

I originally thought that the hot-water bottles were… well, to be used as functional water bottles to keep my brother and his mate warm in their cell. What else would you use them for? I was about to find out. Different rules in prison, remember. One was filled with the vodka and the other with whisky. I was also instructed to put the hash and LSD in between the hot-water bottles and then tape them both up but keep the handles clear for throwing – over the prison wall at a certain time and a certain place where the outside garden party were working and would pick it up.

I got the hot-water bottles myself and then went back to see Davie the biker to see about the rest.

When I parked in his street in the Ruchazie area of Glasgow it was full of police and Davie was being arrested, so I just drove on a bit. I bailed out the car when I parked up cos I never had a driving license at the time. I stood at the top of the street and had 'a butcher's' at what was going on. It was a safe enough distance away. I saw Davie being let go from the police vehicle and headed down to his flat to see what the script was. He was cursing and swearing and throwing his anger about and then suddenly stopped and looked at me.

'Here. You'll need this,' he said – throwing me a crash helmet.

Now this was a big problem – I don't like bikes. Too dangerous. Cars, fine. Bikes, no. It didn't look like it was up for discussion as he fired up his two-wheeled beast. It's not much fun being on the back of a bike when the one in control is in a bad fucking mood. Talk about your life flashing in front of you – 'kin ell, Davie. He rode that bike like... well, like a stolen bike, as it happens. It probably wasn't, cos the police would've nabbed it, but we were ducking and weaving in and out of everything, before flooring it til we were miles away up near the famous Campsies. And that meant my plan to decline a ride home and to catch a bus or taxi was dashed cos we were slap bang in the middle of nowhere. If I'd been brought there on any other occasion, I'd be fucking worried. There was this wee farm house and around 15 or so motorbikes with some big dudes sat outside listening to music. I say listening to, but it's not like you could avoid it. It was like T in the Park had arrived early. There were dogs barking, beers on the go – all the standard things you'd expect from such a scene. It was a total clash of cultures... car chases and knife fights in the scheme on a Friday to this mad lot. Bizarre AF. And there I'd been actually wondering how and when I'd get home. This wasn't a flying visit. Other than the people I was introduced to that night, I was also introduced to weed and beer and vowed ever since that never again actually turns into 'never *ever* again'. Well, you know. How many times have you said that and you're back on it as soon as you realise you didn't die? It was a good night. I know that if not for Davie, these blokes would never give me the time of day. And I get that – we were from different worlds. I was really unsure at first though. I just followed behind Davie without asking too many questions. You don't wanna come across as an excited puppy; you just keep your cool and assess what's what. We headed over to the farmhouse and one of the other bikers who was definitely a double for whichever one in ZZ Top had the biggest beard, put his leg out across the door frame to stop me getting in. He was firmly propped up against it and there was no getting through.

'It's a club meeting, wee man. Club members only. You're not allowed in,' he said.

Fair enough. Davie didn't turn to try to get me in anyway. He'd have known the score. I stood and made small talk with ZZ Top. And then Davie appeared at the door, points at me and indicates me to come in and ZZ Top was none too pleased about it. What could I do? I just smiled until he moved out the way and said I wouldn't be long.

I was introduced to some of the other guys in there. Again, it was all way too out of my comfort zone, but we were there for a reason. Or so I thought. Davie had only really grunted at me so far, so I wasn't completely sure why I was there until he turned to the main guy and told him that I was after two ounces of hash and some LSD. And what he thought of that, fuck only knows. I was a young kid in an alien situation, but they were hospitable all the same. It was one of those things, after enjoying the craic over a few beers and when given the opportunity to tell all those petrolheads the story of how fast and hair-raising the bike journey up the hill was... well, they just shrugged. They laughed in the end and it was good banter. There was one in particular who called me a pussy under his beard, but failed to repeat it when my mate Davie glared at him – a biker's stand-off right enough, but there was no daft shenanigans to be had. I'm sure he was just a bit put out that I was there and I wasn't one of them. I agreed, but like, just go with the flow.

At one point I thought they had a dry ice machine on. I could hardly see anything and it was making me feel a bit wonky. I sat down on the floor to try to find some air before I noticed everyone doing joints and there were bongs everywhere, being passed around and – well, you know what must have happened. Of course I gave it a go. When in biker gang farmhouses, and all that. I took one puff and knew I was going to start coughing – right at that moment when the main guy asked me if I wanted anything else added to the shopping list. I tried my best to answer. I thought I was talking sense, but when I started to explain, it was like I'd had a fucking stroke. Davie started to copy what I was trying to say and I laughed... then he laughed... so he turned and asked me and I suppose the seriousness of the situation was completely lost on me –I had a fit of the giggles and couldn't stop. I couldn't tell if he was getting pissed off with me, but he couldn't fight the giggles for a second longer either. None of us knew what we were laughing about, but it didn't matter. It was a good ice-breaker. Once we calmed down, he asked me about all the stuff on the list again and asked me how I planned on getting it in to prison during a visit. I said it's not getting passed on a visit and was then asked to explain further. By this point, the smoke had cleared and all eyes were on me, intrigued. I felt uneasy going into the details of it all. I said I was not prepared to tell them where, when and how.

'Sorry, can't tell you,' I said.

Silence.

Then the whole room erupted in laughter, except for me as this was serious. Looking back now I can see how funny it was – the cheek of a young kid telling the main biker that in his own gang hut. The truth was more that I couldn't string a sentence together or think properly by then.

You know what? I ended up having a brilliant night there. The next day, I still had Davie's riding to contend with – which was a fucking ordeal with such a bad head – but I secured all that was needed on the list and the bikers never took a penny from me – a right nice touch.

Right. There was still a plan to execute. Clear head, young Ferris. I was running it over and over and over in my head cos I never wanted to let my brother down. I got a return ticket for one from Glasgow Central to London Euston and, from there, I'd get one down to Kent. If Mum had known what I was really doing she would never have made my sandwiches up for the journey. To me, it was a lot more than a journey – it was an adventure. No one other than me and Billy knew about it. It was a brilliant way of bonding with him – he may have been locked up and hundreds of miles away, but here we were doing a job together.

I think the reality of it hit me when I packed my bag for the overnight sleeper down to Euston and then Kent for the visit. I took my football kit out from my holdall and eased the hot-water bottles in, then put a towel, some clothes and my sandwiches in on top. I picked the bag up and weighed it up, you know, seeing if it was easy to carry. It always feels weird when you've got a bag full of dodgy stuff and you're the only one who knows about it. You start to walk differently and everything, so I knew I just needed to act as normally as possible. I don't remember much of the journey because I was going through the procedure so many times. I was probably a bit skitsy, but my interpretation is that I was focused. I knew I had a job to do and I was just playing it over: prison wall at 10.30am, third lamp post, launch the hot-water bottles over. Easy. Ish.

I was nervous, but I'd been through enough fear in my life. This was not something that could physically hurt me. I didn't need to be scared. I gained confidence in every step right up to the main marker – I could do this. I reached the third post. I got the water bottles out, drew my arm right back and launched it with all that I had. And I stood back and watched as it soared right over the wall in a perfect arc. Job done, I walked on towards the main gate to visit Billy. Tony Petch was serving time with him and we got to have a chat during the visit. They were grateful for the delivery – couldn't stop grinning. And that was *before* even sampling any of it! Tony was a mad one; he was an armed robber who once nicked Mike Yarwood's Rolls Royce to rob a jeweller's in Hatton Garden. He told me that he got more heat over nicking Yarwood's Roller than he did for actually robbing the jeweller's shop!

It felt good knowing that I'd completed my mission. For all it took a few seconds to do the job itself, I was imagining the hours of fun that package would have created for Billy and Tony. It had taken me on a bizarre adventure at the same time. It was things like that which made the visits enjoyable and took away that bitter taste when leaving a loved one locked up.

ARTHUR THOMPSON

Right. Before you start sighing cos you already know the history of gangland Glasgow, hang on a second. We need some context to my story and, if there are new readers, they'll not know what the fuck I'm going on about. To tell the story of Thompson, you need to know a bit of background to the city and to another bloke who was known at the same time.

So, Glasgow. Two men blazed the trail for gangsterism in the city. They more or less invented organised crime. Their names were Arthur Thompson and Walter Norval. And already you're wondering: *how the fuck can you rule Glasgow with names like Arthur and Walter?* You may well ask. As with everything like this, there is the real truth and the mythology. These blokes wouldn't be known if they hadn't made a name for themselves, but you always need to be careful with the facts. There are things that have been written, not only about these two, but the whole evolution of Glasgow's so-called underworld, and there's about as much campfire fodder as there are the real stories. There were so many big street-players around at the time, but you'd only think Glasgow was big enough for these two if you believe everything you read.

The old man was born in 1925 and Norval was born in 1928. They had their differences in that Norval was totally old school with the crimes he was known for and Thompson was, I suppose, more into the drug side and looking to move more with the times.

Like everyone within these pages, Norval ran with gangs and made a name for himself before drifting into the more serious side of protection rackets, pubs and clubs, holding up bookies and then into lucrative armed robberies. His first taste for that was in his mid to late teens when he held up a tobacconist shop with a gun. It was only a young girl who was working there at the time. Regardless of any criticism towards him for that, it was probably singled out as an easier hit to start with, and he progressed from there while doing time in and out of Borstal. He honed his skills and was a fucking handy fighter.

The war could have ended the careers of a lot of criminals. Famously the twins and Frankie Fraser managed to swerve it and Walter was no different. He was drafted, chinned people, escaped. He served a year and a half for carving a soldier's face up, but it meant avoiding the war. It was a small price to pay – he had real work to attend.

The history of organised crime in Glasgow after the Second World War threw up a dilemma for social sciences as well as the contentious issue of the flourishing black markets. My dad and his gang were well placed to exploit this in order to put food on the table. This wasn't youth disorder, running around and slashing each other – men were organising themselves to make a living from crime. There was a big difference.

Then, *The War of Norval's Ear* was a bit of a game-changer for Walter. I'm not taking the piss here, it's part of gangland folklore. A huge fucker called Mick Gibson wanted to get in on things and he had a slightly unorthodox approach to it – he'd muscle in on established areas and challenge the main man to a square go. And that was it; his plan would either work or get put on its arse. It's said he crossed paths with Norval in a bar in around 1963. Mick introduced himself and told Walter in no uncertain terms what he wanted and, this being Walter's patch, he wasn't gonna give it up without a fight.

It went to the floor with Walter gaining the upper hand, until Mick bit half Walter's left ear off. In retaliation, Walter tried to stab Mick's eyes out and it resulted in a stalemate situation. That didn't sit well with old Walt. He'd been challenged, he saw it off... but for him it wasn't quite over til the fat man screamed. Their bloody rematch was no contest for Walter. He caught Mick unaware and he had no chance against the frenzied attack. He was done in the neck, the head and body and only just survived. If that didn't secure his reputation, nothing would. Apart from doing someone like Mick Gibson, he had a battle scar to be proud of.

After his next stretch, Norval's Glasgow was a different place. This was the time when all the rehousing had taken place. All the total shithole slums that were overcrowded had been pulled down and all the new slums like good old

Blackhill were popping up. With his mob that became known as the XYY Gang, they hit fuck knows how many post offices and organisations through the 1970s. Payroll was where the big money was at and that's what they went for. Hospitals were the biggest payout, but anywhere with a sizeable workforce would be in his sights. They did dozens of shotgun raids – it wasn't about the massive one-off retirement jobs, it was decent bundles and they were doing it a few times a week.

The mob was brought to justice in 1977 after one of them, Paul Henry, got nicked and sung like a canary. There were four different trials going on at the same time; the crew members were given names like Mr X and Mr Y, and then the gang had a name to operate under. After loads of false starts, delays because of intimidation, threats, physical attacks and arson attacks on the High Court in Glasgow, Norval finally got handed a 14-year stretch. It was the end of an era for him in many ways because Glasgow changed even more the next time round. He may as well have been released onto the fucking moon for all the use he'd be as a gangster. And that's no disrespect. The city itself was the same, but the way criminals worked was on a totally different level now. He was a hard man; a fighter. His name was made on the streets, not the way the new breed fought. It was all about drugs and with that came multi-million pound deals and lives mean fuck all when that much is at stake. A dispute is finished with a bullet, rather than a black eye.

He was a typical battler. His last court battle was a daft one where he admitted the possession of cannabis for his arthritis. His last personal battles were ones that you can never really walk away from: bowel cancer then lung cancer before he died of pneumonia August, 2014. He was 85. Not a bad criminal legacy for someone who started out nicking and selling potatoes and coal before he was 10. He was one of the originals; a man the streets will never forget.

Norval and Thompson's criminal careers ran almost in parallel, but surprisingly they never overlapped. Thompson started out with protection rackets, hitting up local businesses for money in return for their windows not being smashed overnight. Yep, you guessed it – anyone who didn't pay up would start the next day sweeping up and, as if by magic, Arthur would appear at the door to offer his services to the 'grateful' shopkeeper. With his own gang to work with, they used to do bank jobs; blowing safes and making off with the loot like something out of a black and white movie. I always say I never want to glamorise crime, but who wouldn't want to blow up a safe? Just that once, to see what it was like, eh? His first sloppy mistake was that he dropped a set of keys outside a country property when they were counting up and they were traced right back to him. It was a costly one – he did four years of bird for it but used to his advantage, building up his rep, learning and networking.

Like Norval, he was a snappy dresser and was every inch the archetypal businessman. He knew you'd always get taken a lot more seriously if you looked the part. There was an eerily strange similarity to gangs like the Krays and the Richardsons in London. They were into the protection rackets, moneylending, bookies, clubs and scrapyards collectively, whereas Thompson had them all up in Glasgow singlehandedly. He'd take anything by extreme force and didn't think twice about blowing shit up. And speaking of the Krays, they used to bring him in as a freelancer to do their dirty work – that's how hardcore he was. Or that's how hardcore *I* was because old man Thompson brought me in to deal with stuff down in London on his behalf years later. He must've recognised a bit of himself in me, eh?

With his moneylending business, he'd crucify anyone who didn't pay up. I mean *literally*. The word is that in those early days, making a name for himself, he'd fucking crucify them by nailing them to a door or to the floor. His portfolio also included pubs, dance-halls, betting shops, gaming clubs, car salesrooms and a timber yard as well as all the usual extortion stuff. Thompson's game-changer came in the mid-60s when he killed two men by ramming their car off the road. They'd been giving shit to one of the bookies he was protecting, and that was seen as a personal attack. If you're protecting someone, you need to make sure that they *are* protected; otherwise you lose all credibility and respect. If you couldn't run your own protection racket properly you may as well pack up and leave town and Thompson was never gonna do that. He drove after them in his Jag and caught up with them quick enough. He had one thing on his mind and the other car ended up smashed into a wall. The two men were killed instantly: James Goldie and Patrick Welsh. Unluckily for Thompson, there were witnesses and he'd end up on trial for double murder.

Another similarity we shared was a feud with the family of nutcases I was having problems with. What started out as a random altercation at the bookies triggered a relentless grudge resulting in years of bloodshed between the two clans. Sound familiar? In a revenge attack, three of the brothers planted a bomb under Arthur's car. He used it to drive his mother-in-law home the next day, but the car blew up before he even got it into first gear. His mother-in-law was killed. Her name was Maggie Johnston – I don't think the media have ever mentioned that. Arthur escaped without a scratch. It was obvious who was behind it and they were soon picked up and remanded for trial. Bizarrely, it went to court the same time Arthur was on trial for the double murder – both at Glasgow High Court, so he was defence as well as a prosecution witness simultaneously. His own trial fell through when a witness (non-copper) disagreed with the other witness's (a copper) account and said it wasn't Thompson who was seen driving the car. It was a first for a Scottish court – not proven. It was strange, mainly because Thompson hadn't influenced the trial in any way and he walked free. What was even more peculiar was that *the family who'd bombed his fucking car and killed his wife's mother* also walked free because Thompson kept schtum in court. So, it seems all were lucky that day... well, apart from the ones that had been needlessly killed and saw no justice. But everyone else was lucky, eh? People thought Arthur must have had something in mind for them. It's been said that he was totally unmoved by the murder of Maggie. I can't really comment on that. Maybe he was saving face, showing that she was an unfortunate casualty and that he'd sort it out. Only he will know the reasoning.

Rita Thompson was fucking moved alright, and she bided her time. After her mum was killed, she smashed her way through the front door of the family's house and stuck one of their wives (I think it was the wife of the one who Arthur had killed). I've no idea of the ins and outs. With stuff like this, it's what you hear on the streets. It sounded more like a frenzied and not-so-well-planned attack. She was after revenge and got it. She also did time for it. I think this was around the time Arthur was away for his involvement in a warehouse robbery.

It was always the long game for Arthur. Putting the time in was an investment to retire on. He was clever and progressive and saw the value in taking the younger upcoming types, like me for instance, and nurturing them. With his reputation well and truly secure, he could've dined out on that alone for the rest of his days, but he was interested in growing his business all the time.

DECISIONS, DECISIONS

I left school without qualifications. I didn't sit any because I'd missed maybe a year with being in hospital with psoriasis. When I'd gone back to school I was a year behind but a year older, so when they were gonna do exams for the summer, I was 16 the November before it and I just thought, I'm 16, I'm not doing this. I'd encourage my own kids to sit exams cos I know the importance of them now. Back then, it wasn't so much their importance, it was their irrelevance.

I hadn't consciously sought out my criminal career path then. Far from it. I was just happy with the fact that I was 16 and wasn't going to school. There wasn't a plan, but that was the first decision! The second decision was influenced by my mum and dad. The kind of, *You're big enough to get a fucking job, you're not gonna lie in bed all fucking week* influence that most kids have needed at least once in their life.

I got my first job as a van boy for Scottish & Newcastle Breweries, in their Waverley Vintners offshoot which did spirits and wines. I remember the green overalls with the big gold badge and I thought, *fucking great*! It was pretty hard graft up and down the stairs to the cellars. Sometimes you had good drivers and sometimes bad and I'm not talking about their driving skills. I mean, some would be like, 'Right. There's sixteen cases to go there,' and they'd pull out the fucking newspaper and let you get on with it! And there were others

90

who'd give you a hand. There was this bastard, can't remember his name, he was always shouting, 'Are you not finished yet?!' and it was really fucking annoying. I'd barely have started when he'd be getting impatient. Even if I had to do four fucking sets of stairs, I'd get it done but just not necessarily in three minutes. There was one time when his attitude was just too much for me and I reached the end of my tether. I kicked the four boxes off a trolley down the stairs when he turned his back. It was the fastest I'd ever seen him move! He was saying 'grab this' and 'hold that' and he pulled this plastic bin, and told me to shut my eyes and turn my head. A few cases of whisky went in the bin, which I apparently didn't see. He had to fill a report out and he's telling them what happened and I'm thinking, *fucking arsehole*!

Going out the door, it was like, 'Keep your fucking mouth shut, young man.'

It was my turn to wash the van that day. I got the power hose out and I got him with it 'by accident'. I knew I'd got him cos I heard him scream, then he came around and hit me. Someone from the office saw us and I was asked to go in.

'We're not having any bullying in here, tell us what happened, what did he hit you for?

'I dunno, I sprayed him. Accidentally. He thinks I did it deliberately, so it was just one of them things,' I said.

They got him in and he told an entirely different story. He said I was lazy and that was only the second time I'd washed the van, apparently. So they decided no further action. The two of us got let out at the same time and we were walking down the corridor. It was one of those moments where you know they're gonna say something. He just couldn't keep his fucking trap shut.

'You're lucky you kept your mouth shut, wee'un.'

'Am I? *Really*? And how the *fuck* do you get that? You do that again and you're getting *this*!' I snarled. I took a blade out.

'What the fuck you doing with that in work?'

'It's for cunts like you. You're a lazy bastard,' I replied. It was gonna kick off at work, but I was getting £180 a week; good wages at the time. I gave my mum around half of it, something like that.

One Friday, I heard the beep of a car horn outside. It was annoying cos I was still in bed. I took a look out the window and saw a big fucking flash BMW. I didn't know anyone with a BMW, but they beeped again. Then my mate's at the door. He had a beamer on his face as well as a beamer on the road.

'Is that your BMW? How did you get it, did you nick it?'

'No, I bought it,' he said.

'Fuck off! How much?'

We made our way upstairs and he told me he'd paid a couple of grand for it. We got to my room and sat down.

'Look. We want somebody to do a bit of driving. All you do is sit on the corner. Easy work for a good driver like yourself,' he said. But he counted out five hundred quid and put it on the edge of my bed as he said it.

'What's that for? I can't take that.'

'Well I'm not taking it back, so let me know when you're ready,' he said, smiling.

What a bastard! I knew I had a job already. So did he. But come on... And then right as I was sat looking at the money, my bedroom door swung open and it was my mum. I bundled the cash away before she knew what was going on but it was a close call.

Monday morning came. I got up ready to go to work, overalls on, Mum made sandwiches and then the dilemma: do I go left or right out the gate. Left was where the temptation was and right was staying on the straight and narrow. I remember just walking down the stairs, out the gate, and going right. My mate was parked up at the top of the street, where the van used to sit, he had the same grin on his face; a £500 grin... And that was it. From that day, that was it.

It was around 1980. The job in question was a jeweller's shop. They used to go and look in the shop window. Every tray in the window had a tray number and every tray number had a value. The highest value would be in their sights. One was armed with a sledgehammer and the other with a pickaxe handle. There was one shop that they'd been after for a while. It was in a shopping precinct and I thought I could do it but there'd been a few unsuccessful attempts already. In the end, we took the whole window out. We had gardening gloves, goggles and a postman's sack and we just got the whole lot in – cleared the whole window display in one go.

From something like this, if there was say £20k worth of stuff, what you'd do is half that to 10 grand, then divide it by three! That's what it was worth. People were getting big sentences for stealing at the time – it was an '80s thing to steal like that because of the amount you could make in one single blag. It didn't need a shitload of planning or gangs and all the rest of it – it was essentially a smash and grab. And doing it in smaller mobs meant there was more money to be had. I was fully aware I was doing wrong, but it was a month's wages, without any drama, without working like a dog every day. The temptation was too much for me – I actually pretended to go to work for about three months.

I had a few friends from secondary school that opened up the other parts of the city to me. There were kids like Jim Kelly and Bernie Gallagher, people who were a bit rebellious in their own right. The times that we weren't chasing the birds, we were probably taking solvents and beer. I wasn't too keen on the beer but the solvents were alright – some things click with you and others don't. I think if there were drugs available to us, I would've probably given it a try. If you did solvents you would have done drugs and that was a fact. Let's not get on our moral high horse here; we were bored teenagers on a housing scheme in Glasgow and were typical as fuck. I missed the drug scene when I was growing up. I can understand how somebody could get caught in it and it's a blessing that I didn't. Besides, there were loads more exciting things to get hooked on at the time. Life was about getting into mischief. It wasn't always totally legal mischief, but it's just what was going on at the time. I'm a big fan of The Jam. I think to sum up the mood at that time, you could quote Weller's lyrics to say 'Life is a drink and you get drunk when you're young' – it's exactly how we rolled back then. I remember that song from the late '70s and it was probably when I was heading into my teens. It was great back then, but looking over the lyrics now, they resonate so much with what my life was, or what life was for many of us. Very poignant.

PAUL FERRIS: AN OPEN LETTER

Hopefully what you are about to read comes from me – your future self. I suppose, I see this as a unique way in which to show that even though you are still a young lad at 16, you are old enough to understand where you are heading in life. Even advice from Dad went in one ear and out the other. Pay attention – stay sharp and use the skills of survival that you've learnt so far.

Not many kids at 16 years of age listen. Sometimes I want to give you a shake, but most of the time I want to shake your hand. But you will realise that this path you're on is not for you. It holds no medals, personal achievements or even an accreditation from school. Both you and I know it's all about how we learn to survive on the streets from now on in. Let's just call it the university of life and you're in your first year of study. The place you are right now, reading this, locked up, is just the start of something else too.

That bitter taste you've become familiar with is called revenge. Be careful of feeling the need to administer any forms of retribution cos it may well escalate into a lifetime battle that we both know we can do without.

Life is not just a simple set of hypothetical questions. It's up to you to make it – to discover your end goal and get there. Your destination and path is in your own hands. Live your life well – free from revenge, free from prison and do something so unique that makes you stand out in a crowd. Do what you have to and, more importantly, stay alive to tell the tale to your grandchildren.

Be a lion, son, and never be a sheep. Always do the right thing – only you will know best in the end. Never give up what you believe in and work hard to achieve something else in life other than a prison number. The choice is yours. I know you can do it and I know you're strong enough to get to where you want to be.

INTO THE SYSTEM

My foray into the prison regime is well documented. There aren't that many prisons I haven't lived in, really. The amount of books like this I've read with tales of *how good we had it in HMP Wherever...* it's not like they're making it up, it's just that you make the best of a shitty situation. You can either take it on the chin and get on with your punishment and still live a life, or let the whole thing bring you down and destroy you. I think time inside is only as bad as you create it: power through and don't show them that it's really doing you in. Cry on a night if you need to – when no one can see or hear, cos any weakness shown in there is a big fucking mistake.

My first sentence was one of those short, sharp shocks you used to hear about that was supposed to prevent you from reoffending and scare the life out of you. I'd already had the life fucking scared out of me anyway, there was nothing left in me to scare. That's how I looked at it. And I actually enjoyed it. People will wonder, *how could you enjoy something like that?* but that was me making the best of my own shitty situation. I was there cos I'd fucked up and got caught. It was no one else's fault but my own. I could cry about it or fucking well get on with it. I enjoyed the marching, I enjoyed the discipline. I saw some incredible scenes there. It was fascinating: total silence in a dining hall before anybody was allowed to sit down. This was a hundred or so kids, all of them potential career criminals. Then you heard that one click from the clock, exactly on the hour, and that was it. If everyone wasn't there and silent, you didn't get fed. Then the marching and all the rest of it – as mesmerising as it was surreal. That first stint lasted for 12 weeks, then you were out and back on the streets, fit as fuck. I didn't smoke, drink, nothing, just did what I had to do.

I didn't think there was any real attempt to stop people from reoffending while in there. I can only speak from my own experiences. The next step up was the remand centre for young offenders awaiting trial in Longriggend; the equivalent to a university. You met others from different areas and it was just one big networking exercise. Most of the lads in there had already been to Young Offender Institutions such as Glenochil, which housed prisoners serving six months to life. From there, you're through the YOIs and, before you know it, you're a young man and held in an adult prison surrounded by your mates. Young offenders were kept separate to the other inmates in Bar-L, on the top floor, in D Hall. This was because Barlinnie was an adult prison and not a YOI.

I was in there for nicking a car. I never knew there were four gears and I burnt the clutch out. As you may have guessed, I didn't have any formal lessons and I didn't actually pass my test until I was 21. By then, I could've done it with my eyes closed, but up until, you just learned how to drive by... well, by first being in stolen cars and seeing what was what. Thinking back, it was Pickles who taught me to drive. He was a right character – he used to smash palettes up and remove the big wooden blocks in the middle of them and tape them to his shoes. He'd be walking round with them on like a dodgy Marc Bolan from car to car. I was driving quite well in my early teens, so by the time I got to 16 I was pretty decent, but it didn't stop me from getting nabbed. Although saying that, it hadn't been a high-speed car chase or anything even remotely dramatic. One of the lads had abandoned a car and I'd been all over it and going through the glove compartment looking for goods. They've dumped it, so I'm taking it. They just used to run them into the ground for 10 minutes or so and fuck off once they got bored. I'd come along and get seconds on it – anything left was there for the taking. The guy who took it gave me the 'key'. He was a couple of years older than me and gave me a crash course on how to move the gears before he did off. As I looked up from having my beak in the glove box, a police car approached. I knew I couldn't outrun them so I just started the car up and fucking drove off, or I should say *crunched off* and that was it. Busted pretty much immediately and with nothing to show for it. Annoyingly, I was charged with stealing the vehicle. I was a bit put out by that. Not that I was claiming to be totally innocent, but technically, I hadn't stolen the car. Someone else had nicked it, I'd got seconds on it and that's not a real offence.

When I spoke to the lawyer about it, he was a court-appointed bloke called, wait for it... Peter Forbes. Auld Forbesy, I could tell from the off that he knew his shit. And speaking of which, he could obviously smell a bit of bullshit. He said he'd heard lies and excuses from people who were a lot more experienced in the system than me. So, I didn't have to go all-out *woe is me* with him, it would have been a pointless charade – I could tell nothing would get past this fucker.

'If you've done it, tell me and we'll sort something out. If you've not done it, also tell me.'

When I explained to him that the charge sheet specified that I'd stolen the vehicle from this address, I said I hadn't.

'So tell me the story.'

When I'd gone through it all, there was a bit of a pause.

'Well, we'll plead not guilty to that,' he said.

I felt like I had the right support around me from day one, in that respect. All I had to do now was get on with my remand until it went to court. What could go wrong, eh? Nothing. At first.

I felt *welcomed* into the system – if that's the right word to use. I walked in there and people were like, *How's things? Do you need Mars bars, sweets*? and all the rest of it. And that's when I met Joe Hanlon's brother, Paul. We just clicked immediately and became lifelong friends. Not long into my stay there, Paul kicked off while in the dinner queue. You get a steel tray with three spaces on it for your grub; one for your soup, one for your main meal and one for your dessert. In a typical Oliver Twist moment, somebody asked for more. Thing is, it's other prisoners that are giving the food out, not like screws running everything, but there was a screw stood there in charge of the hot plate in the kitchen. So when the lad asked for more, the inmate serving said, 'You've got enough,' acting like a screw, or thinking he's a screw cos he's got a fucking white jacket on. It was a bit pathetic, really – totally fucking pointless. So then next thing I know, Paul Hanlon shoved his tray into the bridge of the guy's nose and broke it open. I'd never seen anything like it... it was just hanging there, flapping. And then it all kicked off, and everyone threw their dinners around the room. It was mental. There was a bloke who we all knew was gonna get smashed up in the exercise yard later, so it was a prime opportunity to just do him there and get it over with quicker. I had my tray of food, so I frisbeed the thing over at him – yeah... then it missed and hit a screw right on the side of his napper. Luckily, he didn't see me and he'd have no way of knowing who it was with all the shit going on. That is, until that fucker who'd been serving the food grassed me up and I got dragged all the way to my cell on the top floor. They gave me another kicking when we got there. There's nothing you can do in that situation other than go to the ground, try to use a wall to protect yourself and wait it out until they decide to stop. It was a fucking terrible position to be in, but that's the way it is. But this one screw hoofed me right in the bollocks and I've never felt pain like it. The kind of *pass-out pain* that only a kick in the stones can produce.

'I hope you go back and tell your wife or your girlfriend how you fucking beat up young boys!'

And they all stopped and walked. They were embarrassed. Really though, I'm not a big physical guy anyway, but when I was 16 I probably looked about 12. They had a right to be embarrassed.

The cops were called and they came up to charge me for assault on the screw. It was like prison Cluedo: Ferris, in the dining room, with the tray. And that was how easily stuff could happen in there; any slight thing could be taken out of context and, before you know it, you're in the frame for shooting JF-fucking-K. All I'd been trying to do was even the score and crack that inmate on the head. I just kept wishing I was home, away from all this mounting shit. A freak accident was on its way to becoming assault and I was only in there on remand while waiting to go to court for the fucking car thing. And, bearing in mind that I'd only been in there for five minutes before all this went off, it's no wonder my card was marked as a bit of a troublemaker.

You know, life's full of regrets and you just have to get on with it and deal with the consequences of your actions. I wasn't all *woe is me*, but yeah, looking back and knowing it was rifling the car's glove box that was the cause to being there... you know what I mean. I'm not sure if the regret at the time was getting caught or actually doing it. All I know was that I was glad I had friends in there. You show your friendship in different ways when locked up and I had all the tobacco and the sweets I could've wanted.

I went to court three weeks later and got told more or less to not do it again. It felt like I'd been locked up for no reason. That was it? There was a social worker's report by some bloke and the stuff that Peter Forbes said, then three weeks of remand to just walk. What the fuck was that about?

THUG LIFE

I ended up living over at our Cath's in Barrowfield for a wee while. There was too much heat at my mum's and I didn't like either having to lie to her about things or have the polis round the door. It just wasn't fair all round. Barrowfield made Blackhill seem posh. I used to either have a jog along to Blackhill on a night or get the bus. The other thing about it was, my sister stayed on this invisible borderline between two of the main gangs; The Torch and The Spur. Then, right in the middle of them – 159 Stanford Street – us. Fucking no-man's-land. So, if you walk out and turn left, you're in The Torch; turn right, you're in The Spur! Fucking hell. As was the norm, there was a gang at each side and they'd frequently meet up in the middle or invade the other, and beat the living shite out of each other. I never interfered with either – you can't ride two horses with one arse, can you? They respected me and I respected them. I was just a tourist there anyway; I wasn't there long enough to have to pick a side. I'd still never let my guard down though, I'd always be carrying. It's just how it was cos you never knew what might happen and you didn't want to get caught out. I knew most of the lads from each gang – not as friends, but we all knew each other from sight. With all that going on, it certainly kept me on my toes. It was better to be a bit jumpy round there rather than complacent. I suppose this was why I seemed to jog everywhere

– you were less likely to get jumped if you were running. But sometimes I felt double-vulnerable. You know, all this gang business was about which street belonged to which gang and there I was, unaffiliated to either and walking through two territories any time I left the house. There was always the threat of attack and the odd reminder that I was one against many would always come my way every now and then. But it was their fight, not mine. I couldn't care less about their half of the street.

Luckily, I was honing my skills and was becoming more and more capable. My reputation was growing. This was helped a lot by the fact that I started retaliating against the Welshes. Not only that, I was attacking them at any given opportunity as well. In turn, the Thompsons were getting to know what was happening to the Welshes, so they got to know who I was – I was doing all the people that they didn't want to be doing. I mean, let's not beat around the bush: the Thompson's could do fuck all against the Welshes and they all knew it. In our part of Glasgow, word travelled quickly. I never knew about the politics and I was never fucking interested. Whatever it was, I was like a one-man war machine taking scalps whenever I could. After years of violence against me, once I realised they were human (well, kind of) and could bleed, I knew they weren't indestructible. I had a lot of anger towards these fuckers. They knew it, I knew it, *everyone* knew it. It was obviously never going to end naturally. I went from someone who didn't like violence to not giving a fuck. I think that's what set me on that path. People would think, *He's fucking mad* and maybe I was, but what is sanity? I call it the University of Life, what you learn on the streets. It first started when a few of them attacked me with hammers – they were cracking them into my head and I just kind of lost it and zoned out. It was like I switched the pain off and just started laughing. It really freaked them out. They stopped what they were doing and didn't know how to handle it. I'm not too sure I knew. It was a real *dark as fuck new Joker from the Batman movies* scene, but it worked. It worked very well. There was a shift in power that started from then on. I could see there was fear in their eyes. Once I saw that, I knew they were mine. There'd still be clashes, still loads of clashes. But it's a lot different when you know you stand more of a chance.

Thug life, back then, before it became a Tupac Shakur tattoo, was something kids wanted – it was an aspiration. I don't think most of them were ever cut out for proper stuff we all ended up involved with. They were still going to school and doing their homework. They'd scrap with a kid from a different street and then sit next to him in class and borrow a fucking pen off him. For a lot of kids though, it's all there was cos there were no youth clubs and all the rest of it. Thugs were not street-players; they were dabblers, they'd wear a scar like a medal. Wear it with pride by all means, but then leave the comfort of your own street and see what it's like up against a proper team. I'm not knocking them. Many became street fighters from those earlier days. I think for many it was a lifestyle thing – something to be a part of and we all know there's a sense of belonging with being part of a gang. It was a time to find their feet.

The street talk then was stuff like saying Mars bar to mean a scar and, if you'd been done over, you were *a seconder* cos you'd come off second best in a fight.

By the '70s Glasgow was a PR nightmare. There was a *Nationwide* thing on the BBC about the gangs and it was even referred to as Little Chicago. I talk about media myths throughout this book and stuff like this is a classic example. *Little Chicago* – are you for fucking real? In 1972 there'd been 12 murders in Glasgow compared to 968 in Chicago. Hardly a cause to link the two together, but that's the press for you. I think it always got written about and reported on cos no one could understand it all. I'm by no means qualified to do that either – leave it to the professors. But why was Glasgow so different? There wasn't really the same level of 'problem' in other cities in Scotland. This is what had all the academics scratching their heads.

The thuggish behaviour has been linked to domestic violence cos it's all that the kids saw in the home and they learnt from it. A *sort that problem out first and you'll sort the problem out on the streets* thing was uttered amongst the authorities. That may be true, but it's easier said than done. Another and more bizarre way of sorting the problem out came in 1968. The singer, Frankie Vaughan, helped organise a weapons amnesty in Easterhouse. He'd heard about gang violence when he played a gig up here and helped to build a new community centre by putting money into it. Now that was a fucking nice thing to do. Some of it may have been a publicity thing, but pop stars aren't always in it just for the PR. He was brought up in Liverpool and was known to have ran with gangs in his time – it was pretty ground-breaking stuff. I don't know if his actions had much of an impact, but the Easterhouse Project was a step in the right direction and highlighted a need.

There's been some really good movies made about gang culture in Glasgow. *Small Faces* by Gillies MacKinnon about Tongland in the '60s and *NEDs* by Peter Mullan set in the '70s. I love Peter and his work. The film was close to his heart cos he was part of the gang, the Young Car-D when he was growing up.

'I remember consciously thinking, *Fuck it*. I honestly believe that for a lot of kids it's as simple as that. No initiation, just someone saying: 'Come and hang around with us'. Before you know it, you're identifying with them and graffiti-ing walls – it gives you a label and, weirdly, a sense of belonging,' he said.

I found this quote from a mother in Barrowfield in the 1970s:

'It used to be a scheme where you could walk in safety. But now you take a chance every time you walk down the road. We used to go out every Saturday night, now you are scared to cross the doorstep. There are two gangs in one street, the Torch and the Spur, and when they are on the prowl life's just not worth living.'

And then in 1977, police in Glasgow launched an urgent investigation cos of stuff that was going on between The Torch and The Spur in Barrowfield. It seemed that they'd got their hands on guns. If this is true, it's a massive leap. Was it about actually shooting each other or just the kudos that they had a gun? The legend goes that a gun was found to be inscribed with *Torch kill for fun* on the barrel and *To Spur from Torch* was on another. If we believe that this was going on, it was a significant step up from fighting in the street. What we thought was street rivalry – even if it was just a bit of *boys will be boys* shit on a weekend – was now a deadly game. As the saying goes, you don't bring a knife to a gun fight. The stakes on the street were raised and there'd be no going back from it.

AN OFFER I COULDN'T REFUSE

There was a point where two situations came together to lead me in another direction. Ian 'Blink' McDonald was robbing jeweller's shops and we'd arranged to meet up in a local pub. The second situation was that I had some jewellery to shift and I was asked to take it to Arthur Thompson who'd buy it. The meeting place for both was the Provanmill pub; Thompson's place. Thompson junior was there. I tried to keep a low profile cos I just couldn't be arsed with any big fanfare and shenanigans. You know when you can sense getting dragged into a conversation with people who've had a few drinks, but you have no interest in it? Well, that. But they made a big deal of getting me a drink and stuff. I didn't want one. Arty was loud and boisterous. He probably thought he was buying me a drink I couldn't refuse. He loved to let everyone know he was there. Then it became more or less another offer, *We know what you're doing with the jewellery and all the rest of it, but you could earn a bit more if you want to* – and then – *Torch this guy's motor for us.* And I'm thinking, *What's this crackpot on about?* You know, you can tell when someone loves talking the talk and that was certainly the impression I got with him. You learn how to deal with people, and you smile and you let them say their thing and everyone goes home happy: he thinks you think he's Mr Bigtime and you think he's someone who talks for the sake of making a noise.

But then he turned around and goes, 'That'll be a thousand pounds if you're interested.'

Fucking well done! Two quid for a gallon of petrol! Done. What's next? I mean, there were so many little jobs like that, it was unreal. That's just how people would make money – certainly how I did, anyway. Little jobs here and there soon mounted up. It got to the stage where I could go back at any point and it was like a shopping list of crime; this one needs that sorting out, and this one needs to be rammed off the road, this money needs to be collected, he needs to be given a message, that property needs sorting out and whatever else. I thought, *I'm gonna see how much I can actually do*. It was just fucking nuts! But I was brought up to believe that you prove your worth and that's what I was trying to do. But there's a big difference between working *for* somebody and working *with* them. Working for someone you're on wages, working with them you're earning profits; so I ended up as a glorified debt collector. We helped out with that and we got a couple of grand every week. It was like Christmas every day having such an expendable income as that. A lot of people lost their friends through it, lots lost their lives through it, but a lot of people changed their lives as well through it. Money's not everything, but it is when you haven't got it. Bearing in mind that I didn't have many legitimate job offers and didn't have the qualifications to get any, I was drifting into something I found easy and that paid well. What more could a youngster want?

I was an obvious choice for the old man because I was exactly the type of youngster he needed in his firm. I'd earned my reputation quickly. For me, it wasn't about who he was or anything like that. To me it was about earning money and Thompson provided a way of doing it – an easy way of doing it. I'm not gonna downplay him though – he had a reputation and having that connection was never going to do me any harm. It went hand in hand – I was picked out cos they knew my reputation and what I could bring to the table. Blink wasn't really interested in working for Thompson.

He was like, 'Why the fuck's he want kids working for him when he reckons he's the fucking Godfather of Glasgow? It's bollocks.'

And I was more, 'Let's see what might happen, eh?'

It was just a *Wanna make some money*? conversation in a pub.

Was it an active decision? No.

Was it a conscious decision? No.

Was it a bad decision? Who knows? I'd rather find out than not find out. You've got to knock on every door, eh?

REG McKAY

There was a social worker's report by some bloke and the stuff that Peter Forbes said...

The first time I met Reg he was the senior social worker for Blackhill. It was a prominent, unforgiving job. We eventually called him the *Champion of Lost Causes* because of the kind of person he was; a one-off, someone who gave a shit. In fact, at that time and being in the system at an early age, he was the only one who did give a shit. It throws you in that situation when you find out someone cares, cos the care system back then was built on anything but care. When you meet someone like Reg, it restores your faith. In time, the others would always let you down, but not him. With Reg, nothing was 'just a job.' He went above all that because, at the time, the system wasn't really much of a system. Not then. Complaints or whatever were all just brushed under the carpet; but Reg was somebody who took a lot of things on board. I was 16 and into the second day of my three-week remand at Longriggend for nicking that car. I'd not had any dealings with him prior to that. It was good just to get out the cell and actually meet him, what with everything that was going on at the time. It was a weird situation to be thrown into, then the dinner time riot – it all happened so quickly before there was any real initiation into the system.

114

I met police officers, prison officers, court people, legal people... it seemed endless. In that respect, all I would have been to Reg was another face from the scheme. He'd seen my type before as well. I remember him saying something along the lines of, *You'll end up in prison if you keep going on like you are* kind of thing. And that was just a typical thing people like him said to people like me. He was legally bound to work with me because I was from Blackhill – his jurisdiction. So he was tasked with writing a report. He had to visit my mum at home and make sure there was a home for me to return to and that kind of thing. It was basic information, I think, and a pretty standard thing to do for anyone new to being locked up. I suppose much like your dental or medical records, that information then follows you around. There was no need to do any of it again unless there was a family house move. I was still in school at the time, so there were children's panels and all kinds of professionals who had to read through stuff and confer and nod and all the other things they do.

Reg's face was just another one in a long list.

LITTLE GREEN BAG

A blood-curdling scream broke everything. It saved my life. Anne-Marie. If she'd not been there, I'd be dead.

Her scream brought total disarray all over again by the time it had finished. It seemed to go on for a while but it was over in probably three seconds.

They'd been watching the place for hours. They knew we were in there. We'd been shopping and rented a couple of films to watch. I'd also been given the keys to the old man's car, so that was parked to the side and was further proof that we were in the flat. When they chose their moment, they'd hammered on the door. We were startled because no one knew we were there and no one should have knocked – not like that, anyway. Anne-Marie jumped up to see who it was. I was straight up after her; it was obvious that it wasn't a social call, and that was when we heard them shout my name. They were through the door and surrounded me with guns to my head. This was not typical at all. They were doing their best not to act like police but, in doing so, they may as well have been in uniform. It stood out a mile. If they weren't coppers, Anne-Marie would have got it and then they'd have finished me off. It would have just been another bullet, a slight deviation to shut a witness up permanently.

After a stabbing incident in Glasgow involving Raymond Bonnar, the head of a team who had apparently ripped the Thompson's off for £50k in a drug deal, the heat was on me. The cops had been to the Ponderosa looking for me and it was time to get out of town quick smart. I was already awaiting trial for possession of offensive weapons, ffs. Arty Thompson gave me a set of keys for the hideaway and the keys to his Daimler. I was off. Anne-Marie was on and off then on, so I went up there by myself in the car and met up with her.

The family holiday home, or the so-called family holiday home was not the big country manor that's in the movie. The reality was a tiny two-bedroomed flat. It had a decent sea view, but was basic all the same. In short: it served a purpose. I think the perception we have from all the other films is that you go on the run and escape to luxury; whereas a regular modest flat does not arouse suspicion and is the most likely option (I checked the address while writing this. You can see the property listed online. It sold for less than £50k a few years ago. It was weird seeing where it all happened again). Of course, the three plain-clothed detectives who had guns pointed at me also knew where I was, so it was a no-brainer who had tipped them off. What none of these people knew though, was that my then-heavily pregnant girlfriend, Anne-Marie, was with me. If it was a tip-off from Joe Public, the coppers would have known she was there. They'd have been prepared. This was crucial evidence for me: if they knew a woman was present, they'd have had to have a female copper at the scene. And, more than likely, they wouldn't have just barged through the door to shoot me in front of her. A typical technique they used was to phone up just before bursting in. Not to tell me what they were doing, but to distract me – the element of surprise, misdirection, call it what you will. Anne-Marie being there sent them reeling – totally spooked them into action and shouting for someone to get a WPC to the house, pronto.

It was only when she'd come back through from another room to see if I was ok that she screamed, stopping them in their tracks. I smiled inwardly when I twigged that the hit wasn't about to go down. I probably sneered a bit, but I knew I wasn't out of the woods completely. A complication could still be dealt with if they were prepared to.

There's the old cliché of things like this happening in slow-motion. To me, it didn't. It never does. There was no time to do anything, no time to think. As a man who'd lived a life fighting on the streets and reacting to attacks, this felt so different. I'm never completely off guard, but I was as close to it as I'd ever been for an active criminal. We'd gone there to relax, to live as civvies and let the dust settle on things at home. We weren't there like Bonnie and Clyde to plan jobs and count our ammo, but we may as well have been in a horror film with me saying, 'I'll be right back.' The whole atmosphere of the house turned that instant. Strangely, it still felt peaceful beneath the shouting and chaos, like it was just playing out. With my face pushed into the carpet, even with my eyes bulging, straining and my neck bulging, I felt a release. I relaxed. I was aware of my breathing. Just my breathing. Filtering out all the chaos. Breathing... drifting... I couldn't help but think the carpet still had a slightly new smell to it. Ha! The end of the line for the wee man and he's wondering if they used Shake 'n' fucking Vac! How mad is that? Thinking back now, it was a familiar smell in amongst it all that enabled me to take my mind elsewhere, to a nicer place, almost seeing the light like in *Gladiator* when he has visions of walking through cornfields to see his wife and kid. A bit out-of-bodyish... a scene so out of the ordinary. I'd accepted the situation, but not the fate. The surroundings looked different from this angle – juxtaposition of calm against the chaos. I'd relaxed for that one second, and then in the next instant, I hated the police for snatching it away from us. It's a totally different feeling to get busted when you're not up to anything. It leaves a bitter taste. We were away from all that shite without a care in the world. It was like I'd suddenly been shocked back to life with a defibrillator, back into the commotion.

If you've had your house raided, you'll know what I'm talking about here. The extreme shouting is to disorientate you. Shout loud and fast and in their face – like a drill sergeant barking in your ear in the army. Dish the orders before they've got time to think or react. Shove them around knowing that any retaliation ends in them assaulting a police officer, take your problems out on them, your inadequacies, and know you have licence to fuck with people's lives whether you actually are serving the public or have a vendetta against them.

I knew I wasn't going to get shot that night. Not with her there. So, no matter how hard or often the big man jammed a gun into my head or my back, we all knew it was just an empty threat. It gave me some power back. With my hands cuffed behind my back, I was lifted off the floor and into a bedroom. They wanted me and Anne-Marie kept apart. They bundled me onto the bed and searched me for any concealed weapons. As this big copper, the snowy-haired George Dickson patted me down, he took my bank card holder and some cash from my pocket and threw them to the floor and continued searching down to my ankles. At that point his gun fell from his pocket or holster onto the bed. Very amateurish for a policeman, never mind a would-be hitman. I kicked it to the floor and called him a fucking idiot. It could easily have gone off by accident at that point. *Come on*! Last thing you want is to get whacked out by fucking accident!

The sound of something else, something light, hit the floor next to my card holder and Dickson asked, 'Whose is the brown powder?'

No answer.

'Whose is the brown *fuckin' powder*, son?'

I hadn't twigged at the time, but it could well have belonged to Arthur's other son or his daughter. I'm not even sure which of them was using at the time – they were both totally unconnected to the family business and must have been a total embarrassment to the old man. Degenerate fucks. Something wasn't right. It seemed too convenient for them to come in like that and then find a bag of stuff – especially as we'd been there a while and hadn't noticed it. I was probably more bothered at this piece of shit calling me son. I've never liked that. My dad can call me son. I'm my dad's son.

'Well if this isn't yours, it must be your pal Arthur Thompson's then, eh?'

No answer.

Regardless, it was put with my things and passed off as mine – bagged up as evidence. That's how easy it happens. You've seen it in films or TV a million times – it isn't made up, people get shot by accident in struggles and detainees fall down stairs all the time. Fit-ups are just sly. I wasn't taking that kind of shit and started kicking off; calling him a drug dealer and saying he was supplying me with drugs. I couldn't get the words out quick enough – I gave the same anger as he'd shown only minutes earlier; lashing out as much as I could in that position. *Brown fucking powder*? A bag so small that it could only have been for personal use and it offended me that they'd try to make it stick that I used heroin. Knowing that they were now there to fit me up, fuck knows what they were prepared to plant. They'd try to make me look like Pablo Escobar if I wasn't careful. During all this, I knew I threatened him. I'd probably threatened them all. If any man did the same to me and my girl, they'd be getting carried out of there in a body bag. It's just how it is. Someone taking a liberty like that and planting drugs on me was no man of the law – he was a lowlife dealer and I treated him with the same contempt. My threat wasn't to a serving police officer, because a serving police officer is there to prevent crime not to *create* it.

Not much of it stacked up: were they there to shoot me or to nab me for attempted murder? And why did they have a warrant to search the place for drugs? Seemed a bit odd that they were out to get me for something I had no association with – and managed to find them. What a lucky break, eh? Another thing that didn't add up in this fucked-up equation was the question of whose brown powder it was. The problem here was that the 'brown powder' was in a little green baggie; a coin bag that they use in banks – how the fuck would anyone be able to determine a colour through that? You'd only know if you planted it. He hadn't even opened the bag at that point. He put it in with my card holder and I heard muffled talk in the other room of him asking Annie-Marie about it. What a fucking piece of work this bloke was.

I saw one of them walk past with evidence bags sealed up. They contained items like telephone books, bits and pieces that had been lying around the place, envelopes and papers and one had a wad of money – around £400 survival money. They'd be planning their Christmas party on that. The reason for the raid was the apparent attempted murder of Raymond Bonnar and they were looking into 13 other attempted murder cases.

There were things I didn't know at the time. Maybe I was blinded by my own loyalty. I can look back and know it was them who initiated the raid. They were in cahoots with the cops and that's what happened. At the time, that would have been the last explanation I'd believe. The next thing was that while I was on remand, the Thompsons did not visit Anne-Marie to check on her and help her out. It was a given – wasn't even up for discussion. But this was another thing that gave them up. Arty Thompson did come to visit me, though. He came to tell me that I was sharing the big house with another of the gang that had ripped his old man off. Mark Watt, a fucking huge lump of a man. He was like a fucking bear. The order was to let him know that Arthur hadn't forgotten about the £50k. I knew challenging him to a fight was a suicide mission, but it was all part of the job. He'd left me in a crumpled and bloody heap in my cell but I found a weapon and staggered out after him to cave his head in with it.

The whole thing was a Ferris Conspiracy and fucking catchy title for a book. It was a game-changer. They knew what they were doing; they knew they were setting me up. What they didn't know was that Anne-Marie was there. The reason why they didn't know? I never told them. So the Godfather of Glasgow revealed himself as the one behind it. Albeit indirectly. You see, in our game-what am I saying here? You're reading this, you know the score. Whether you know my story or not, it's pretty much accepted that gangsters and the law don't mix. When they do, it's usually the gangster giving up information about people in order to protect themselves and operate hassle-free; favour for favour and a blind eye turned – everyone happy. So, once a career criminal or a Godfather creates an alliance with the law, then they'll do anything to carry on their business with no risk of arrest. Whether you're close to them or just an associate, it doesn't matter. You assume there's loyalty until it's tested like this, but believe me – they'll give you up in a second to save their own skin. This was the Thompsons' way of illuminating me once and for all. By getting rid of me, they were illuminating a threat to their own throne in Glasgow and the police were getting rid of the one who was always slipping through their fingers. With me out the way they could all breathe easy for a bit. If you go after someone you've got to do the job properly because that person will come after you and will do the same to you. If you join forces with the police to do it and they don't do the job properly, then you've not only put yourself in the firing line, but you've admitted your affiliation to them. Big mistake.

It was only when the whole debacle came to trial that it was revealed that only two guns were signed out at the station. With three guns present at the raid, that meant that there was one unaccounted for… one unknown gun that was off the radar that could have been used in a murder and easily covered up. It was really only at that point where it sunk in properly. It had been a conspiracy to kill and they had free reign as legitimate gangsters. I told my solicitor about what I'd heard them saying and that I was certain they were going to kill me. Another tactic would have been to plant it on me. They'd kill me, put it in my mitt and shoot it a couple of times to say that I'd opened fire first. Then the gun would be dirty and I'd be responsible for whatever the fuck else and they'd all receive medals. Without evidence, it was just my word against that of the police. 'No, no… he didn't have the gun, honest,' and all that. These were Glasgow's dirty squad – a dangerous gang to take seriously. They were bigger criminals than the criminals they went after – I had no chance of being believed. That was, until Anne-Marie had been questioned and said the same number of guns were present. She barely even knew what I did for a living because I didn't want her involved. So this kind of thing was etched in her memory forever. Three guns.

THE TRIAL

I'd used Peter Forbes of Forbes & Co Solicitors in Glasgow, for years. He was good. He said that Bonnar had dropped the attempted murder charge against me. *Thank fuck*, I thought. I was on seven days' remand pending further enquiries and I thought that was it. Whatever happened in Glasgow with Bonnar – these things tend to get sorted on the streets. It wasn't a legal matter at all. I thought I was just gonna turn up to court a week later and be freed. Instead, I was presented with an indictment (charge sheet) which said I did have the drugs in my possession. To have drugs on you, to go on the fucking run and to stay on an island, the last thing you want to be doing is selling drugs. Who would? Where do you escape to? If you're on the run and if you've got a stash of drugs, then it's surely for personal use. The charge sheet stated that the drugs were found in my pocket.

They'd seized the clothes that I'd been wearing for any traces of blood, DNA or whatever it was. At that point Forbes ordered a high end toxicology report from Glasgow University. He knew what he was doing – we wanted the best result to prove a point.

In court, I was asked to explain what happened during the raid again. The lawyer then turned my attention to the charge that stated specifically that I had a new position and he looked at me and asked if I understood the significance of it. I didn't. 'The police are saying that you physically had that bag of powder on you.'

So, the card holder from my pocket should have minute particles from the green bag on it, around 1,000 times thinner than human hair – it did. It had to because the copper had held them together. It would be impossible not to. But it would also have been impossible for fibres from the bag to not be in my pocket as well, given the amount of pushing, pulling and throwing me around that had gone on. There were no fibres from the bag in my trackie bottoms at all. He didn't even go to the bother of putting it in there to take it out and fit me up like a smug TV detective. So it was left to the jury to listen to the toxicology report and then Donald Finlay, who was defending me, played a blinder: he asked the toxicologist if he could get his professional opinion on another matter. This bloke was widely regarded in Glasgow University as being at the top of his game, so he was very credible to have in the witness box. 'Ok,' was the rather apprehensive reply. Donald asked him to put his finger inside the green bag (he did) and then asked him, 'What colour is your finger through the plastic of the bag?'

'Light green,' he said.

'Thank you. So, if you put a glass vial of diamorphine [heroin] in the green bag, would it have an effect on determining the colour of the powder in the vial?'

'No, because it's a glass vial.'

And so, the vial was placed in the green coin bag and he was asked, under oath, what colour it was.

'Dark green,' he replied.

If *Liar Liar* had been out at that point, I'd have been tempted to do a Jim Carrey impression and shout out, 'And the truth shall set you freeeee!'

Again we're back to the question: *how on fucking earth could anyone tell it was brown powder*?!

It was down to the jury to consider. Under Scots law, as you may know, there's a verdict which basically means they believe it was you but they don't have enough evidence to convict you. In that instance, the Crown has failed in their obligations to convict you under that process. It was all coming down to who the jury believed: me or the coppers. In my mind, I knew I was not guilty, if it was based on the attempted murder of Bonnar. But he dropped the charges.

Was I carrying heroin? Was I fuck! Who wants to take it on the chin and say heroin's for personal use? The stuff they were trying to do me for was 86 per cent pure. That's pretty heavy shit – they didn't just get this on street level. If I was selling it, it could have probably stretched to make around £3k. To me, it wouldn't have been worth the hassle. The thing here was that anyone caught with heroin of such purity would get a big sentence because the higher the purity, the further you must be up the chain. Having that kind of purity would be signalling me as a major player in the heroin game. Sneaky fuckers, eh? If we don't get you one way, we'll make sure we get you in another way.

After my story, I left the box and the police officers went in and told their 'stories'… which just happened to be entirely different to what had actually taken place. The only agreement I could come up with was that we were all under the same roof at Thompson's place. Seriously, if you think that the police uphold the law and tell the truth in court, you're very wrong. They couldn't give a fuck about the truth as long as they nail you. You can't be naive enough to think that the truth will win, because the truth from a blue uniform is whatever they want it to be. Maybe they had a masterplan, maybe they all just let their mouths and imaginations run wild… maybe they thought the jury would buy it all. Who knows? I think their lies were designed to dismantle anything I said, to get me angry and to breaking point. I was consistent and calm throughout – that definitely helped. The charge sheet backed up everything I said. I knew it would be very difficult for me to sit down and make people understand what actually happened that day. It was off its fucking head. Reg found it difficult, most people I told found it difficult… maybe the jury did, but the police came unstuck with their different versions and the impossible science. To look at it another way, if they were on a major drugs bust like they said they were, then they'd have the phones tapped and they'd know that Anne-Marie was with me. Another thing that makes it all less believable is that the warrant was issued on the fucking island before I even got on it. It was surreal. The fact that they knew I was going to be there before I arrived was more evidence of Thompson's involvement. Even a blind man could see what was going on.

I'm smiling slightly as I recall this, but at the time it was serious. I genuinely believed it was Thompson junior that set me up. I was unsure about the old man. I was keeping an open mind. During the raid, they found an A4 envelope and a note that could have meant something. I saw it – it had some writing in biro on it, courtesy of Arty's own chubby hand. It was a list of drugs:

Black 50
Sulph 10
Coke 4
£50,000
£75,000

No one would quite know other than Arty himself, but it's a pretty certain bet that it was drugs and not a weird shopping list.

Now *everything* was to play for because allegiances changed and the knock-on was that the course of my life changed. If not for Anne-Marie being there, it would have been game over for me. Now being fitted-up, I couldn't just roll over and accept my fate. They were trying to send me down for a long time by any means necessary. Fair play – I was a bad man that they wanted off the streets. This was their opportunity. Dirty tricks are always used to get a result and no one ever plays by the book. I get that. Whatever it takes, make something stick. What I didn't know before then was that the Thompsons were a) with the police and b) willing to have me shot.

The Thompsons didn't know my suspicions, so at least I had that on my side. I could keep my head down and plan my retaliation if I found out it actually *had* been them. Whether it was Arty acting alone or the instruction of the old man, it didn't matter if it still came from 'the Thompsons'. This wasn't just a case of, 'Oh, no. The boss is being a pain in the arse today.' This was an event that would change the course of my life, the Thompson's... and the whole makeup of Glasgow's underworld. When things like this are initiated, they need to reach their conclusion... or else there'd be deadly consequences to pay.

The burning questions were, had the Thompsons set me up and had they tried to have me killed?

TAM McGRAW

There's not much to think about when you're locked up in a cell. The other way of looking at it is that you've got everything to think about. It's not like you've got any other pressing engagements to attend. One of the dangers can be that you'll overthink stuff. And that's not a healthy thing to do inside because there's very little you can do about anything. Your mind is the scariest fucking prison you'll ever know.

I worried about Anne-Marie, I worried about young Paul as well. He was only just born on 29th April while I was awaiting trial. It was a small comfort to know that both Anne-Marie and Paul were living with Anne-Marie's mum up in the north of Glasgow.

There were all the parallels of the situation with my dad. Was this all just history repeating? At this point, maybe. But the thing is, it's not like I got all existential about the whole thing. I tended not to worry about stuff I had no control over. So questioning myself about why I was there and my past wasn't even a thing. It wasn't something to sit around philosophising about and sticking it in a fucking journal. My mind had to stay active in more productive ways.

The stuff with the Thompsons was obviously my biggest concern. And my wandering mind led me to thinking about another known informant whose name I heard just before being remanded: Tam McGraw.

In every city, in every town, there's a McGraw. Part weasel, part eel, part snake, and part rat, they scavenge around in other people's rubbish, looking for scraps to feed on. Usually, these people run an organised crime empire by getting in with the police to inform on other criminals, giving themselves an Access All Areas pass in the process. They'll stop at nothing to save their own skin, they'll give anyone up and they'll profit from the misery of others. And it's those fuckers who always seem to make it to the other side unscathed, leaving a trail of destruction in their wake. But at what cost? They rarely leave the house. When they do, they surround themselves with minders, get driven around everywhere while hiding on the backseat and are always looking over their shoulder.

Everyone knew he was with the police. *Everyone.* The press knew, we all knew. Even straight-goers knew. It goes without saying that the entire police force knew because they were the ones allowing him to operate. It was almost a fucking comedy in the end. He was trading in flesh while being allowed to trade in arms. Whether they still despised him because of his activities or not, it was a working relationship and they were colleagues. The Licensee. I mean, come on. You don't get called that for nothing. It wasn't because he owned the Caravel pub either, cos everyone knew that it was his missus that ran it.

There may be a misconception about McGraw because of how he was portrayed in *The Wee Man*. He was played by John Hannah and a few people have asked me about it. Maybe because of what John brings to a role, I don't know, but this is what I've been told. The perception of McGraw from the film is that he was just some slippery fucker, a bit of a non-entity, not a serious player, not a lot about him – certainly not a top-of-his game gangster. I can see why you'd think that. McGraw, regardless of my opinion of him, had made a name for himself as a decent armed robber. He was an organised criminal, ran a team, was into everything and, if you believe all you read in the press, made a lot of money from his empire. And made even more once old man Thompson was off the scene.

McGraw was around when the ice cream wars raged and seemingly got away with killing a whole family of innocent people in a house fire. I knew all of that was going on, but it wasn't anything I was involved in and wasn't really on my radar. The wars hit the press in 1984, while my little green bag predicament was playing out, so it had been raging for a while before. The press said it was to do with drugs and *The Ice Cream Wars* was their tag, but a fitting one all the same. The vans operated around the schemes of Glasgow and, because they also sold stuff that shops sold miles away, there was money to be made and demand was high. And with that, as ever, came the fight for power and control to secure rounds. The local amenities back then weren't anything like we have today, so by taking produce to the people, you could make a tidy profit a week. You could make even more if most of the stuff you were selling had just been robbed from town. A lot of people reading this who are over say 35 years old, may remember things like the bread van (selling bits and bobs other than just bread) or the pop van (they sold pop). The ice cream vans were the same. Knock-off cigarettes were a massive seller and there were no *mind that child* trading restrictions in selling to the schemes. The ice cream aspect of it became almost a sideline to the produce-selling side. And with so many people trying to make a living, competition was big.

There was unfriendly rivalry and intimidation. Rock up on the wrong street corner and you could get bricked, beaten up, petrol bombed or shot. I think it's very plausible that knock-off ciggies were sold cos they're easy to get hold of and replenish. The downside: if you got spun by the polis selling anything in a tiny van, it would be an easy find and expensive to keep losing... and you'd never make a getaway doing 20mph while *Green Sleeves* was blasting out of a loudspeaker.

Six members of the Doyle family were killed in the fire, including a baby. If a blind eye had been turned to what was happening on the streets, there was no getting away from something like that once it was reported nationally. The entire city was shocked that stuff like this was going on; it exposed the criminal element behind something anyone would think was an innocent enterprise. I'd heard on the grapevine that Billy Love, serving time in Bar-L, had invented a story as an alibi to save his own skin and the police bought it. He told them he heard Thomas TC Campbell and Joe Steele's names in a pub and that, apparently, was enough to jail them for 18 years. He wasn't even in the pub – it was all a tale and the coppers lapped it up. They were scapegoats; sacrificed. It was all lies, it was all a trade-off with the police and there was one man behind it...

MEMBERS OF THE JURY...

My charge sheet that the case was based on:
Carrying a pickaxe handle, a wooden stave and
two knives, attempted murder of Raymond
Bonnar who was sitting in a parked motor vehicle
stabbing him repeatedly, unlawful possession of a
controlled drug, namely diamorphine, a Class A
drug with intent to supply it to another, and
failure to comply with my bail conditions and
committing offences.

I was known by the police and by Joe Public as
a criminal. There was no denying any of that. It
was fair to assume that the jury knew I was a
criminal. That was the worrying part, the
preconceptions. I know that most of my
readership is not naive. Many of you out there
may have had a brush with the law, you may be
reading this while residing in your luxury suite at
Her Majesty's Pleasure or you may be sat on a
bus on your way to your nine to five nightmare.
Whichever. I'm not the judge here.

So, here's the thing: criminals are generally a
bit dishonest. I know, *I know*. Criminals make a
living by bending the rules and living outside the
law. That's pretty standard practice, you'd agree.
A police officer also has a set of values, you
would think. They're in a trusted position where
they are proud to protect and do so by using the
powers at their disposal to apprehend and
maintain order while operating within the law.
It's a basic job description, you'd agree. In the

real world, we all mix it up a bit. I'm a criminal one minute, yet I live within the law because there are rules and conventions within society. If we didn't adhere to all that stuff, we'd just go around shooting people rather than talking things out or taking whatever we want from Sainsbury's whenever we want. That just wouldn't work. Coppers live within the same conventions outside of their role and they uphold the law when they're on their shift. What some of you may not know is that some coppers, only some, also bend the rules of the law to their own advantage. It may be hard to believe, but it goes on. So, to spell it out a bit clearer – some coppers are *bent as fuck*. Whether they tell a tiny white lie or invent something in court, it all amounts to the same thing. For example, a less serious case may be a copper telling a few lies on a statement to get a conviction. It means nothing to them; the guy in question is irrelevant, not even a name. The consequence is that whoever they did it to could be a generally decent bloke who has now lost his driving license or his job... which will then have serious consequences to his life. Copper gets a pat on the back from the sarge and the bloke has to deal with life-changing situations. A more serious example (the seriousness being relative to the accused's life), an entire police force goes after one man who operates within the criminal fraternity; the man refused to be part of their team and has a good record of victories against them. That criminal could also be a generally decent bloke with a family. Regardless, they build a case on him based on second-hand information passed to them by other criminals doing them a favour. They aren't just going for a fine and losing a license for a few months; they've netted their biggest adversary and they'll stop at nothing to make sure he gets sent to the country's toughest prison for the rest of his life or turn a blind eye to the culprit if he is set up for gangland execution. In this situation, they will think nothing of lying, creating their own evidence, mixing with criminals, paying informants, arranging murders or looking the other way when they happen. Officers, sergeants, whoever get promotions or earn their retirement from shit like that. They still don't lose any sleep over it. Some people are just *sketchy as fuck* whatever they do or don't do for a living.

I don't mean to be condescending here. We can't be naive enough to think that corruption doesn't exist. It isn't invented for the sake of films, but if you want one of the best examples as a recommendation from yours truly, try *The Departed* by Martin Scorsese. Brilliant cast. Anyway, I'm not fucking Blockbuster Videos (one for the oldies, kids) and let's not water down the severity of corruption. It is very common practice and it is an abuse of power to fuck people over. The uniform, the title, it gives license to use the law and go above it to get what they want. The only real rules with corruption are: cover your tracks, don't get caught and don't grass –

which is, more or less, how criminals operate: bend the rules, break the rules, there are no rules. It doesn't matter. If they get the result they wanted, then who gives a fuck? It's another criminal off the streets.

Even as I read through court documents again for this book (the ones referred to are reprinted in the back), the whole thing stinks of shit. I had no idea what Thompson's shite smelled like, but it must have been this. None of it adds up. It's impossible that they'd have known I was there by a casual tip off. I hadn't even been there long enough to change my clothes, so it's not like I'd been seen out and about, other than getting some supplies in. In court situations like this, the police know they're lying. It's their act though. That's all you have to keep in mind. They're lying to cover stuff up and it's up to my team to pull them apart. All the while the jury are watching their body language and the way they talk.

I will highlight some of the bits I said in court here, in case it's not that easy to make out in the scans in the back of the book.

Fiscal: Is there any comment or explanation you would wish to give regarding that charge today.
Me: Yes there is.
Fiscal: What would you like to say about that Mr Ferris?
[Fucking brace yourselves...]

140

Me: I would like to state from the beginning to when the police came to the house in question. The police came to the door while I was watching TV with my girlfriend, a football match was on the TV, that's when I heard the banging at the door. There were several bangs and I quite distinctly heard a voice from inside the house stating that they were the police and that they were armed. My girlfriend got up off the couch and walked towards the door leading to the hallway. She looked along and saw police officers standing there, there was 3 of them, each one had a gun. My girlfriend told me that there was men at the door and they were all armed. I then went out into the hallway myself and seen them standing there in a position with their arms outstretched and the guns were pointing at my head. They then said to me 'Get on the floor and put your hands behind your back'. There was one officer in particular the tall one with the grey hair I believe his name is Mr. Dickson, he put the gun at the back of my head and said to me 'You know what this is' and 'Don't attempt to move'. I was then handcuffed taken into the adjoining room across from the living room where I was searched. All the officers in question came into the room while another officer sent down for a police woman to come up to look after my girlfriend. They were searching around the room and I asked them what they were looking for, they said it was in connection with an attempted murder in Glasgow and that they believed they were looking for either a knife or a gun.

While searching the house it seemed to be Mr. Dickson who seemed to be in charge. He pulled out a package from somewhere, I didn't see what it was, he had his back to me and within seconds of each other all the CID officers asked him what it was he had. He then searched me, put the stuff out of my pockets on to the ground next to the wall unit and I asked him again what it was he found, he says 'It's just powder', he then took the sachet of powder and put it inside my wallet, it wasn't in any folder it was just inside the outer covers. He then took me from that room and asked me where Mr. Thomson was, I replied that Mr. Thomson wasn't down, he says, he then said to me 'Whose stuff is this? I says 'What stuff?' he says 'The brown powder' I says 'It's not mine I don't know nothing about it', 'Well it must be Mr. Thomson's then, where is Arthur?' I replied to them that Arthur wasn't down, they then said to me 'His car's round the back' 'I says 'I am using the car, it's me that's driving the car' when I replied that all the officers looked at each other and then took me into the other room.

While I was in the other room I was strip searched and they seemed to be searching inside my pockets for anything else that I had, they then left me, went into the living room to see if my girlfriend had been dressed yet. They took a statement off her I believe and while one of the uniformed officers was watching over me in the room the CID came back in and explained to me that I was being held in Rothesay to be taken up to Glasgow the next day as there wasn't a ferry. I was taken to Rothesay Police Station and I was cautioned and charged with attempted murder which I replied I didn't know nothing about it.

While I got took to Glasgow they took the tracksuit that I had on from me and gave me a change of clothing, they never gave me any explanation why they were taking the tracksuit. I was then taken to court and that's all I have to say about the drugs charge.

Fiscal: When you were arrested and cautioned by those same police officers, again said 'They're tools of the trade.' Did you say that?

Me: Yes. I did say that.

Fiscal: Alright. Do you want to explain why you said these things?

Me: Yes. While I was asked if I admitted the charge I said yes. That was to the Procurator Fiscal, the reason for the first explanation of self-defence I was referring to one of the offensive weapons mentioned namely a wooden stave. The wooden stave is in fact a martial arts stick and it's used for the purpose of self-defence. That was why I had mentioned self-defence; it was nothing to do with any other offensive weapons that was in the car, that's why that statement was made, self-defence.

On the second reply that I made 'They're tools of the trade' which is true, I work for a garage

143

which is Triangle Garage it's in Birkenshaw Street, Dennistoun, I use the pick axe handle and the both knives that were mentioned on the charge are in fact two Stanley knives which I use in due course of my work along with the pick axe. I have witnesses to say that I do and have been using them in my work. There was also a number of other offensive weapons in the car which they could have taken there was also items like hammers, screw drivers, iron bars, jack levers that they could have taken as well and classed them as offensive weapons but they didn't. The only ones that they took from the car were the ones that were at the back seat of the driver's seat. The second reply that I made 'They're the tools of the trade' was because that I do use the items in question in work.

You need to get a balance in these situations. I was still learning the ropes, still honing my various characters. It was a courtroom drama – every case is. Lawyers, solicitors, QCs, whatever legal the legal people are – they're all playing a part. You think they're like that all the time? They elevate the drama in all the right places. You need to be credible, consistent, be a sympathetic character and inject some pathos into the role. An act is different to a lie though. You can still perform the truth. In most cases, it's a lot easier to 'act' the truth because you fucking well believe in it. For my first biggie, I think I did pretty well.

There I was in the dock. I tried not to look at the jury who were sat to my left next to the prosecution. My defence was sat to the right. The judge was right in front of me as I sat in between two police officers. It was a weird scene. The coppers were wearing white gloves and each had a wooden baton, like they were ready to clump whoever disrespected the court. Needless to say, no one disrespected the court.

So, bear in mind that Lord Murray is, how shall I say, *a bit of a talker*. I've got his entire summing up to the jury here. Sometimes it may be difficult to understand what he's going on about. I get that and apologise in advance if it gets on your nerves. I've included the whole thing because, although it is difficult to follow at times, I think it puts you in a similar state of mind to what I or the jury was going through. If you start zoning out or skimming it – imagine being there and having to listen and concentrate on what he was saying. If you follow bits of it – again, you're in the same boat as many others. If you're the only one who can follow all of it – Hello, Lord Murray! Thanks for buying my new book!

I've also included some of the original documentation provided by William Hodge & Pollock Ltd, Shorthand writers, 26 North Fredrick Street, Glasgow, G1 2BT. The transcripts may not look too good when reprinted. The main aim was so you'd know they actually exist and I'm not just talking out of my arse. Strap yourself in...

<u>Wednesday, 27th March, 1985</u>

Lord Murray: Members of the jury, you have now heard the whole evidence in the case and you have listened to persuasive argument by counsel for the Prosecution and counsel for the Defence. When I have addressed you will retire to consider your verdicts.

I start with our respective functions here as Judge and Jury. The decision on the facts in the case is a matter for the Jury, while issues of law are for the Judge. The assessment of the evidence and its evaluation are your province. They are matters for you and for you alone. It is for you to judge the credibility of those who have given evidence before you, and the reliability of the testimony which they gave. You have to consider which witnesses to accept or reject, or what parts of their evidence you will dismiss from your mind as tending to prove anything. If you conclude that something is a lie or not to be relied upon, that doesn't establish that a competing version of the facts is true. On question of fact then, including any inferences from facts, and these are vital in this case, are entirely for you to decide fairly and impartially in accordance with your oath on the evidence which has been led before you in this court.

146

Now, ladies and gentlemen, you proceed on the evidence. You don't proceed on elements of sympathy on the one hand or prejudice on the other hand, whether these are sympathy for the accused or prejudice against the accused, and having said that, you will specifically remember something Mr. Findlay mentioned a moment ago. There has been mention in this case of an attempted murder charge. The accused is not charged with that and it is not an issue here so you will put out of your minds any suggestion of prejudice against the accused arising out of that, or any other mention of criminal activities which are not the subject of the present indictment, and I am sure you will follow that.

On the other hand, questions of law which arise in the trial are my responsibility and mine alone. On questions of law you have to accept my directions and apply them in your consideration of the evidence. You accept them not because I am infallible on the law, but simply because you have got to have one person setting the context, a referee setting the context. Having said that, this is not an issue in which there is much dispute between the two sides in the present case, so I set the legal context for you to view the evidence.

I start with certain general directions of law. Firstly, by our law an accused person has the benefit of the presumption of innocence. An accused is presumed innocent unless and until guilt is brought home to him. If that presumption is not displaced by the evidence in the case then the accused must be acquitted.

Secondly, the burden of bringing home guilt to an accused person rests upon the Crown, the Prosecution, and it rests on the Crown throughout, not just during the Crown part of the case.

The standard of proof which the law requires of the prosecution is a high one, namely proof beyond reasonable doubt. It is not for an accused to prove his innocence. If, having heard the whole evidence, you are left therefore with reasonable doubt then you must acquit the accused. You will notice that the test is that of reasonable doubt. This does not mean a speculative or a theoretical or fanciful doubt. It doesn't mean mere hesitancy. It means the kind of real doubt might affect you in making a major decision in the practical conduct of your own lives. It means, if you like, a doubt based on reason, not an impulse or feeling or anything of that kind, so when I refer to the Crown satisfying you on certain evidence or proving certain facts, please bear in mind that the standard set for the Crown is proof beyond reasonable doubt in that sense. I am sure you will see these two principles alone take you to the position that there is no burden of proof on the accused person at all.

Thirdly, by the law of Scotland an accused person cannot be convicted on the unsupported testimony of only one single witness, however credible or reliable that witness may be. There has to be corroboration, that is supporting evidence, confirmation if you like, from some other independent source. Now, that other source may be another eye-witness, for example, if one policeman speaks to something it may be there is another policeman or two or three other policemen who speak to the same matter. If you believe them, that would be corroboration. The other source on the other hand may be a fact or facts established independently by other testimony, for example, identification or fingerprint evidence, and we have had some of that in this case obviously relating to the contents of various things that are produced, and that kind of thing is circumstantial evidence and that is perfectly satisfactory also as corroboration of what you take as primary evidence, namely a witness that you accept. Corroboration is required only to prove the essentials of crimes that are charged, and ladies and gentlemen, I will give you a little bit more information on that because in a moment or two I will refer you the indictment and indicate to you what are the essentials of each of the crimes charged here, and although there are just five numbered on the indictment, in substance I think four is in two parts and really there are two alternatives to that, so there are six items you have to deal with there.

Fourthly, if the Defence seek to establish any fact, whether by cross-examination or by leading evidence, and you have had both in this case, in order to found on that fact, the Defence do not have to satisfy you by proof beyond reasonable doubt, nor do the Defence require corroboration. If an accused's account exculpates him and you believe him, then you must acquit him on the particular charge that you are dealing with, but even if his account taken by itself or along with the bits of the other evidence or along with all the other evidence gives rise to reasonable doubt, then you give the accused the benefit of that doubt and again acquit on the particular charge that you are considering.

Fifthly, if a person involved in an incident says something about it at the time or very shortly afterwards, or says something to police who are making enquiries into what they find, then if that statement is freely given, it may be used to incriminate him if it contains incriminating matter. Now ladies and gentlemen, such a statement is the more readily admitted if an accused person has been cautioned beforehand and told that the police are making certain enquiries so that he has got an indication of what they are about and also warned that if he does say anything it will be taken down, noted and may be used in evidence subsequently, so these are matters to bear in mind. Obviously if someone is cautioned and charged, that is an even more formal stage at which the accused has full notice of what the police may charge against him because he then knows the nature of the charge that is likely to be preferred in subsequent criminal proceedings.

Sixthly, at judicial examination – you have heard a reference to the judicial examination in this case. It is founded upon mainly by the Defence, but was founded upon in some respects by the Crown. As I indicated to you before it was read out by the Clerk of Court, a judicial examination provides evidence of an accused person taken by the Prosecution before a Sheriff on a limited basis and not on oath at a relatively early stage of criminal proceedings against him. An accused need not answer questions put to him although this may give rise to an adverse comment later on, and he may consult his solicitor before giving any answer. Questions may be put by the Defence only at the end and then just to clarify, not to cross-examine or to state a positive defence. In that sense the proceedings are somewhat one-sided. By Act of Parliament, the transcript of the evidence at the judicial examination is part of the evidence at the subsequent trial, that is the trial you are sitting in judgement on today.

You have, therefore, to take the transcript of evidence into account, whether it favours the Prosecution – the Prosecution found upon it in certain minor matters – or the Defence, and Mr. Findlay founded upon it very specifically and asked the Clerk of Court to read it to you, so it is part of the evidence in the case to be taken into account along with the testimony which you have heard on oath, but it is right to point out evidence on oath given in court is entitled to greater weight than what is said in this rather one-sided procedure and not on oath before the Sheriff, but bearing that in mind, there is also this point to be borne in mind, that as a judicial examination takes place at a relatively early stage, there was criticism from Mr. Findlay that it didn't take place earlier, but nevertheless, it was a week or so after some of the incidents which are charged, and the important point about it is something that is said very shortly after an incident may be made at a time when what is said is likely to be true because it may later be forgotten or be the result of some confusion because a lot of time may pass before the criminal proceedings come into court, so take these two factors, one slightly adverse at judicial examinations, that is the fact it is one-sided and not on oath, but the time element is important in the other direction, something that is said there and consistently maintained later is of special importance and entitled to special weight.

With these preliminaries, there is only one other preliminary I would point out to you, and it is important you have this point at this stage, that Charge 4 is in alternatives. Unfortunately, alternatives are really quite simple in their common sense point of view, but they do give rise to slight complication because of the alternatives posed to you. You can convict of one or of the other. You can acquit of both. What you can't do is convict of both, so please bear that in mind there are a number of choices here before you, but whatever you do in the end of the day

152

you cannot convict of both the options in Charge 4. You have got to choose one or the other, so please bear that firmly in mind. I will have more to say about that matter when I come to the facts relating to that charge.

Please look at the indictment you have got before you and let's consider the various charges on it, and having looked at that, I will then endeavour to indicate to you what the essentials are of these charges, and remember that is important because that gives you the measure which you have got to apply when you look at the facts to see whether they come up to that standard.

The first charge and second charge are both offences of having an offensive weapon in a public place, and then there is a reference to the Prevention of Crime Act 1953, Section 1(i). They are on different dates, and the first one is one the 2nd of August. Please bear in mind the registration number of the car has been altered. That was amended. It is FSX. I just mention that because Mr. Findlay went back to the old letter in his address to you but it is now X, and it is not important because I am sure you will remember the car incident that relates to, and it is a very minor matter, and then you go on Charge 2, which is a similar offence relating obviously to a different implement. The Prevention of Crime Act provides in section 1(i) that any person who without lawful authority or reasonable excuse, the proof whereof shall lie on him, has with him in any public place any offensive weapon, shall be guilty of an offence. Now, the wording of that provision is unfortunately not as simple as it may be. I'm afraid that it is sometimes a fault of Statute. The same fault applies about the Misuse of Drugs Act, which is in many ways less attractive to read, but the gist of it is that it is an offence and you may be found guilty of it if it is proved. It is an offence to have an offensive weapon in a public place without lawful authority or reasonable excuse.

In the present case nobody is suggesting that the accused had lawful authority to have any particular article with him, although do bear in mind that whether or not something is an offensive weapon is critical, so if you decide any of the implements charged are offensive weapons, it is suggested that lawful authority existed, but what is said by the Defence is there is a reasonable excuse. I will amplify that a little bit later, but that is the general proposition. Sub-section 4 of the same section of the 1952 act says that 'A public place includes any highway' and so on, and it also provides that offensive weapon means any article – Now, this is an important point, so please listen to it carefully – 'Offensive weapon means any article made or adapted for used for causing injury to the person'. That is one leg, and the other leg is 'Or intended by the person having it with him for such use by him'.

Now, ladies and gentlemen, I think that you could easily look at the first two charges and consider very briefly as a preliminary the particular facts in relation to those two because of the definition of offensive weapon, as I have put to you, bears immediately upon the articles which are named in the two charges. The first charge relates to a pickaxe handle, a wooden stave and two knives. Let's take the pick-axe handle first of all. Is that an offensive weapon? An offensive weapon is an article made or adapted for use for causing injury, and I think you would probably have very little difficulty taking the view that a pickaxe handle wasn't made for that purpose. It is made for holding the sharp end of an axe so it wouldn't be an offensive weapon in terms of the first leg at all if you take that view. It is for you, not for me, but I think you would find that easy. When you come to the two knives, you have seen them produced and heard they are ordinary household Stanley knives, and again you must ask yourselves is that an offensive weapon? It is made or adapted for causing injury, and I think you will have very little difficulty saying it is not. They are not daggers like the production in regard of the other charge, so if that is your position, and I imagine it will be, you will be saying the pickaxe handle and the two knives certainly wouldn't be offensive weapons in terms of the first leg of the definition. They may or may not be in terms of the second leg, but I'll come to that. What about the stave?

You have heard evidence about that and it seems to be, although the history of this particular bit of wood seems to be shrouded in some mystery after all the evidence has been led, it would seem to be the case that is regarded by everybody who knows anything about it as probably a martial art tool, instrument, weapon, something that is intended for martial arts. If you take the view that means it is an article made or adapted for causing injury, it may be difficult to reach that view. You may say it is essentially a sporting implement like boxing gloves or perhaps the fencing sword. Is that an offensive weapon in terms of the definition or not? It is perhaps a bit difficult, but you could take the view that a martial arts wooden sword is meant for hitting people with if you can get at them but the art is to be able to get at them with the other stave the other chap has, and it would be open to you to take the view that is something designed for causing injury, although if you do sporting activities no injury is caused, and it's equally open for you to say it's a fencing type of thing and therefore not an offensive weapon in terms of the first leg either. I wouldn't take a great deal of time about that because, as Mr. Findlay fairly pointed out, the issue is very, very narrow and the charge is not the major charge on this indictment at all, but ladies and gentlemen, when you deal with that charge you might want to approach it that way, and if you reach the view that none of these items are offensive weapons within the first leg of the

156

definition, you have got to ask yourself about the second leg, and that says that 'An offensive weapon may be an article intended by the person having it with them for such use', that means for causing injury to the person, and you have then got to ask yourselves whether these articles in the car at that time, where the accused undoubtedly was, were intended by him to be weapons. That's where the reply, when there is an explanation sought, self-defence encapsulates two features in it. On the one hand, what is the point of having something for self-defence if you don't intend to use it as a weapon, so that would seem to suggest all of these articles, though not intended for use, nevertheless were intended by the possessor to be used for that purpose, but by the same token, saying self-defence puts forward something that is referred to as an excuse for having the article, and then you have to ask yourselves, and again it may be a matter which would take you very much time, is there anything in the facts here to justify the accused having these things and intending to use them for self-defence? If you think there is, there is no offence and you acquit, but if you think there isn't, and it may be difficult to see anything very obvious justifying self-defence, you would be entitled, if you are satisfied beyond reasonable doubt on the elements I have put to you, to convict. That's of the whole lot, simply on the basis the excuse put forward, self-defence, contains within it an intention to use as a weapon, an explanation or excuse because of some threat

157

there to defend myself. It's as simple as that and I needn't say anything more about it except one minor caution. You may recollect that when the Judicial Examination was read out to you in regard to this charge of possessing a pickaxe handle, a wooden stave and two knives in contravention of Section 1 of the Prevention of crime Act, the accused was asked if he understood the charge. He said 'Yes, I do.' The Fiscal then said 'Do you deny the charge?', and the accused said 'No'. In case you think that is conclusive of the matter it's not, because I think it was clear the accused's evidence on oath in the witness box what he meant by that, but it is a matter for you because you heard all the evidence. If you reach the view that what he was saying was 'I admit these things in the car and I had them, but I don't admit it was an offence', it's not conclusive, but that's one of the factors you are entitled to take into account in considering whether that charge has been proved or not.

That is Charge 1, and I say no more about the facts relating to that, and that brings me on to the next charge which I can also deal with fairly simply. That's another charge of the same kind. I said that an offensive weapon means exactly what it says, having it with you, and when you come to the second charge the elements that are involved in having a weapon perhaps begins to have more importance. The first one has no difficulty. The second one does raise difficulties because quite obviously to have an offensive weapon with you in a public place you first of all have to have some proximity to the weapon. Obviously the normal sort of thing would be to have it on your person so that the question of – there must be a physical link of some kind quite obviously. The normal physical link probably would be to have it in your pocket, or if you are dealing with the article to which Charge 2 refers, that is the sheath knife – you remember everybody agrees there is a little clip on it so you can clip it onto your belt – it would be quite understandable if you had it in its sheath clipped to your belt, that would be in your possession. Such a weapon can equally be in your possession if it is in a car beside you, so there is a physical element connecting the accused to that knife, and that isn't challenged by the Defence, but what is said by the Defence is this, that the police officer had some difficulty finding it. You remember that knife which was shown to you by the Advocate Depute – I think it was Label 6 – you may take the view it is very easy to conclude beyond reasonable doubt that is designed as a weapon and therefore it is an offensive weapon within the first leg of the definition that I have already put to you. I'm sure you will have very little difficulty with that. It's plainly designed as a weapon. Well, ladies and gentlemen, it's for you to decide that, but if you decide that, then the issue is did the accused have it within the meaning of the Act? There is the physical link there beside him next to the driving seat and there is the question of – I suppose you could say this –

although the police had difficulty in finding it, its proximity is perhaps convenient for the driver because I think the evidence was it was on the left-hand side of the driver in between the driver's seat and passenger's seat although under the surface fairly totally concealed, but you may feel that would be the sort of place somebody who was driving a car might put something if they were wanting to have it for self-defence or any other defence, and as far as this particular weapon is concerned, it isn't a question of the accused saying self-defence because he doesn't say much in regard to that. What he says here is I didn't know anything about it. It must have come from one of the others. That takes you to the critical question did the accused know that it was there or not? If you take the view that he did not know it was there – that's what he said on oath – then you acquit him of that charge because that's the end of it. It may be something has the physical proximity to me that would make it in my possession, and I'm sure you will see the sense of that, so if you accept the accused version he didn't know it was there or if that gives rise to doubt in your minds about whether he knew it was there, it's out and you acquit him of that charge, but if you don't believe the accused and you reject all that, and there are other elements in the case I'm not going into that support it to some extent – you remember the account of how it could have got there, and the man McFadyen that hasn't been able to be brought – all that helps the accused's position even though you haven't heard McFadyen, so if you reject all that the Defence found on relation to this charge, there would be sufficient, just sufficient, but there would be sufficient for you to reach the view as a matter of inference that if a driver is in a car with a weapon of that sort, an offensive weapon if you hold it to be such, conveniently placed for him, even if concealed, if you take the view that is the sort of thing, if the driver is in charge of that car, if you take the view therefore that the circumstances are such that it is less convenient for a passenger in the back, because that is the McFadyen account, less convenient for him, therefore not likely to be in his practical possession at the time, if that is the view, there is just sufficient for you to draw the inference that it was the accused and that he knew it was there, and despite what he says, but that would be a matter of inference, and remember the inference would have to be one drawn beyond reasonable doubt and therefore before you got to a conviction on that charge you would have to be excluding all the elements on which the Defence founded as pointing away from conviction on Charge 2.

Again, I need to say nothing more about that charge so I will say no more about the facts on that, and let me turn to the third charge, and that I can deal with very shortly, facts and all, because it is not contested in this case that the accused did have the cocaine in question in his possession. It is a charge of simple possession. I will tell you in a moment what is involved in that in relation to the fourth charge, but it is a matter of course for you. You have to be satisfied beyond reasonable doubt. Even if the accused admits it in the witness box, you still have to be satisfied of his guilt beyond reasonable doubt, but you will have little difficulty with that, and Mr. Findlay addressed you rightly in saying it is just a theoretical point that you could acquit on that. You would obviously be fully entitled to return with a verdict of guilty as libelled on Charge 3, but it is a matter for you and you alone and you are entitled to acquit if you are not satisfied.

Now, we then turn to the fourth charge, and let me say in regard to this in case it isn't already obvious to you, this of course is also a charge of two parts dealing with the Misuse of Drugs Act 1971, so if for any reason it was necessary for you to consider the precise nature of Charge 3, you would get the essentials from what I am now telling you about in regard to Charge 4. The only difference is that Charge 3 is simple possession which is the weaker alternative of Charge 4 apart from place and time. The only other difference is that Charge 3 deals with cocaine which is a Class A drug whereas Charge 4 in both its alternatives deals with heroin as a Class A controlled drug.

Now, ladies and gentlemen, the Misuse of Drugs Act 1971 makes provision for the control of dangerous or otherwise harmful drugs with a view to preventing misuse and abuse. It categorises various controlled drugs according to

162

their harmful potential and it creates as essential certain criminal provisions. Section 4 which is mentioned relates the production or supply of controlled drugs. Supply includes distribution and distribution simply means handing over, and handing over doesn't have to involve money, although it often does, and the street value of what is handed over may be very significant in deciding whether there is supply or whether there is mere possession. The Act provides for regulations permitting people lawfully to use the drugs for the purposes of which they are produced because most of the drugs with which we are concerned have perfectly proper therapeutic use, and doctors, dentists, chemists, vets and surgeons are entitled to have drugs at various times lawfully and properly, but if you are not authorised in that sort of way, and the Act specifies those authorised, Sub-section 1 of Section 4 makes it unlawful to produce and supply, and Sub-section 3 makes it an offence to supply such a controlled drug.

We now turn to Section 5, and perhaps you can see in passing all the references to schedules and so on I have mentioned, but we now come to the actual criminal provision with which you are primarily concerned. Section 5 makes it unlawful for any unauthorised person to have a controlled drug in his possession. Two offences are created, Sub-section 2, that is in the weaker second alternative, makes mere possession in such circumstances an offence, and Sub-section 3, which is the earlier alternative and the one that is the more serious, makes it a separate and more serious offence for anyone to have such a drug in his possession with intent to supply it to another.

Now, ladies and gentlemen, what does possession mean in this statutory context? It means a physical connection. In this case there is no problem in regard to either of the drugs in 3 or 4 because there is ample evidence, if you accept it, of possession in the sense of physical connection, then indeed there have to be two other factors. There has to be knowledge and there has to be control. Knowledge, which is a matter that has no difficulty in regard to the cocaine because you have heard the accused's position on that, but in regard to the heroin which is the subject of the very hotly contested issue, whether that was really in the accused's possession or whether it was planted by the police, the serious charge that is made by the Defence, that of course is very much in issue. You are not in possession of something unless you know you have it even if you do have it, so knowledge is important. Physical possession, physical connection is vitally important here because that is challenged, and control is also necessary. That may not be a matter giving rise to so much difficulty, but if you were satisfied for example the police were telling the truth, I think you would have very little difficulty in reaching the view beyond reasonable doubt that there was a physical connection, knowledge and the necessary control. Well, all of these are necessary to the second or weaker alternative of simple possession. When you come to the first alternative, there, not only have you got to be satisfied that all these three elements that go to simple possession are established beyond reasonable doubt. You also have to be satisfied beyond reasonable doubt on evidence satisfying you of intent to supply to another.

Now, ladies and gentlemen, where do you get evidence of that kind? You get it by inference. Sometimes something is said. Sometimes there is ancillary equipment like scales which make it pretty obvious something was intended to be supplied. Let me stress first of all that you don't have to establish any other particular person to whom it was intended to supply. That is not necessary, just the same way as if somebody selling newspapers would not be required to prove to whom he was proposing to sell them. It is obviously something you draw as inference from the fact of standing at the street corner shouting 'Evening Times' or from having a stall with newspapers laid out in front of them, so look to other circumstances to find out where inference may be drawn. Here, there isn't much. What is founded upon by the Crown is first and foremost the amount of the heroin mentioned in the charge, and although it is a fairly small amount from the point of view of kitchen materials like salt or baking powder, from the point of view of the drugs scene this constitutes a large amount. You may consider, because although it's only 1.3 grams or thereabouts of a certain purity, fairly high purity, you heard in evidence this is something that would fetch, divided up and packaged properly, as much as £2,000 average. It might be £100 or £200 to buy in bulk, but sold on the street you could multiply your profit in that kind of way, therefore the fact you have got something in bulk that can be split up to produce that may be a factor of importance in deciding whether the possessor had it with intent to do that, to make a profit. That's one factor. Street value, quantity are really two facets of the same thing.

What else is there? Ladies and gentlemen, if there is supply, you would not be surprised to find large sums of money in association with drugs, and if you believe the police evidence, and I don't think there is any contest about the money that was found, there is corroboration of it, but you have got £60 or thereby wrapped around the green bag. That is a sum of money. There has been corroboration of it, but by itself the finding of that money in association with the drugs may be another factor which would take you to the inference that the drugs weren't intended for use, but rather were the product of some supply proposal or part of the system of supply.

What else is there, ladies and gentlemen? The only other thing that appears to me to be relevant there, and it is a matter entirely for you, is this Production16, the envelope with all the markings of fingerprinting on it. That is found, if you

166

accept the evidence, and I don't think any very strong contest is made by the Defence – you will remember the accused evidence on the matter – he didn't really know where it had come from, but had his suspicions, but Miss McCafferty puts suspicion away because she saw it being found and you may take it was obviously there in the house. It is quite true no specific connection can be drawn, none you could found on beyond reasonable doubt can be drawn between the accused and that envelope. It's not suggested that the writing was his or anything like it, and certainly his fingerprints are not on it, and let me mention that point the Advocate Depute suggested, that there was something odd about the suggestion that the accused made that he was really being invited to inspect the envelope when his hands were handcuffed behind his back, but that is not my recollection of the evidence – of course it is your recollection that matters – but my recollection of the evidence is that the accused said indeed, that his handcuffs were behind his back at a certain stage, but at another stage he was strip searched, and the police said that too, and his clothes were taken off, and his clothes could hardly be taken off without the handcuffs being taken off, so although that matter wasn't canvassed, you may think the accused was right about that, at some stage he was invited to handle the envelope when the handcuffs weren't on, but it is a minor matter. The important matter is it may be a very small piece of evidence, but in this house where the accused was with his girlfriend, an envelope is found. Looking at that envelope, whatever significance it may have, it does appear everybody accepts the apparently innocent words 'Black', 'Sulph', and 'Coke' which, to you or I black could be anything, sulph could be sulphur used for weedkilling, coke could be Coca-Cola, and the figures could be anything or nothing, but everybody accepts the figures have a drug connotation, but that is another element. In the house in Rothesay there is an envelope which seems to have some significance to drugs, not drugs in relation to this indictment, but drugs and a large sum of money. The accused is there, £400 in one room, £60 wrapped round a green bag attributed to him by the police, and if you accept that evidence, that is the vital issue between the two sides. If you accept the police evidence there would be sufficient there for you to draw the inference of possession, if you find that established in this case, not a great deal, but sufficient for you to draw the inference that the possession was with intent to supply.

Two other minor matters, ladies and gentlemen, and I'll then be able to relieve you about how matters are progressing in terms of time. Two other matters – first of all I have mentioned to you already that, whatever you do, you cannot convict of both alternatives of Charge 4. You've got to choose one or the other or you acquit of both. Look at it this way – the greater alternative, the first charge, the greater includes the less. The second charge is the lesser. If you find the facts sufficient to prove the first charge then you have already found the facts relating to the second proved, but as the greater includes the lesser, you convict of the first and the second drops because it includes the second. If you find that there is reasonable doubt about intent to possess, then you forget the first one altogether, the first alternative, and if you are satisfied of possession, you convict of the second alternative and the first falls away, so if you return a guilty verdict, that is easy. You choose one or the other. If you are acquitting you acquit of both. You can return your verdict a different way by acquitting of one and convicting of the other, but I think the simpler approach was the way I indicated.

Lastly for tonight, because in a moment I'll be suggesting we adjourn, but lastly for tonight, there is the fifth charge which, from the point of view of statutory drafting, is the least simple of the lot, and if you were somewhat puzzled by that wording – I think the Advocate Depute found it difficult to put in a clear way to you when he was reading it out – but the drafting of these provisions is unfortunately not as satisfactory as it could be. That is not criticism of the Prosecution here. It's just a fact that Parliament has done it in a way which doesn't make it easy for us in court proceedings. What it means has been put to you very clearly by both counsel and although you may have difficulty in understanding what it says, what it means is that the accused was on bail.

There was a police officer spoke to that. Production 4 is the production saying the accused was on bail when the incident charged in 4 occurred, and the Bail order, which I have before me because it is part of the court documents, the Bail order says the court granted bail on a certain date, the 24th of October 1984, and one of the conditions was the accused does not commit an offence while on bail. We have passed on from the days when money bail was the rule and you now have bail with conditions like that, so ladies and gentlemen, if you find Charge 4 proved on one or other of those alternatives, the situation is that there is evidence already before you that the accused was on bail at the time. If he was, then he has committed an offence against the Bail Act because that's what the conditions says. You must not commit any offence. If you do, you are committing an offence under the Bail Act, so despite the difficult wording, it is easy. If you convict on one of the alternatives of 4, you convict of 5 also. If you acquit of both alternatives in 4, in other words 4 is an entire acquittal, you must acquit of 5, so 5 stands or falls with 4, and having said that, you need to pay obviously very little attention to it. Of course you have got to be satisfied beyond reasonable doubt that 5 is established, just as you'd have to be satisfied beyond reasonable doubt that 4 is established. Subject to that, it is entirely a matter for you.

Now, ladies and gentlemen, I have mentioned many of the facts in addressing you so far. However, I have left for a good reason the strenuously contested issue of facts, the central one relating to Charge 4, and I am leaving that to tomorrow, because I think it would be quite wrong for me to charge you for another 15 minutes or so and you would retire to consider your verdict. You've got virtually six charges and all the facts relating to them to consider even although some of them are easier than others, and I think it would be quite wrong to put you in a situation where you were getting tired and perhaps hungry and feeling you ought to be home. This is too important a case, as both counsel indicated to you, for you to proceed in that way, so I'm sure you will accept it as the proper thing to do, that we'll adjourn at this point and I'll complete my charge to you tomorrow, and very shortly after that you will retire to consider your verdict.

Let me caution you again, ladies and gentlemen. I haven't finished my charge to you, so still reserve judgement and do not discuss the merits of the case with anybody else. Keep that for the jury room tomorrow when my charge is completed.

Adjourned.

REFLECTION

I know many cases in which individuals are offered deals to put down others for their police handlers. I saw this from a very early stage in my life. I saw what people can do and say to save their own skin. It was tough enough surviving out there on a daily basis, without having to wonder if your friends were also your enemies. You don't need that kind of shit. It's the ones who live like recluses with more CCTV cameras than the *Big Brother* house that you needed to be wary of. Sure, we all need to protect ourselves, but if you live a constant lie of giving people up and telling tales to the police, you'll also be paranoid about it all unravelling one day and people acting upon the rumours. I'd decided that dealing with the police was not for me. It was not what I was brought up to believe in.

The reason that both Thompson and McGraw were working hand in glove with the police is that they had given information in the past and were credible snitches. That's why deals were being done all the time – it was an ongoing working relationship. I didn't know it when I first met Thompson, but that's how he was able to operate so freely. His survival wasn't all just by lucky coincidence, cunning and stealth; he was protected because he was an informant.

I know how it all played out now, but at the time it was a totally different story. I wasn't wet behind the ears at all. The stuff with Thompson

172

just didn't add up. At this point, we didn't really know each other well enough to have had a falling out. We were acquaintances, sure, but that's as far as it went. I wasn't in his pocket; he wasn't my *boss* so to speak. I did some jobs for him and I know I was seen as *one of his* in that respect. Our working relationship was only that: see if there were any jobs on the go if and when I wanted to earn from him. There wasn't a gangster annex at the Ponderosa where wise guys would sit around all day waiting to be called up. It was just that we were on side with each other. So, as much as we'd never had a crossed word, it was because there wasn't enough time spent in each other's company to get to that point. It was stilted conversation of no real substance other than business.

This whole green bag situation, though. It didn't smell too good. The Thompsons were absent from the trial, but that was because it would have become a media circus and made it a bigger thing than it was needed to be. But, were they not there because they'd already done their bit? Their part of the bargain was over, why'd they need to waste time seeing the result when they'd be told it? The more I thought about it, the more confusing it was – every time I'd get to my conclusion, I'd ask myself why, and then I'd go back to square one. The fucking warrant was the biggest clumsiest thing about it. Issued on the day at 1pm, Anne-Marie didn't even know at that point. Our plans were changing by the minute and we didn't even know what was going on. That's pretty staggering police work, wouldn't you agree? And why a warrant for drugs? Unless they knew they'd find them – because they were fucking well bringing them along! Again, the alarm bells rang through my head... at 1pm, the only people who knew I'd be there were the Thompsons. And now the police.

And then I'd remember snippets from what people had said. My dad told me Thompson was a grass ages ago, but I knew better. Blink had asked why the Godfather was on a constant recruitment drive and I chose to ignore it. I could see now that there was a lifecycle – a life expectancy – for his employees and the countdown began as soon as you agreed to work for him. When you reached that point of maturity, of realisation, of outgrowing him, you'd be set up, sent down or killed. And that would make way for the next one, while all the time Arthur gets older and richer until the time comes for Arty to step in. These men were fucking dangerous because of their ruthlessness in getting rid of people.

The penny was beginning to drop:

Why the fuck's he want kids working for him when he reckons he's the fucking Godfather of Glasgow?

Looks like I was about to find out.

THREE POSSIBLE VERDICTS

Thursday, 28th of March, 1985

Lord Murray: Well ladies and gentlemen, I now resume my charge to you, and I have no doubt you will recollect the main general points that I put to you yesterday, and bearing these principles in mind let me turn and deal briefly with some of what I think are the central issues. Of course, it's for you to decide what are the issues that are critical and contested here, but I would, I think, require to draw your attention to some of the issues that I think are important ones. Whether they are the important ones of course, it's for you to decide.

Well now, first of all the Defence. Now, this consists of a number of items, any one of which perhaps might not carry too much conviction taken by itself, but Mr. Findlay submits powerfully to you that when taken together they carry the necessary conviction, that is to say they prove the positive defence put forward, or if they don't do that, at least give rise to a reasonable doubt. Ladies and gentlemen, what are the principal matters founded upon here? Well, first of all there is the question of the warrants, police warrants. Why was a warrant to search for drugs the basis on which the expedition to Argyll Street, Rothesay, took place? Well, it could be quite innocuous because, as was said by the police officers from the Serious Crime Squad, in

175

particular Mr. Young who seems to have been the officer who authorised the expedition and who proceeded on information given to him by Sergeant Dickson, and no doubt from other sources, he was the person who decided what the warrant should be, but the point put by the Defence is why drugs when perhaps the obvious warrant was to search the house so that a man who was wanted for another crime, not to do with this indictment, could be arrested. Just in case there's any doubt in your minds about it, of course that would be the point of the alternative warrant which has been mentioned in the case, and criticism, you may recollect, was directed at one or two of the police officers for apparently being unduly coy about this, but ladies and gentlemen, the position would certainly appear to be that if the police wanted to arrest somebody who they had grounds to suspect of a serious offence and if that person was thought to be in the house of somebody who wasn't involved – if it was his own house it may be a different matter, but the house of somebody who is not involved, you can well understand it would be desirable to get a warrant, and the warrant would be to go to that address, search it and arrest the man who was suspected, and that would have been sufficient, again as has been pointed out, if there was a suspicion of arms about the place, then that by itself would have been a sufficient ground, you may feel, for the warrant, a warrant of that kind to justify the use of guns being issued to two of the people involved. Well, the suggestion of course that the Defence put forward is that the request for a warrant for drugs was made because Sergeant Dickson, and he's the one at whom the finger is pointed, and I think there's little doubt about that, that Sergeant Dickson had decided before anything formal was done that drugs were going to be found. That's the suggestion, and then it's in that light that the criticism that has been focussed on Sergeant Dickson was put, and I won't narrate it, because you remember that, I am sure. It was mentioned to you in all its detail by Mr. Findlay.

You then come to the next point, the question he put very clearly, who put the green bag inside the folder, and that's a good question. He then, and you remember the evidence about that and the point that Mr. Findlay made, then there's the failure to fingerprint the green bag. If indeed there was an issue from the beginning really of the enquiries in this case about whether that green bag was planted or was genuinely found, what better way to resolve it than by taking fingerprints, then another point – it is put by the Defence that the police, and Sergeant Dickson in particular, because I think make no bones about it, that's the man who is criticised. That's the man at whom the finger is pointed. I think not really any of the others except perhaps as allowing him to get away with it or being party perhaps to saying that they saw something that they didn't quite see, but ladies and gentlemen you will remember the evidence on that and I won't rehearse it. It's said that the police, and Sergeant Dickson in particular, knew that there was brown powder inside the green plastic bag, not because they could see it, although it's said that was the effect of Sergeant Dickson's evidence, but because Sergeant Dickson had put brown powder in beforehand, then again it is said, and this is perhaps less material to the allegation of planting because these other points all go pretty straight, don't they, to the question of possible planting by Sergeant Dickson.

There is a side issue, something that's in a sense a side issue, but it's got an important bearing on credibility. It's said that Sergeant Dickson had a gun although he denies it, and the other police officers deny that he had a gun. It's put on the basis that three police officers had guns, and of course that's what it can be said Anne McCafferty, the accused girlfriend, said, so there you have really three officers with guns. That's what is said, not two, and then you get the detailed criticism pointing the finger who had the extra gun, Sergeant Dickson, the very man who is picked out as being the villain of the piece as it were in regard to planting of the incriminating green plastic bag, then you have got in support of this, and credibility of the accused account supported by the account which he gave to the Sheriff under Judicial Examination at the very first opportunity, and then as a comment on that, it's pointed out that instead of the judicial examination being perhaps within a week or two or three days of the incident, the critical incident, namely the search of 24 Argyll Street, Rothesay, on the 12th of December, it takes place a bit later than that. Why the delay if everything was so clear-cut as the police say in evidence in court? Well, ladies and gentlemen, again I think, and I may have omitted something that you think is significant in what was put to you on behalf of the Defence by Mr. Findlay. If I have missed anything out, that doesn't mean it isn't of importance. You will give full and fair attention to all the points that he made to you in his address to you and indeed all the points that were put for the Defence in evidence, but ladies and gentlemen, summing it up, I think Mr. Findlay indicated that even if no one of these items that he dealt with, including the ones that I have mentioned, even if no one of them by itself gave rise directly to a reasonable doubt, looking at it as a whole, is there not something suspicious about this armed police expedition to Rothesay even if it's difficult to pin-point the precise ground? Well, ladies and gentlemen, that's a point that was put by Mr. Findlay with considerable eloquence, and you may think that has got some force and plausibility in face of an apparently formidable police case, and Mr. Findlay doesn't shrink from that. I think it is quite clear that he is accepting that it is a formidable police case which has to be displaced by the Defence in this positive theory. Well, ladies and gentlemen, you will consider it, but of course the plausibility of the positive case for the Defence is not enough for it to succeed. You have to accept it. You've got to accept this. It's not just a plausible defence. That's not enough. You've got to accept it or it has to give rise, either by itself or along with other parts of the evidence or along with the evidence as a whole, to a reasonable doubt, so ladies and gentlemen, that is the case for the defence, and a case in depth, and even if you don't go so far as to accept this forceful and plausible defence, it may nevertheless give rise to a reasonable doubt, and that is enough for an acquittal on Charge 4. That's really the only one that I am dealing with at the moment because that is the point at which this planting allegation focuses. It's really got nothing to do directly with the other charges because you will remember that was dealt with very quickly by Mr. Findlay at the beginning for that very reason. The earlier charges, the first three, are different altogether, and the last charge is one that hangs entirely on Charge 4.

Well, ladies and gentlemen, it's only right to consider that positive case for the defence in light also of the evidence that there is for the Crown because I'm sure you accept what was said by both counsel, that you want to scrutinise this evidence, the Crown evidence with great care and it's only if you accept the Crown evidence as establishing guilt beyond reasonable doubt that you could proceed to a conviction on Charge 4 as indeed on the other charges.

Well, ladies and gentlemen, Sergeant Dickson, presented by the Defence as the villain of the piece, the police conjurer, is somebody who is picked out, I think, for two reasons, first of all because he is the person most directly involved in the evidence in the charge for which the police were wanting to arrest the accused, and of course that's got nothing to do with the present indictment. I've already warned you about that. Equally I would warn you that you mustn't proceed on any prejudice arising out of the police's judgment that some of the police should be armed on this occasion. You mustn't hold that against the accused. It's got nothing to do with the present indictment directly at all.

Well, ladies and gentlemen, this focuses first of all on the question of, I suppose, warrants, but I'll deal with that, I think, more appropriately at a later stage. That was the first point put by Mr. Findlay but I think it may be more convenient to deal firstly with the somewhat peripheral matter of the guns for reasons which I think will become evident. First of all, it is said Sergeant Dickson had a gun. That is the allegation. It's not disputed that two of the officers had guns and it's not disputed, as I understand it that Mr. Goodall didn't, so we have got some armed and some unarmed officers. That seems to be accepted on all sides. The allegation which matters in connection with the, and it's important for credibility, and that is important in connection with the allegation of planting by Sergeant Dickson, not by anybody else, just by Sergeant Dickson. It is the gun that is significant in regard to that. Now, ladies and gentlemen, how does the matter stand? Well first of all, I think it is only fair, as emphasis was put on this by the Defence, to look at what was said about the gun by the accused at the Judicial Examination. That at page three it was read out to you and it appears in this context the accused says – it's a very long answer, you remember, that's been referred to more than once occupying practically the whole of the page. The accused was watching TV. I'm not quoting it yet. He heard a banging at the door, several bangs, and he heard distinctly a voice from inside the house stating that they were police and that they were armed, then, and I am quoting, 'My girlfriend got up off the couch and walked towards the door leading to the hallway. She looked along and saw police officers standing there. There was three of them. Each one had a gun. My girlfriend told me there was men at the door and they were all armed', and then he refers to men standing with arms outstretched with guns pointing at his head. Well now ladies and gentlemen, that's what the accused said at the Judicial Examination about guns, and you may think it is clear from what he is saying is the product of something that his girlfriend said up to the point where he himself sees people pointing guns at him, so that, ladies and gentlemen, it's a question for you to decide whether the accused is saying at any point there 'I saw three guns', or whether it isn't fairly considered his girlfriend who says there are three guns. Well ladies and gentlemen that's important and it's double-edged because on the one hand I don't think it could perhaps fairly be said that the accused commits himself in Judicial Examination to seeing three guns, and secondly, and this is a point in favour of the accused, in evidence he doesn't end up by saving 'I saw three guns'. He says 'I saw two and there may have been a third', something of that sort, but you will remember what he said about the matter, so ladies and gentlemen, the accused doesn't come forward and as it were try to pitch the case too high. The accused himself accepts that two police officers had guns and he saw two with guns, and therefore the evidence of Miss McCafferty may really be peripheral and part of the background. It's there for you to consider and give what weight you please, but I think it might be wrong for you to proceed on the footing that Mr. Findlay put to you, that the Crown has conceded, by failing to cross-examine Anne McCafferty, conceded that there were three guns. I don't think that that would be perhaps a balanced way to look at it, but it is a matter for you. In any event, at the highest pitch, Anne McCafferty, you may think, is simply saying to you in effect that she thought there were about three guns. Well anyway, ladies and gentlemen, the accused's position is clear. He in the end of the day in evidence on oath says two guns and therefore the important point isn't so much the number of guns. There's no dispute, as I pointed out to you, that two police officers were armed and at least one was not. The important point – is the accused correct in giving evidence that Sergeant Dickson had a gun at some point and pointed it at his head in the hall when he was on the floor? Now, that of course is a different matter altogether and you have got to weigh the evidence on that because it's obviously a possibility that despite what he said, Sergeant Dickson took one of the guns at one point and did exactly that, but of course in reaching a conclusion on that matter, which I point out to you is a background matter. It is not directly concerned with the question of planting. That stands on different evidence, but you would want to consider the evidence relating to that first episode when the police break into the hall. Remember the evidence. There's a conflict obviously between what the accused says happened and what the other police officers say happened, and I would merely point out that Sergeant Dickson is billed as the villain of the piece. Do you think that the Special Crime Squad officers are put in the same role? Two of them are sergeants and there's some criticism directed against at least one of these, Sergeant Trimmer. I think Sergeant McIntyre is in rather a somewhat different position. I'll come to that later. I'm not really very clear that criticism was directed against Constable Goodall, the junior constable, the junior officer who was there. Well ladies and gentlemen, if that's right, then when you are weighing the criticism of Sergeant Dickson, I think you would want to take account of the fact the Serious Crime Squad clearly would not be in the picture in the same way on this evidence, if you accept it, and you may feel that the evidence of what happened when the door was opened by force at the beginning, that the evidence on that given for example by Constable Goodall and Detective Sergeant McIntyre and indeed Sergeant Dickson, but he is in issue very much, that that is evidence you would want to consider very carefully to see if it's consistent with what the accused said. If you accept the police officers, Constable Goodall, or if you accept Sergeant McIntyre on that, then of course it contradicts the accused. Equally, if you accept the accused's evidence or it gives rise to a reasonable doubt and in the end of the day, looking at the evidence as a whole, you come to the view Sergeant Dickson did have a gun, well that would be a step forward for the accused and would take you on the road to acquittal.

Well, ladies and gentlemen, the next point – I'm not taking them in the order that Mr. Findlay put them – but rather I am trying to put them in a logical order. I'm not saying that this was illogical, but I am rather looking at it from the point of view of taking together things that may naturally go together. There's the question of the possible delay in the judicial examination, you remember the point I touched upon a moment ago. Well ladies and gentlemen, was there a delay? The incident took place, as charged on the indictment, on 12th of December 1984. You will remember that the centre of what happened in fact at 24 Argyll Street was the finding or the alleged finding of drugs. Well, it was a powder strictly inside a green plastic package. Well you heard the evidence that this required to be analysed by forensic scientists before the police could be confident that there was a controlled drug therein. Well, the production for the Crown, the production for the Crown which deals with this examination is Production 10 and that shows that the date on which the report was made by the forensic scientists was the 18th of December. The Judicial examination takes place three days later on the 21st of December, so it's a matter for you whether you think that it is a substantial delay or whether what happened was that once the police had the forensic scientific report on that powder confirming that it was heroin – that was their suspicion – whether they didn't act with perfectly reasonable promptitude in them having the Judicial examination because that by that time was the only serious charge that could be related to that particular episode, that is the search of the house on the 12th of December, so ladies and gentlemen, that is a matter of course for you to decide. You will bear in mind the view which I have already put and was stressed by the Defence that there was something wrong about that. Well was there or was there not? Was that reasonable or was that an unreasonable delay, then we come to the question of the warrants, and this of course is going back to the very start. This is Sergeant Dickson, the man at whom the finger of suspicion is pointed by the Defence, going to get a warrant in order to arrest because of grounds that he has, but these are nothing to do with this case, and also for wanting a warrant, or giving information to Mr. Young which he decides justifies a warrant for the search of drugs.

Now, ladies and gentlemen, I think you ought to be realistic when you look at this matter rather than pedantic because it is quite obvious that police officers making enquiries into suspicion of crime may go there because they have a number of different lines of enquiry, perhaps all focusing in one house or in one person, and either is enough to get a warrant obviously, and ladies and gentlemen, you may feel that law and order would be extremely difficult to enforce if the police had to get warrants for every conceivable vicissitude. Instead of going with guns they would be going with folders full of paper. I don't want to exaggerate the matter, but obviously a certain amount of commonsense has to be applied here and you may feel it is only proper that the officer who decides what warrant is to be issued applies a discretion which of course gives room for error and of course can be criticised afterwards, but applies discretion, and what he may do is to ensure that proper authority is given to the police officers, and that they are sent out on a proper mission with proper power, not with something to cover every possible contingency. Well, if that's so, looking at the issue of a drug warrant here, you have really not got to start on the supposition that it should be exactly right, the warrant, for what happens afterwards. You've got to ask yourself whether you can accept reasonably that Sergeant Dickson, and he's the man at whom the finger is pointed, and Superintendent Young who apparently makes the actual decision, that there was something sinister about that. Well ladies and gentlemen, whatever view you reach on the evidence, and you have heard Mr. Young and you have heard Sergeant Dickson and of course you heard the accused and the defence – whatever view you reach, you may say to yourself this – suppose that a warrant had been issued to search that house and apprehend a man suspected of having committed an attempted murder, suppose that had been the warrant and drugs had been found, would the Defence not be making exactly the same criticism? They go there to arrest a man and they find drugs. The drugs were planted so they would get him anyway, so you see the same sort of criticism would be put, you may feel, at almost any warrant that was selected unless the police went with a whole sheaf of warrants to cover every contingency.

Another point, and I only make two in regard to this – what in fact was found in the house? Well, the sinister issue, the matter which is at the focus of the Defence criticism, and it's a powerful one, is this green plastic bag, but what else was found in the house? Well ladies and gentlemen, there is no dispute that a large sum of money was found and that's the kind of thing you may feel you may well expect to find when you go to search a house on suspicion that drugs are trafficked there. What about the envelope that was found? At the beginning it looked as if this might be seriously contested whether that was planted too, but in the end of the day I don't think it was seriously challenged that that was found, and I think Miss McCafferty saw it being found by the police. Well ladies and gentlemen, whichever way you look at that it seems to be accepted by both sides of the bar that this envelope has writing on it, not connected with the present charge in any way, but which reasonably construed indicates drugs, controlled drugs, and has reference to large sums of money. Ladies and gentlemen, if that wasn't planted, would could be wrong then with issuing a warrant to search for drugs, so there may be nothing sinister at all then in that warrant even looking at it from the point of view of the Defence and approaching it in the way that Mr. Findlay approached it. The critical issue of course is still open and it's the vital issue. Despite all that, was this green package planted by Sergeant Dickson or was it found when the police searched? Well ladies and gentlemen, I make the same point about the other criticism of Sergeant Dickson. He found heroin because he decided drugs would be found and he asked for a drugs warrant so that the drugs would be found. Well, all that goes on the preposition doesn't it, that at some point Sergeant Dickson armed with heroin or brown powder, armed with it, puts it into the possessions of the accused. Well, does the evidence really give room for that when you look at the Crown side of the case, if you accept it. Sergeant McIntyre, and the accused significantly was willing to give the benefit of the doubt to that member of the Serious Crime Squad – who is it that finds something in the pocket of the accused? It's Sergeant McIntyre on his evidence, and it's the evidence too according to my recollection, but it's a matter for you of course, but according to my recollection Constable Goodall says the same, that the search, the preliminary search, the frisking at the beginning in the bedroom was done by Sergeant McIntyre, and Sergeant McIntyre himself said that he unzipped the track suit trouser pocket. Did somebody zip it up beforehand? Is it said that Sergeant Dickson put something in there before it was zipped up? I don't think it is. Well ladies and gentlemen, the pocket is unzipped by Sergeant McIntyre and he takes out the folder and puts it on the bed. That's what he said according to my recollection. That's what Constable Goodall said according to my recollection, but it's yours that matters for all these matters, what Sergeant McIntyre said, what Constable Goodall said, what Sergeant Trimmer said and of course what Sergeant Dickson said.

He is the man at whom the finger is pointed. The police officers all, you may think, give the clear evidence that the contents of that folder were put on the bed not by Sergeant Dickson, but by Sergeant McIntyre, put on the bed by him and they then fell open. Do you remember the folder comes open the way everybody described very vividly and the green packet is seen inside? Now, that's what they say if you accept that evidence and our recollection of it indeed is to that effect.

Well, ladies and gentlemen, I'll come back to that because Mr. Findlay put a very powerful question and it is important right at the centre 'Who put the green bag in the folder?', so I'll come to that in a moment, but there is another important matter because the Defence say well, Sergeant Dickson knew, and he is the man who is said to have done the planting, Sergeant Dickson knew there was a brown powder in the bag at the time when he couldn't yet have seen it because he refers to a brown powder, and you will remember the evidence he gave upon that. Well ladies and gentlemen, again it's my impression, but it's your recollection that matters, that when Sergeant Dickson first gave evidence about that, he didn't in fact give a description of the colour of the powder, but simply said that he saw a powder in the bag. It's quite true that later on and certainly in cross-examination he referred to that as a brown powder which he suspected because of its colour as being heroin, and that's the strength of the criticism that the Defence put forward. Well, is that a fair inference to draw? Ladies and gentlemen, you have seen that green bag and you have seen the contents of the little bottle inside it. You have also heard the evidence and it was mentioned by Mr. Findlay very properly. It's an important point, that the expert brought by the Defence, and you will give full and due weight to all that he said, and it helps the Defence, that he couldn't really see the colour. He thought it was a grey powder until the top was opened and he looked inside and could see it had a brown quality when he did that. Well ladies and gentlemen, that again is something that cuts two ways because the fact of the matter is, if your recollection of what happened in court is the same as mine, that nobody ever poured the contents of that little glass phial into the green bag so none of us have seen what Sergeant Dickson actually says he saw, namely the powder in the plastic bag when it was found disclosed in the bedroom of the house, so that is a matter you would no doubt wish to take into account.

Well now, ladies and gentlemen, let me turn then to what is really the critical question 'Who put the green bag in the folder?' That's a perfectly reasonable question put by Mr. Findlay, and put in that way in isolation it carries an implication which is clear, but is the implication necessarily a reasonable one, for example you could put that question along with other questions. Who put the cash line card in the folder? Who put the insurance cover note in the folder? Who put the

HORT 1 form in the folder? Who put the banknotes in the folder? Who put the folder in the tracksuit pocket? Who zipped it up?, and then ladies and gentlemen you go on to the questions I have already dealt with, the police evidence, to the effect of how they say the green plastic bag was found by them. Well, if you accept that police evidence and you reject the Defence positive case, ladies and gentlemen, there is evidence there which would entitle you to take the view that the police did indeed find that green bag, as Sergeant Dickson says he did, and you don't have to go on Sergeant Dickson alone, because if you are doubting his truthfulness, his good faith, you've got these other police officers, but remember that the accused himself is prepared to give Sergeant McIntyre the benefit of the doubt and you may feel it is difficult to withhold the benefit of the doubt from Constable Goodall, and then there is only Sergeant Trimmer. Do you think he was cooking up a case? Remember the demeanour of these witnesses, ladies and gentlemen. That's a matter that you are entitled to consider, and then of course there's Sergeant Dickson himself. Do you really, having heard him and having seen him in court, do you really think he did plant this evidence in that way?

One other matter ladies and gentlemen that's important to the central question, certainly in my view. It's a matter for you whether it is the central question, but for the Defence it was said that the accused had all along given substantially the account that he gave in the witness box and that in particular that's what he said had happened, this planting, as he stated it, was how he put it to the Sheriff. Well now, ladies and gentlemen, I leave it to you to decide because I'm going to quote again what he said in this long answer, whether what he said to the Sheriff is indeed the same as what he said in evidence in this court. The important point is that in the middle of this long answer he indicates – I'm not quoting yet – that he believed that the police officers were looking in the house for either a knife or a gun. 'While searching the house' – now I'm going to quote – 'While searching the house it was Mr. Dickson who seemed to be in charge. He pulled out a package from somewhere. I didn't see what it was. He had his back to me and within seconds of each other all the CID officers asked him what it was he had. He then searched me' and that would seem to be Sergeant Dickson. 'He then searched me, put the stuff out of my pockets onto the ground next to the wall unit and I asked him again what it was he found and he says 'It's just powder.' He then took the sachet of powder and put it inside my wallet. It wasn't in any folder. It was just put inside the outer covers.' Well ladies and gentlemen, that's what the transcript says he said to the Sheriff. Is that the same as what he said in court? If it's the same, well that's consistent. If it's not the same, what inference do you draw from that? Is that a picture entirely different from the one presented now or is it not different in such a way that it would carry any implication for or against the truthfulness of the positive case that the Defence make, then I come, and I am nearly finished, ladies and gentlemen, to another criticism which isn't perhaps in the foreground but is an important criticism put by the Defence. It's the failure to fingerprint the green plastic package. Well ladies and gentlemen, if the police looking for a pickpocket who has stolen a plain gold cigarette case, very valuable, beautiful plain polished surface, if they find such a cigarette case in the pocket of a suspect, do you think they are going to fingerprint it? They have actually found it in the possession of the pickpocket. Why fingerprint it even though it would take perfect fingerprints? There is a limit perhaps to the extent at which the police could properly go on fingerprinting suspects. If they find something genuinely on somebody, what more do you need to show that it was his or that he had it, and the charge is one of possession of drugs. It doesn't need to be anything more proprietary than that.

Well, ladies and gentlemen, take another point into account. Looking at the practical realities of it, the green bag, by the time that the forensic report is made, and that's the only time that the police definitely know that this was heroin. They had their suspicions before, but of course if it's not heroin then there's no serious charge and no need for fingerprints because that would be a dead waste of time, you may think. On the other hand, if it is heroin then the question of possible fingerprints will arise, but by that time ladies and gentlemen not only have police handled the green bag, but the forensic experts have handled it and you will remember there was some criticism from the Defence expert that perhaps the powder on the outside and some parts of the inside would come when it was poured into the bottle. Well ladies and gentlemen, after all that, what would be the point of fingerprinting, and ladies and gentlemen, until the Judicial Examination that follows that, why should the Crown have reason to suspect that this green package is going to be said to be planted? So looking at it realistically ladies and gentlemen, is there force in that criticism or is that a criticism on which you can indeed proceed and say well, it would have been decisive. If fingerprints had been found, that would have been pretty conclusive. Well ladies and gentlemen on any view, there would have been a lot of fingerprints if any had been detected at all and indeed at best for this point, it's accepted by the Defence expert that this is a plastic bag with his powder on it, so anything that was there before the powder got there would presumably be less easy to detect than it was before.

Now, ladies and gentlemen, I have focussed some of the issues, contentious issues in this case for you, not all of them. You will pay fair and full attention to all the issues and in particular to those so cogently and persuasively put before you by Mr. Findlay. I think it would be useful, because it is a somewhat complicated indictment unfortunately, if I briefly recapitulate to you what is open to you on the various charges:

Charge 1, if you are satisfied beyond reasonable doubt that what the accused called his tools of the trade were nonetheless intended or one of them was intended for use as a weapon you are entitled to convict. However, you acquit if you accept self-defence as a reasonable excuse in the circumstances or if you have a reasonable doubt arising from any of the evidence on that matter. Equally, you can delete a particular item or items of the tools of trade if you consider that such an item definitely wasn't intended as a weapon.

Charge 2, if you are satisfied beyond reasonable doubt that the dagger or throwing knife was an offensive weapon designed to cause injury, and it may be difficult to avoid if you consider that the accused, despite his denial and the story about McFadyen in the back seat, had it there for his own purposes. If you accept that he did not know that it was there or that it may well have been McFadyen's or if you have reasonable doubt, you will acquit.

Charge 3, this is the cocaine one, the accused admits this and there is ample evidence of guilt. It is, however, a matter for you and you are entitled if you are not satisfied beyond reasonable doubt to acquit.

Charge 4, this is the alternatives, you may acquit of both alternatives. Now, if you accept the defence positive case, then you will acquit of both alternatives. There is sufficient evidence, if you accept the Crown case, to convict of the more serious first alternative. Obviously therefore there is sufficient evidence if you accept it to convict of the less serious second alternative, but as I have indicated to you previously, if it's a conviction on Charge 4, one is accepted and the other falls, so whatever else you do, ladies and gentlemen, if you are coming back with a verdict of guilty on Charge 4, please remember to make it clear beyond per adventure which alternative you are finding proved, and you could do that easily by making it clear that you are convicting of possession with intent under Section 5/3 or that you are finding simple possession under 5/2. If you accept the accused positive defence, you would acquit of both alternatives. You would equally acquit of both alternatives if you have reasonable doubt on the basis that Mr. Findlay put to you. If you have a reasonable doubt looking at the Defence evidence as a whole or taking it or part of it along with the rest of the evidence, the Crown evidence, if any of that gives rise to reasonable doubt, or any bit of that gives rise to a reasonable doubt in the sense in which I have defined it, not just a feeling that there is something fishy, but a doubt based on reason, then of course you acquit.

Finally **Charge 5**, if you convict under 4 of one alternative or the other, you are entitled to proceed on the unchallenged evidence to a conviction on Charge 5, but if you acquit of both alternatives of 4, you will acquit in respect of Charge 5 also and the appropriate verdict in that event on Charge 5 would be not guilty because that's the one that can only proceed on the hypothesis that there is a conviction on Charge 4.

Finally ladies and gentlemen, you will consider each of these charges separately and weigh the evidence relating to them separately in the scales of justice, and only if you are satisfied beyond reasonable doubt of each will you return a verdict of guilty on that charge. There are three verdicts open to you, namely guilty, not guilty and not proven and I have put these in alphabetical order so that there should be no prejudice. The last two, not guilty and not proven, are both verdicts of acquittal, not guilty being the more forceful acquittal, and of course it follows from what I have said to you that you return separate verdicts on each of the charges, as I have already charged you. Your verdicts can be given unanimously or by a majority, but if the verdict is to be guilty of anything criminal, there must be at least eight of your number in favour of that view, and that is really quite obvious if you think about it. There has got to be an absolute majority of the 15 of you before you can convict, at least eight out of 15. You could in theory have a majority for guilty with seven only because there are two other verdicts. That's not enough for a conviction. You've got to have eight. If you do not have eight for guilty of any particular charge, then you must substitute an acquittal on that charge.

When you retire you may care to select one of your number to be foreman or forewoman, to collect your views, to act as chairman and to speak for you when you return. The foreman will be asked in respect of each charge whether you are agreed on your verdict, and if so, what the verdict is, so please make that clear particularly in regard to Charge 4, and if you are striking out something in regard for example to Charge 1, please make it clear what you are striking out. You will also be asked whether your verdict in each case is unanimous or by a majority so please will the foreman note that, or the forewoman note that. We are not concerned about the actual arithmetic, but simply whether the result is a unanimous or a majority result. Now, I can take the verdicts from you at any time when you have resolved all the issued.

Are there any other points counsel wish to put to me before they duly retire?

The Advocate Depute: No, my lord.
Mr. Findlay: No, my lord.
Lord Murray: Very well ladies and gentlemen, retire please and consider your verdicts.

The jury retired at 10.49 a.m.

UNDER MY SKIN

The bullying had gone on for, I don't know, maybe three years on and off. I remember the point where I was leaving primary school to go to secondary school and, to me, that was just too much of a leap. I'd dealt with enough from that fucking family. Now, here in the big school, there were older ones to deal with. That's when the psoriasis kicked in.

I was taken to the doctors cos they thought I'd picked up an infection at school. They thought it was scabies or something. They looked at it and treated it and decided it wasn't. I felt even more alienated, having people examining me and trying different stuff only for it not to work. It was like it was my fault; I was feeling lower and lower all the time. I ended up in hospital for a considerable amount of time and I remember missing near enough the first year at secondary school. When I went into hospital I was in the children's ward with babies. And the treatment I was getting was like thick, cold tar or paint. It actually smelled like tar, like when you go past road works or a building site and they're doing the roof. They put that all over me three times a day and then wrapped it all up. I couldn't bear it: bath, showered, bath, showered. Then there came a time when they moved me from the kid's section to the older section and I saw older men with psoriasis. I was just like a zombie. I walked through on autopilot and sat down next to my bed. It was like I wasn't really there. I sussed it was because I'd become a man, but I just shrugged at it.

It all calmed down eventually and I got back to school, met my old friends, made some new friends and then discovered that the family had been sent to another school further away. The fucking relief. It was fucking magic! Getting back to school, sport was a bit of a problem, people were ignorant and didn't know what psoriasis was. In fairness, I wouldn't have known what it was either. I was so self-aware, because we all know how cruel kids can be. I was so terrified that it would leave me prone to being singled out and bullied all over again. Fortunately for me, you couldn't see any of my blotchy red skin because I never had it on my hands or my feet. In PE, I became the default goalie so I could wear a tracksuit.

I had various bouts of it through my teens. I spent a couple more months in hospital while I was locked up. I noticed a girl while I was there; Anne-Marie. She also had psoriasis and was in the female side. We used to meet up and sit in the day room, and our romance blossomed. Knowing she had it, I felt a lot better. Maybe more at ease, had some confidence, because I knew I didn't have something to hide that she may have been repulsed by. I think there's a shock aspect and ignorance when some silly fucker says something like, *Can I catch that*? And because you've got it, it magnifies situations because the thing becomes the centre of attention and creates embarrassment. The relationship was so much easier meeting in there. I mean, it's not the most common place to meet someone, is it?

One day the doctor appeared at my bed with a few students. I didn't know they were at the time. They were in to look at my psoriasis and try to find the cause of it. People were baffled because normally it's a hereditary condition and nobody else in the family had it. I was frustrated at the 'experts' not knowing what was causing it, but they were a bit stumped. To be stuck there when no one has a fucking clue is difficult to put into words. It *felt* like they were making progress, but were they? How long would I be there for? Without any obvious answers, they started asking more questions. The next step was to find out if I was getting physically or mentally abused at home.

'How do you get on with your dad?'

'Well, he's in prison.'

'How do you get on with your mum?

'Mum goes to work.'

'What about school?'

As I told them they turned and looked at each other. I saw that Eureka moment in their eyes, and then it dawned on me as well.

They'd been the cause of it. That fucking family of degenerates who were terrorising me. It's like being detective and going back to certain triggers, matching events up. The psoriasis represented that family even when they weren't giving me a kicking. It meant they were always there, always on me, making my life unbearable. That's what they were; the thing that was causing me agony and making me withdraw, making me feel like a leper, making me cover up, recoil at the slightest touch – it was all them.

Was I going to sit back and let a bunch of cunts do this to me? How long was I going to let them get away with it?

I decided to do something about it and that's what I did.

THE VERDICT

Fucking hell, 46 minutes to reach their verdict.
You can never tell if it's a good or a bad thing.
With the judge going on about the villain of the
piece, I thought he meant me at first. It was nice
to know he meant Dickson. That was a big thing
in my favour. And the toxicology report. I just
need to keep stuff like that in my mind and stay
positive.

Upon their return at 11.35 a.m.

The Clerk of Court: Ladies and gentlemen, who
speaks for you?
The Foreman of The Jury: I do.
The Clerk: Would you stand up please? Have you
reached your verdicts?
The Foreman: Yes.
The Clerk: What is your verdict in respect of
Charge No. 1?
The Foreman: Charge No. 1, guilty.
The Clerk: Is that unanimous or by a majority?
The Foreman: Majority.
The Clerk: Charge No. 2?
The Foreman: Not guilty, unanimous.
The Clerk: Charge No. 3?
The Foreman: Guilty.
The Clerk: Unanimous or by a majority?
The Foreman: Unanimous.
The Clerk: Charge No. 4?
The Foreman: By a majority, not guilty.

The Clerk: Now, there are two alternatives. Is that a majority not guilty on each alternative?

The Foreman: On both alternatives.

The Clerk: And Charge No. 5, may I take it that is not guilty?

The Foreman: Not guilty.

The Clerk: And is that unanimous or by a majority?

The Foreman: Majority.

The Clerk: If you sit down I will record your verdict. Ladies and gentlemen, is this a true record of your verdict – the Jury unanimously find the panel not guilty on Charge No.2, guilty on Charge No. 3, and by a majority find the panel guilty on Charge No. 1 and not guilty on each of Charges Nos. 4 and 5?

The Foreman: That is correct.

The Advocate Depute: My lord, I move to sentence in respect of those charges on which a conviction has been returned and I tender a schedule of previous convictions. My lord, it has been drawn to my attention that the terms of the last conviction there recorded and disputed, it has been drawn to my attention, and it is a relatively minor matter, and that is the one on 15th October, 1984, and rather than become involved in any procedure at this stage, I would without prejudice invite your lordship to disregard that previous conviction.

Lord Murray: I shall take that out of the counting.

The Advocate Depute: So far as the schedule of previous convictions is concerned, your lordship will see that in 1981 he was convicted of assault and robbery. In 1982 there is a conviction for attempt to pervert the course of justice, also in 1982 an offence under the Firearms Act and the Prevention of Crime Act, and also in 1982 a further conviction for assault with intent to rob, and in 1983 a further conviction for theft which attracted 9 months' detention in a Young Offenders' Institution. The conviction under the Firearms Act, Section 4/4, is the possession of a sawn-off shotgun. That is what Section 4/4 relates to, and your lordship will see that there is there in these previous convictions evidence of violence and dishonesty and matters relating also to firearms.

Lord Murray: Is the sentence correct on the 20th of May 1982? It must have been 12 months' detention, I would imagine. That is the firearms one.

The Advocate Depute: It must have been 12 months' detention as opposed to imprisonment, yes, and according to my information my lord, Paul Ferris is 21 years of age and he is said to be single. Your lordship has heard of his relationship with Miss McCafferty and your lordship has also heard of the nature of his employment. The only other thing it would be appropriate for me to say is this – that in relation to Charge 1 it is a conviction in respect of the possession of the offensive weapons. So far as the shooting – I think it would perhaps be inappropriate for me to say anything concerning the shooting of the motor car my lord.

Lord Murray: Well, I think that doesn't arise.

The Advocate Depute: It doesn't arise.

Lord Murray: It may have background relevance.

The Advocate Depute: It does indeed, but I think in the circumstances I should take it no further.

Lord Murray: I am perfectly content to take it on the basis that it has got nothing to do with it.

Mr. Findlay: Your lordship has heard my client's personal circumstances both from the Depute and in evidence, and your lordship will bear in mind he has been in custody since his arrest in relation to these matters, and that was effectively the 12th of December. My lord, looking to the very discriminating verdict of the Jury and comparing that with his previous convictions, there is a similarity that cannot be missed and also there is an obvious difference between the charges that have been found not guilty and other matters which don't appear on the record, so that there is a very clear relationship, I would suggest, between the record and the way the Jury have approached this matter, and I say no more about it at this stage than that. In relation to Charge 3 your lordship heard his position. He admitted that charge. He was going through some personal difficulties and he got cocaine to try. It is in the context of these things a comparatively minor matter, in the context of these things. Taking then Charge 1, I would not imagine-

Lord Murray: Mr. Findlay, it is right, is it not, that on the record this is the first drugs offence that he has been found guilty of?

Mr. Findlay: Yes, no history of drugs at all. In relation to Charge 1 I would not conceive that that would have brought him before the High Court, had he faced that charge. Even with Charge 3 it would be unlikely that would come before the High Court. That being so, it's really that I would suggest my lord might feel is the general basis of disposal in relation to that matter.

Lord Murray: Having said that I think perhaps you wouldn't resist the preposition that that charge might nevertheless have been an indictment before the Sheriff.

Mr. Findlay: I think that is right, yes, so it is really perhaps more a Sheriff Court indictment than the High Court as the matter now proceeds. There is really nothing more to say about it than that.

Lord Murray: Thank you, Mr. Findlay. I want to consider this matter as I have to make separate sentences on the statutory matter. I will retire briefly.

I was back downstairs and had a bite to eat before being brought back up into the court.

After an adjournment.

It was tense. Why could it all not just be wrapped up in one go? But, hey, I didn't want to rush him. I had to stay positive, breathe... *breathe*...

Lord Murray: Paul Ferris, I have considered what sentence is appropriate in light of the convictions that the Jury have returned against you. I accept that the incident on the 2nd of August 1984 involved nothing that could be regarded as a weapon except if it was intended to be used as a weapon and I take that into account in mitigation. However, having regard to your previous record, particularly the one of the 20th of May 1982 which resulted in 12 months' detention, I must take a serious view of this conviction. Bearing in mind the points that were put to me by the Defence, I consider that the appropriate sentence on this charge is one of 18 months' imprisonment. That will be backdated to the date of your arrest. So far as the drugs charge is concerned, I am satisfied that this is the first time that you have been involved in drugs, and bearing in mind the amount, I think I can take a lenient view of this offence, and in the circumstances, I am prepared to limit the sentence to one of 12 months' imprisonment. That will also be backdated, and these to run concurrently.

MY VERDICT

I was genuinely delighted with the verdict and, although the minor charges got me at least a year in prison, I was happy that the jury believed my word against that of four senior police officers. The sentence was backdated to my arrest in December, 1994. I say police officers, but I felt that's what they called themselves in court. I knew differently and so did they. On the day in question, they certainly were not officers of the law. The people who took part in the raid were nothing short of what I would call deranged perverts who tried and failed to convict me of something I had not done.

To say that they were seething was an understatement. This was a massive loss for them. A massive and unexpected loss – they weren't used to shit like this. They didn't go to court and lose – the public usually take their word as the truth. Their dirty laundry was hung out in public with the trial and, from that day on, I was a marked man. I knew that when I was going into it. I was young and I was planning on being around for a lot longer so, in my mind, the fight was just warming up. I never saw Dickson in court and I did mean what I'd said to him in the flat. It's now well documented in *The Wee Man*. I think the police already knew the game was up and they were exposed. It became a damage limitation exercise for them, wondering who this little fucker was who won the day in court despite all the odds. Well, that little fucker was me and was I not jumping for joy. After being cleared by the jury, I now had to start a new chapter – no pun intended – on my new life as an adult prisoner, convicted upon what I'd admitted.

The weapons charge would usually have netted me a much lesser sentence in a smaller court. I think the judge was just exercising his right to clip my wings, so to speak. There wasn't much more he could do and he was showing me that he didn't like their collective authority being fucked around with. Fair enough. I didn't like him much either. Or his fucking wig.

At one point, I actually thought that the police were going to be charged with perjury, but it eventually was all swept under the carpet. Or so they thought. I've got a long memory. I was sent down for what I did and not for something that was manufactured to get a conviction. Yeah, as a criminal, it hurts to go to court and admit something. We're not renowned for our honesty, after all. But you've always got to be thinking and use whatever tools at your disposal to wrong-foot the fuckers. It goes back to when I learned to play chess as a kid: you sacrifice a few things to get a win. I admitted to the coke. It'll be on my record, but it's not like I was ever gonna have a clean sheet anyway, is it? And it wasn't like I'd have to update it on my CV. These days, it's probably more unusual to say you've never *had* coke. Auld boy Murray was probably snorting tonnes of it off the arses of hookers backstage when he was waiting to be called in. He must have thought I was a right fucking lightweight. But he must have *thought* – and that's the point. The jury must also have thought.

Hopefully they thought: *If young Ferris here admits to having coke in his possession, then surely he'd admit to the heroin, if it was his*?

And then, *If he's telling the truth about drugs, why would he be lying about that other gun*?

It was my first offence for drugs. I knew they'd be lenient. I wasn't naive, I was taking a hit to deflect a bigger hit and it paid off. The whole thing was a massive learning experience: there was the Thompson clan showing me that they were in with the police and there was all the dishonesty from the police. It showed me how they operated. The Thompsons proved to be sly as fuck and I'd really need to watch my back from then on. The police – well, I now knew exactly how they operated. They were as corrupt as anyone else on the street. The uniform was just a way of trying to legitimise it.

Here I was leaving the High Court in Glasgow after being found not guilty on the main planting of heroin charges. I felt vindicated and knew what I was facing both in and out of prison. I'd made my position clear – *don't fuck with me*. I'm not for playing games with and if people had issues then make sure they are legit. I was and still am well up for voicing my views on it. That included me telling others what Fatboy or his father had done to me; setting me up, sacrificing me on a silver platter to be killed or put in prison for a very long time. It was either one or both who sold me down the river and, despite my best efforts to find out who it was, I concluded that it may well have been both as only they and they alone knew where I was. The warrant being issued even before I even set foot on the island was a bit of a clue. As I've said, you do that and you only get one go at it. If it blows up in your face, you've only got yourself to blame. The police knew my father and, more importantly, they knew me. They knew me as someone who would do whatever it takes by every means necessary to expose them.

I wanted to cheer and shout, *Fuck you*! or something to the coppers. There are loads of things you want to do, but it's best you keep cool and dignified, isn't it? I was in Donald Findlay's environment there and any silliness would have been disrespectful to him. I'm not that kind of man.

Others have since claimed that Fatboy could not have sent the police to the flat as he was in prison, but that's not true. It's another one of those things invented – by someone trying to clear his name. At that point, Fatty Thompson was not in prison. If he was in prison, he couldn't have handed me the keys to his dad's car.

If you don't learn to survive in the scary forest you will never get out of it and, as my dad once told me, be a lion son and don't be a sheep.

My verdict? There was gonna be a war.

BIG HOUSES

Ah, those early days in Longriggend. I suppose I actually do look back on them with fond memories. Being locked up in Glasgow was never those from the north fighting the south. You'd have Glasgow fighting Edinburgh, though. Where I usually describe Longriggend as a university of crime, there's also the analogy of it being like serving an apprenticeship. You'd have city to city conflict or you have some other conflicts locally, and there'd always be someone who wanted to get to someone else. People could step in all the time to prove themselves to others and form alliances that way. It went on all the time, just like it did on the streets. It was a good way for people to make a name and be in with someone once they got out.

I ended up back there for assault and robbery. A friend and I took a bag from somebody who was gonna deposit it into a night safe. It was the usual thing of one distracting the guy while the other takes the bag. As it's usually to a shop you're talking at least a few grand a pop. Me and my mate George 'Geo' Redmond were the ones who used to get offered such jobs. Once you were in the clear, you gave so much over to the guy who was the spotter and the one who found you the work. To keep your own overheads and outgoings down, it was best to work in twos.

On this job, and unfortunately for me, somebody gave chase and I just kept running and running and running until I got rugby tackled. It was right out of the blue and this was the funniest part of it. The blag was in Airdrie in Lanarkshire and the off-duty copper that caught me was the fastest runner in his rugby team. As if that wasn't bonkers enough, the daftest thing about it all was the direction I was running – towards the fucking police station. So, I went up, pleaded guilty, and was carted off to Longriggend. I was taken to Barlinnie again, charged at Airdrie court, back to Barlinnie, picked up and taken to Longriggend.

This is where the real rebels got put. Of course, as soon as I rocked up and they looked at my file it was, *That's him who threw the fucking tray at the screw*! It never leaves you! *You'll not be going near any dining halls, Ferris*! and fucking all the rest of it and I got to the stage where I came clean.

A screw used to come in and give me newspapers, general chit-chat, play a game of chess and I suppose there's good and bad in every environment. Not all of them are thugs and sadists (apparently).

'What was all the carry on the last time you were in? The thing with the tray?' he asked.

I told him the story and he just started laughing.

'It's not fucking funny!' I said as I laughed. It *was* funny and it was a moment to savour. We were both in that screw-con situation, but there was still times where you could share a laugh and still feel human.

'What was it you said to him in your cell, again? We all heard that story when he kicked you in the nuts from someone stood outside the door,' he said.

I was glad that I'd provided them with some entertainment. Before he left, he said:

'In the end, they're all gonna have a kick and that's just the way it is.'

Aye, he was right. I was in for the whole fucking three weeks. It was at a time when my psoriasis was flaring up and I was on an escapee list. That means you put your prison clothes outside your cell door and you get given a set of pyjamas and a pair of slippers to wear. The screws that run most of the segregation units are hard bastards on the inside, but they would be different on the outside. There was medical treatment available to inmates that I never knew I was entitled to – no one told me about it and I didn't ask for it – it just wasn't offered, despite my obvious suffering. So my psoriasis went as high as 90+ body mass. There's always a three-week wait to be taken back to the bus and to court. I'd already pleaded guilty, but the three weeks are to ensure the court knows all of your circumstances, if there's anything taken into account, if you're due for another charge you can bring that in and compress it or go and get the one sentence and whatnot.

On my way to the prison bus, I knew that things weren't right. My arms were getting cut, the backs of my legs were getting cut and I just had to

217

get on with it. I got cuffed to others who were up in court the same day, so it wasn't comfortable at all. In court I was given three months detention; another short, sharp shock. I don't know when they thought the shock would kick in – they knew my face by now. And there was a 12-month sentence to run after detention.

On our way back on the bus, we were all cuffed together and were straight into this military-type setup. It was all *shine your boots, press your trousers and keep your shit tidy* stuff. There was this big Irish screw who was shouting at us to march. March here, march there, quick march, slow march – you never walked anywhere for the first three months. It was fucking gruelling. Some would say it was punishing, then they'd realise it was supposed to be. No prison is soft. No prison treats you like a snowflake. Even less so back then. We were the biggest blight to Scotland's reputation and this regime was designed to essentially beat it all out of us. After a couple of weeks getting into the routine, I thought I'd cracked it. How wrong can you be?

In the gymnasium, you got paired off with somebody who's already there. So I got paired off with someone who was a gym orderly.

The mats were there and the screws were saying, 'Right! Let's see how many press ups you can do in a minute.'

So a button was pressed, a big stop clock thing, and this big Johnny Bravo inmate started going like fuck, like he's doing a world record, so the screw stopped everyone and said we're all gonna start again. Each of us not doing the press-ups had to put a fist on the floor beneath the one doing it so that their chin had to touch the top of it before going back up to complete a full rep.

'Don't do too many,' my gym buddy whispered.

He was right. There was no time for conversation. I took my time. The trick about not doing too many was that next time you're in there, you've got to beat your score. Go slow, do 20 even if you can do 40. The next one was you had to run and touch both sides of the gym, catch the medicine ball, throw it back and then flip onto the mat to do your press-ups again. Then the other guy had your legs while you did your sit-ups. Then we were out on the football fields. And who was the silly cunt who put his hand up when the Physical Training Instructor asked if anyone had ever done any running before? Fucking me, that's who! I was fit enough to run cross-country for the school from running scared through fear. That fear turned into fitness and that fitness turned into running and, because I was light bodied anyway, cross-country was something I was interested in and good at.

'Are you being *fucking funny*, son?!' he shouted. 'Fucking cross-country runner?!'

He made me do a six-minute mile while he booted me up the arse. I was totally demoralised, but you've just got to pull yourself together in that kind of shit. They were there to make you crack and push you to your limit. It probably wasn't far off any real military training, to be fair. Marching and running through the pain barrier with boots that are digging into your ankles in clothes that were unbearable. Forget about that. Fuck pain – it's all in your head. Everyone just wanted to get out of there and you could actually get out early if you behaved. That was the incentive. It was a government-led initiative that was put into Scottish legislation many, many years ago as an impact on fighting for young impressionable kids noted to have so far lived a life of crime.

The next time I was in the young offenders, it was by police escort. You could say I'd gone up in the world since rifling through already-stolen cars. I was charged with five attempted murders and for using a firearm against a family. I got 12 months to be served back in this ex-military situation where they don't take any shit.

I was almost in awe at the way the discipline worked in there. I was amazed that one head screw could control so many people. The dining hall: it was exactly the same drill as the first time I'd been in. It was familiar; it was almost comforting to know what to do. The place was immaculate and top food as well. And you needed the food cos of all the training, but the problem was the whole sitting down to eat thing. There were four of us to each table. When he shouted, you had to grab your chair, swing it round, and sit

220

down all in one go – everyone, not just your table – and nobody ever got it right first time.

'Back up!'

And you just had to keep going until it happened in perfect timing. You'd usually get someone messing it up for a laugh, but after the third take, you'd be likely to get lynched if you weren't careful. When it worked it was like listening to a finely tuned orchestra. It was fucking mad! And it didn't just end with sitting down. I had a big plate of sausages and chips with two slices of bread. I levelled them with butter, loaded the first slice with chips, put the two sausages on it, flattened the other slice on top and was just about to take a bite out of it when it was smacked right out of my hand by a screw. Not violent, but enough for it to fall onto my plate.

His voice was like thunder, 'There'll be no fucking butties in here, lad. Get up!'

So I stood up and he sat down in my chair and he cut a chip in half, put the cutlery back down, took a slice of bread, took a bite from the bread and put it back down.

'You'll learn that before you ever get out of here, son.'

Ok, learn from example. You don't make that mistake twice. Not only were you getting discipline, you got trained how to eat properly. There were a lot of lads in there who didn't really know how to use cutlery.

Being out on parade was another test of resolve. We'd have our shiny boots on, all our trouser creases sorted, and the governor would be walking up and down looking for excuses. You needed to be on your toes and be sharp all the time in there and I was quite happy with the regime and getting myself fit. While I was doing this you'd think it would put me in good favour, but I knew by playing their game I still wouldn't get any preferential treatment. I was never going to get released from the detention centre because I had another outstanding case to go up for from when I took the car chase – the case regarding the shotgun. At the time, I'd only been asked to drop a bag off. It was a farcical police chase. I should have known even then that all my police chases would end up in farce.

We got woken up and taken to the washrooms in the morning – *you better be up, your bed better be made, your towel in your left hand, your plastic mug, your slippers on*. We'd just be wearing slippers, socks and boxers. This ginger haired Irish screw was handing out razors, but I still can't fucking grow a moustache now, never mind way back then.

As I filed past him, he was like, 'Razor,' and I was as polite as possible.

'No, thanks,' I said, and carried on walking.

'Oi, get back here! *Now*!'

As I was stood, he said *razor* to another lad and got the reply, 'No thank you, sir.'

He looked me in the eye. His face was red and straining with anger.

'*Razor*!'

'No thank you, sir,' came my reply.

And that was that. You had to say *sir* after everything. If he even suspected I was taking the piss, he'd have just cracked me in the jaw. I started taking a razor after that – even though I didn't need it! I loved the challenges like that. Whether he was being a total arse on purpose, trying to make me look bad, trying to make me crack, let everyone know who was boss – whatever it was, it didn't bother me at all. The regime presented these challenges and I made it my aim to react accordingly. You need to understand that they never used to employ regular blokes there. These were tough times to be out on the streets and even tougher times to be locked away with teenage maniacs. To deal with them, they'd employ ex-army, the toughest coppers you ever messed with, huge broad-shouldered men who wouldn't look out of place brawling their way through the roughest bar in town. Could you take one of them on to create a name for yourself? Could you fuck. If you had a death wish, maybe. So, on the street if someone talked to you like that you'd cut them without a second thought: inside you just had to grit your teeth and see where you were at fault. With all the rules to adhere to, you generally were at fault as well. One thing that got me through it all was knowing my dad and brother were still in prison and they'd done a *lot* of years. For me to complain about a few months of my life wasn't even an option. My psoriasis meant that my hands, face, ears, feet – luckily never my bollocks – just the rest of my body was covered. That part of it was worth complaining about, but it was my cross to bear, I suppose.

I had a mate in there called Neilie 'The Bomb' cos he was always making devices to blow up people's cars. He used to run HMP Glenochil and, at the time, they targeted all the sex offenders in there. A Home Office enquiry was carried out cos there were around eight deaths. Some of the deaths were suicides and two of the others that I know of were helped along. Neilie earned a lot of respect for his initiative. He was a fantastic guy. I always remember him saying that he was a right crude cunt. If I ever had any doubt about this conclusion, he soon reinforced it. Someone stole a packet of chocolate biscuits from his cell and his revenge was to give himself a stinky finger (stick his finger up his arse), then walk past the culprit and give him a 'moustache'. That was pretty crude. He was always playing pranks on screws to lighten the mood. Some of them wore brown overalls, to identify that they were civilian workers. There was one in particular who would think he was a screw and shout *tools in* if there was any hassle going on. I mean, he was just doing his job, but sometimes he got on our nerves cos he was there pretending to be a screw – and that was a worse crime than actually being one! *Tools in* was kind of the war cry for backup. One time he goes over to question Nealie about something, but Nealie had already got somebody to rub the back of the padlock with shit. As the civilian screw was trying to unlock it to get through the gate to Nealie, the shit ended up all over his hands to the point where he was retching. He went to the toilet to wash it off and Nealie couldn't stop laughing. It was pretty obvious who the culprit was cos he was laughing before he'd even grabbed hold of the padlock.

Next time, he stole the screw's flask from under the table, got a lump of shite (we all had tough shit cos of the steamed food, you never really had a soft one) and... well, you can guess the rest, I'm sure. When they shouted *tea break*, the screw took the cup off the top of the flask and – this is no word of a lie, I saw it with my own eyes – put it down on the table. He was still talking to another screw and wasn't really looking at what he was doing. He unscrewed the flask lid and the shit popped up and we were all howling. It was like a fucking kak-in-the-box. He didn't even notice it until he was pouring his tea into the cup. And it broke in two as he poured and he went fucking nuts! Absolutely nuts!

I used to go over to the hospital wing for a bath cos we only had showers in our bit. One day I went over for a bath and was just about to sit down on the bench when Nealie warned me not to. I looked at his pants and he had stripy shit stains all over them: the screws had only gone and played a shit trick on Nealie by coating the slats of the bench. *Fucking hell*! It could only happen in prison. It was pretty disgusting, like. When we thought back to stuff like that, we'd always wonder and ask Nealie if he had just shat into his hand to do it or shited directly into the flask. He never did give a definitive answer, always kept us guessing. It was just one of his secrets that he'd take to the grave. He died early, due to pneumonia.

I spent a lot of time over in the hospital due to my psoriasis. That's when I had medics trying to suss out what the cause was and the same place I met Anne-Marie.

Inside though, you had to learn, you had to be active, you had to get to know people and make sure people got to know your name – unless you were giving up the game when you got out. But no one was. We were all well and truly in the system now. This was where the real work happened: access to the right people who had the right connections and all the questions like: is their finger on the pulse, why are you here, what did you do, was there a necessity to do it, was there an underlying problem, did you need the money for drugs or did you need it for gambling? And there's a reason for doing everything – is there a common trait between the offences that have gone on? By then I was a serial offender. I'd done Longriggend, Barlinnie, the detention centre. My path was mapped out as far as prison was concerned.

It was fucking hard going. It felt like I'd joined the army without actually knowing about it. It's the kind of thing that's probably been offered up as a reality TV show: send unruly kids at risk of offending to a strict take-no-shit detention centre, have the toughest screws around shout at them and discipline them to breaking point and see what it can turn them into. You could either fight against it or accept it. I had an opportunity to prove things to myself about fitness and about who I was. I was all for healthy mind, healthy body. I was doing quick miles, setting myself goals, using the superfast lads as pacemakers.

I got another armed escort from court to Pentonville. I didn't know I was going there until, well – until I just arrived there. That's the thing once you're in the system: remanded for trial, they don't give you any advance movement order, they just tell you to pack your shit and you're offski. You're a security risk; they can't let you know anything in case you try to arrange a breakout. It's just a mystery tour and that's why it's called ghosting! They ghost you from here to there without a leaving or welcome party.

I was only on a quick visit to Pentonville before I was whisked away to Belmarsh, but what I remember about it was the infestation of cockroaches. All I had to think was, if Oscar Wilde could put up with it, then I'm fucking well sure I could. It was a bit like one of those celebrity jungle challenges on my night there. You know when you wake up and get that *we're not alone* feeling, spot something out the corner of your eye and shit a brick? Well, here was this big fucking thing with feelers wanting to share my pillow. Then, once my eyes had adjusted to the light, I saw they were all over the place. I grabbed my boots, shook out whatever was in there, put them on and river danced the fuck out of the cockroaches. In the morning, the governor came in on his daily round, the patronising fuck.

'How are you this morning, Ferris?'

'The porridge is rank. They put sugar in it, not salt,' I said.

'Well, you're not in bonny Scotland now, you know... anything else?'

'Yeah, the overcrowding in here is terrible. Something needs to be done about it,' I replied.

It struck a nerve. 'Well, how would you know about that? You've only been in here less than a day!' I could see him saddling up his high horse.

'If you'd care to look behind the door, you'll see why.'

And he did. There were about 20 dead cockroaches kicked into the corner. He said something along the lines of, *You won't need to worry about that shortly, son*, as he stormed out with his nose in the air.

'The place is fucking full of criminals as well!'

I don't know if he heard me. And, sure enough, a couple of hours later I was on a bus to HMP fuck-knows-where. I wasn't told where I was being transferred to, but one night in there was enough. They're lucky Trip Advisor wasn't around then. I ended up with toilet tissue in my ears and up my nose, socks tucked into my fucking trousers and gardening gloves on to make sure nothing could go up my sleeves.

From Pentonville to Belmarsh, I could hear a helicopter. I was in a van with a couple of screws and was shackled in an isolated cubicle. They don't wait for red lights; they stick the blues on and you hear sirens and you're through. You'll catch the odd glimpse of people in cars, craning their necks to see if Hannibal Lecter's in there, because of all the excessive security. It was a massive operation each time I went anywhere. Don't give me a hard time about tax payer's money – it wasn't my idea. I was innocent. Well, innocent until proven guilty. I spent a lot of time going from prison to prison like this: Belmarsh to Full Sutton, Full Sutton to Frankland and then from Frankland I was released, re-called, put back into Durham and then transferred after the medical request back to Frankland.

Out of this lot, I remember Full Sutton had a full size football field and they had another field for exercise. They also had the changing rooms for the home and away players, but that seemed to be where all the punishments were dished out and scores settled. It actually had toilets as well – it was a newish build for the time, so like, not something that Victorian fuckers had been hanged in. Full Sutton and Frankland were way, way above anything that Scotland ever had. Durham is probably the closest comparison to a Scottish prison.

Belmarsh was very similar to Barlinnie, Pentonville and Durham because they're feeder prisons, rather than long-term prisons. You'd be in there for short to medium sentences; three to six months to maybe 18-month stints. Frankland and Full Sutton are long-term prisons, so you'd be in there for anything over 18 months. Visitors to Belmarsh had to be vetted otherwise you got a closed visit. This meant that you had a bulletproof screen and you talked through an intercom system – a bit like what you see in American films. So, to have an open visit, the local constabulary had to go to the address that you provided and take a statement, you had to sign it, they'd take photographs and pass to the prison service. Then, when your visitors turn up, they do the internal database stuff which matches up with the police visit and that confirms the visitor's identity. It seemed a bit excessive, I suppose, but rules is rules.

My sister, Carol, said, 'You've got no idea what we've gone through to get in here.'

I tried to keep a straight face, 'You should see what I had to do, sis!'

She told me about the security vetting, but apparently when you go into the visiting room and they call your name, you get taken in a minibus through the normal prison to get to the other prison because it's like a prison within a prison, like a Russian Doll. The place is so fucking big. Cameras are everywhere; brand new, state-of-the-art stuff so although it was a new prison any escapes from there would be as unbelievable as they'd be impossible. There may have been for all I know, but it didn't look like it was worth trying. You couldn't do it now, you couldn't use someone's identity because of all the facial recognition, biometric stuff and Belmarsh is full of biometrics.

Like many I was locked up with, I'd already had experience of prison from visiting my dad and my brother. I've probably been visiting them since I was 12, so for around 40 years. It wears you down after a while. Some people call them unlucky places. For me as a prisoner, watching my family get up and leave is hard. Knowing how hard it is as a prison, you see a member of your family and you can mentally escape. It doesn't matter if you've got PlayStations or Jacuzzis, masseurs or solid gold taps... what you haven't got is your freedom and your family; you can't go down the pub for a pint, go and buy the newspaper, walk the dog, refuel the car, collect your kid from school, sit out in the garden or have a nice lie-in on a Sunday. All these things that you take for granted are no longer there: they're gone.

BAD THINGS

I wasn't a kid anymore. I was serving my time inside as well as on the streets. I was learning all the time; I was meeting people, making good contacts and making strong friendships with reliable people. I was doing everything I needed to be doing in order to make my way in my 'chosen' profession. I never know if I actively chose it or if it chose me. Sometimes it felt like I was being swept along with it and reacting to situations, and others I knew I was the one in the driving seat and making it happen. I knew there was something important I needed to make happen, though – there was something that had been following me around for years. There was a dark cloud in my life and I needed to rid myself of it: the Welshes.

Again, I'm not exactly sure what the catalyst was here. I'd been suffering for years at their hands. There was a time when I was able to balance the odds and I took the opportunity. They'd made me fearful enough, so I felt there was absolutely nothing to lose if I launched an attack. Successful or not, it would be a message to them all.

I had a gun battle with one of their cousins, Jazza while we were driving down a country lane. We'd arranged a proper showdown, but he was too impatient. He nearly killed the bloke who was driving him. There we were, neck-and-neck, trying to shoot each other while hurtling down

232

this quiet road... he's shooting in front of his driver to get at me. The first bullet nearly took half the driver's face off and probably deafened him. He'd shot the fucking window out as well. A gun battle in a car and he didn't even think to let the window down first? For all it was serious, it will have great comedy potential when it's on the big screen. He got slashed in prison because of his name but was not as bad as his cousins. I think he eventually got out and died later. I don't know for certain. I could go on for the rest of the book with stories about these fuckers. Maybe let's put them all to rest (pardon the pun) with a roundup of what inevitably happened to them:

Martin Welsh was scalped on Royston Road and survived, John Welsh had his throat cut from ear to ear on Royston Road and survived. He did die at one point, but then managed to come alive again in another area. I think it was a cousin called John who properly died. George Welsh was partially decapitated on Hogganfield Street and died, Tam Welsh was shot twice in the head on Provanmill Road and survived, and James Welsh was slashed and survived.

Remember... bad things happen to bad people.

OH, BROTHER

Billy and I did some time together. It was in 1985 when I was serving the 18 months for cocaine possession and an offensive weapons charge. I'd always had a single cell or people who I knew in there with me, so it wasn't a hassle for them to move our Billy in with me. Talk about irony – you put up with sharing a room together at home and you can't wait to have your own space. Other than that, prison was like a club with the same familiar faces coming and going all the time. Rehabilitation didn't exist. I still don't think it really does work – certainly not to the extent they want it to. I mean, however you look at it, whatever qualifications you come out with, they'll always go hand in hand with a prison record. There's no escaping it and you can't just erase the fucker. Prison life was and always will be surreal – sometimes you couldn't tell if people were coming back just for the craic or whether they were trying to evade the law. Talk about revolving doors, these people were permanently stuck, for silly offences, usually with a disclaimer of not remembering cos they'd drank too much. It was funny, but a bit tragic at the same time. For those of us where crime was part of our entire being, we didn't know anything else. To have a chance on the outside and mess it up by getting hammered and doing something stupid is such a waste.

On the wing the screws liked to keep good order and discipline, that's all they want to do. So I said look just get my brother up here with me and we'll be fine. But we did have a clash of personality. I don't suppose you can avoid it as brothers. In general, we were ok. Again, as the younger brother and even though he'd done his fair share of bird, I always did feel like I was the one looking out for him. And that's fine – I knew he'd always have my back when I needed him.

We got into a few funny scrapes, like. One of the boys that had been in the young offenders came in with a bag of sawdust. When I first saw it I thought it was a bag of gear, but then... What do you want sawdust for? Of course – he had it to knock up a load of superglue and he did the locks on the next landing. He did locks all over the place cos he had so much of the stuff and loads of people couldn't get out or in that night. Billy had his routine like everyone else does in there. He got his tea with his plastic mug and had a wee bite of his sandwich. His toothbrush and toothpaste were on the table cos he'd have a wash during the night. So while he was out having a natter, I did the inside handle and the rim of his cup. I glued his toothpaste and toothbrush to the locker. He came in and I watched him as he had five or six gulps of tea. Then he got that inquisitive and confused look on his face – he couldn't understand how, when he put his cup down, it wasn't leaving his hand! And I couldn't stop laughing. *Fucking hell*!

'You think this is funny?' he shouted.

I couldn't answer. My laughter was a giveaway.

He thought it was his skin, but it was the plastic that was melting and it probably would pull his fucking skin off if it had time to set longer. It was just enough to stick and cause him some grief. He jumped up and started swearing at me and it's the first time I remember nearly having a go with him and I thought I can't do it – it's not right! Anyway he walked past – flounced, even – like a right drama queen, grabbed his toothbrush and the fucking locker fell down with the toothbrush still stuck to the side of it! Well, that just set me off further. I was roaring from side to side on my bed and he was getting madder by the second. He couldn't understand what was happening. It was blowing his mind. How could nothing fall off stuff? He got the gist of it after I showed him the superglue. After he calmed down, I gave him a go of it with the proviso that he wasn't allowed to do any of my stuff. He reluctantly agreed.

He didn't give anything away until there was shouting and screaming coming from a cell. We were making some hooch, minding our own business and heard the screws go running to where the commotion was. The screaming came from a bloke called Scullion. It sounded like he was smashing his cell up. We made our way to our door to get a better look. There were a few screws outside his cell – some of them stifling laughter, others looking a bit angry at the whole scene. The ones inside were trying to hold him down as he lashed out. A minute or so later – one screw walked out backwards holding Scullion's arms and another followed behind holding his legs. In the middle was poor old Scullion – his pants round his ankles and a toilet seat stuck firmly to his hairy arse! Well, I nearly coughed a lung up laughing. So did Billy. It was a good way for us to bond (no pun intended) after the recent little niggles. They carried him downstairs to the surgery to dissolve the glue. No diggity? No doubt.

We were always at it – little things like that helped pass the time. I know the screws hated it all at the time – I mean, who would enjoy having to disconnect a toilet seat after a 20 stone inmate had been for a dump and carry him downstairs to have the thing surgically removed from his arse? But – and this is a *big butt* (definite pun intended with double t) – I bet they're still talking about it now. We were just making their job a bit more bearable. It can't be riots and stabbings every day – you've got to have a laugh every now and then. Billy said that he wasn't well one day and he wanted to stay in bed.

'That's fine. Stay in bed, mate. Get well,' I said.

When I got to the workshop, I told the screw that Billy wasn't working and wasn't feeling too grand. Six or seven extra blankets later, he was still freezing cold. Sounds strange to say, but lucky bastard – being ill and getting a couple of days in bed was a lot better than working. The next day he was still no better and I had to go to the cell downstairs for something in the afternoon and I heard Billy's laughter. He must be feeling a bit more chirpy, I thought. I left it for a bit and went back up at teatime. I was like his personal skivvy getting his breakfast, lunch, dinner, and supper while he was lying in his pit feeling sorry for himself. I got back from my days' graft and there he was, milking the fuck out of it. I looked at him and I thought, he's my brother and I love him and I want to look after him but... he's taking the piss.

'How you feeling then, Billy?' I asked, while standing over him with a full beaker of ice cold water...

BLUFF AND COUNTER BLUFF

My last criminal case was behind me, but the events that surrounded this episode were still there and very raw.

I was nearing the end of my 18-month stint in Barlinnie and I knew I'd be a marked man for police retaliation over the exposure of the fit-up in Rothesay. An important challenge for me was to bond with my son, Paul, and try to make up for lost time. What I didn't know at that stage was that my time to do that was running out.

Russell Stirton appeared on the radar. He was eager to speak to me about something serious and left word at my parents' house and that I had to contact him. It sounded ominous. Russell was known to me. He wasn't a mate or anything, but we eventually met up. When he finished talking, I wasn't sure what to do; other than pay attention to the details: Russell told me he'd been contacted by members of an elite police unit and they'd offered him a deal. Quite simply, Russell Stirton was an aid in the fabrication of evidence against me, to then enable the police to arrest me.

This time I was well up for the fight. I was invited to meet crime reporter, Don Lindsay. At that time, he worked for STV news. Both Lindsay and Stirton had convinced me that this threat from the police, and whatever plans they had for me, were genuine. Mentally, it was not a nice place to be in. I was generally on high alert, but this kept me very wary of anything and everything and I reported it to Peter Forbes.

A second meeting with Stirton took place at a petrol garage in Barmulloch. We were being observed by an off-duty cop as we discussed the next trip to STV headquarters in Cowcaddens. At the next visit, we'd arranged to meet with David Scott, head of news and current affairs. I went over to pay for my fuel and the off-duty cop went over to Stirton and introduced himself as Graeme Mitchell.

What I didn't know at the time was that Mitchell had failed his sergeant examinations and was an ambitious uniform cop who wanted to be one of the big boys in CID. He saw an opportunity to use me as a ticket to get to the top at Baird Street, the cop shop where he was based.

Mitchell offered to be my eyes and ears within Baird Street and wanted a favour in return. I made it clear to him that I wouldn't give him any info on others as I was not a grass, nor would I supply him with anything that would result in the arrest of anyone. Mitchell said that the 'favour' was not of that kind, so I presumed that he wanted money. I made a mental note of how much I was prepared to give him in order to meet again and to record the whole conversation. I had a substantial amount in mind. The recording would have been worth every penny.

PC Graeme Mitchell told me what the favour was:

'Can you get me a shotgun? A good yin?'

I agreed. It was a big saving, bearing in mind that the shotgun he was looking for was £100.

Mitchell was no honest cop. Whatever he intended to do with the shotgun, I was prepared to take the risk. I needed to get what he said about Stirton on audio tape – recorded evidence was the only way to get anyone to believe me. Mitchell told me I was the prime target for a police fit-up.

There has always been speculation as to what he meant that night by warning me. The second night was a different ballgame and I was armed with a hidden tape recorder. I recorded at least 30 minutes of our conversation.

Here's a flavour of events as they unfolded in that conversation, quoted directly from Graeme Mitchell in the transcriptions:

'I'll tell y'something else that came back. Somebody in the Drug Squad is supposed to have given somebody who's been in Russell's car – some wee guy – the stuff to plant in his car, right. At first they said they'd found it in Russell's car because they need statements. But if it goes to trial, it'll be that he dropped it out in a matchbox under his motor. The wee guy that's been in Russell's motor is a tout for another Mitchell and they are claiming tout money to pay him off for Russell getting done. That's the story. Nobody knows that… you know.'

I was astonished at what he said and I was also fully aware of now having proof. My proof would be the recordings – you cannot argue with taped conversations – that confirmed a plot where the police were again trying to fit me up and send me back to prison.

What happened in Rothesay and the Arty Thompson trial were still fresh in my mind. I decided to stand my ground and fight. I could've ran, but I'd done enough running from violence. I hated being bullied and this situation was no different from my younger years.

I was aware of what Mitchell was saying to me. He took a sudden aggressive tone – a *right in your face* sort of thing.

This is what Mitchell also said:

'He's mouthing off that eh some cop he says he thinks it's Blackhill or Baird Street is telling Russell everything he needs tae know aboot the polis and the goings on an everythin', but the thing goes back to tha' he better fucking hope the ground can open up and swallow him ye know cos there'll be fuck all left of him tae go tae court.'

This reminded me of the threat from DS George Dickson – not even a year had passed since then!

Mitchell carried on talking and I nodded and engaged in small talk, knowing I was recording it all. I let him blow off some steam. If he thought I felt threatened by his statements, he had another thing coming.

My alarm bells were going off like mad; and then came another bombshell. The other Mitchell mentioned earlier was Eric Mitchell. PC Graeme Mitchell continued:

'Eric Mitchell told me wis they got a phone call right. They phoned the Drug Squad's room detective sergeants, but Eric says that a phone call came in and all it said wis – if yer wantin' Russell Stirton he's gonna be dealin' smack. Red Road Court, he's there the noo or he's due to arrive or something like that, a cannae mind whit the words were, but whoever it wis that phoned obviously knew he was fuckin' goin' wherever it wis, he was goin' ye know an' a few nights after they got Russell. Eric thinks he's been set up. See Eric's wife or ex-wife is a DS in the Drug Squad an' she hates his fuckin' guts and she's tryin' tae have him blown away. Ye know which if Russell takes this y'know, that Eric's set him up and wanted tae get him blown away would fuckin' suit her doon tae the ground y'know.'

So, there were two Mitchells on the scene at the same time: Graeme and Eric. Russell Stirton had been pulled over by Eric Mitchell, who was also a detective sergeant based at Baird Street police station.

Russell Stirton was sorted. With what he'd secretly recorded, the proof was there to be heard. It said everything. But what about me, have I got enough proof? Can anyone facing the same set of circumstances ever have enough independent proof?

Eric Mitchell was caught on the secret audio tapes and this is what was said next:

'Pull in through the lights for a quick word Russell. Ok, jist a wee word of friendly advice. There's a lot can happen between now and when it goes to trial, ok. Just leave it at that just now, but don't ever start threatening police because, like I said, wee Paul very nearly went for a walk up the Campsies one night and if I thought you were gonna start playing these games, I'd take you on a night fishing trip and you won't be coming back. If I thought for one minute that y' meant tae make threats I'd open up the open season on Russell Stirton, okay. Right, now all ah'm saying is we do our job and you've got to accept you're in a high risk occupation and every so often people like you and Ferris, they'll all go some time sooner or later. They all go, it's a high risk occupation but the one thing that you do not do is go aboot threatening polis.

Now, wee Paul made a threat to George Dickson and ah can tell you here and now that wee Paul was very nearly wasted; he was nearly away for a walk in the Campsies one night; he was never nearer going. All ah'm gonna say's that these tables can be turned sooner or later or sometime there's a long time between now and when you go tae jail or when you go tae go tae trial. Everything that's gonna happen tae you is gonna be down tae Constable Gilligan and maself. We go intae court and put the mix in for you you'll go tae jail; if we go intae court and don't put the mix in and you've got a decent lawyer, you'll walk away fae this but awright. Gilligan and I arnae all that happy about the way every things worked out.

We're going into court an' say that we saw you flung it under the motor, right. There's a lot can happen between now and when it goes to trial okay.'

That's what you call a Glasgow shakedown – no money demanded, just the threat of murder and being sent to prison like some fucking game of real life chess. This time round I thought I better find out the rules of the game, as there didn't seem to be many choices for me. I also needed to make sure that I played better than anyone else cos my life and my freedom were at stake. I managed to hold myself together as I sat in the STV studios and listened to all of this.

Both Russell and I handed over our audio tapes to STV and I found out about another recording; this one was made visually by STV:

Don Lindsay: First of all Russell, just take your time, relax tell me the whole story, starting from eh, when you were, eh pulled up, eh, I think at the pub, is that right?

Russell Stirton: Yes, at the Brig.

Don Lindsay: First tell us the whole story.

245

Russell Stirton: Well, ah just came out the Brig with my friend an' his wife and her friend and they walked up to the – it's a – off ramp an' the two cars were there, two Cortinas. There wur two Cortinas... he had a Cortina an' ah had a Cortina and he was takin' his wife and his friend home an' ah wis speaking to a man across the road, who owned a cobbler's shop. Ah's speaking away tae him and he's went away so ah went over and returned to ma car, opened ma car door an' ah've went in ma car, started the car up, sat there fur aboot half a minute, a minute, an' then the police car drew in. Ah've seen 'im in ma mirror, the drivers got out an' came over and asked me would ah step out ma car. Ah says yes, stepped out ma car and ah says, 'Whit's this all aboot?' He says, 'We want tae search yer car.' (cough). Ah says no problem and he asked me would ah go intae the police car. Ah says yes, so ah walked intae the police car an' this other wan come over – Mitchell his name – and says tae me, 'We'll need to take this car away for a thorough examination.' No problem, ah say.

So we got intae Baird Street, strip-searched me, thirty pounds in ma possessions or sumthin', an' took ma clothes. Took me out and held me under section two ah think it was, of the drugs act or sumthin' and they kept {ommission}, they be present when they search ma car, they says naw {ommission} back into the detention room.

246

Ah lay there and as ah wis lying there ah wis half sleepin' and ah went up to the windae looking out, jistae see whit wis happenin'. Went back into the, the corner where ah was sleepin' and ah put ma head down and next minute, four police officers came in.

Ah says, 'Ah wis done fur having drugs in the car (cough). Ah said not drugs in ma car {omission}, says yes, you're done and ah looked at em' shook ma head plus ah started tae get angry wi' one of the police officers. Ah threatened 'im fur whit they done tae me (cough). They jist laughed at me, said, 'Ah'll see ye in ten years,' an' then as ah wis down tae the Sheriff Court goin' up they wanted me up they know. That night, two of the drug squad officers came in thairsels, wanted me tae make a deal wi' them – put people down fur them an' asked me aboot a Teddy Hughes, a Paul Ferris and a Terry Monaghan. Would ah help them out?

Ah says, 'Whit can you do fur me?' He says 'Ah'll get you out on bail,' so ah says ah'll do it. So , ah wis in the Sheriff Court, they've come up, another wan, ah Smith, Ronald Smith an' Ingles, ah think his name wis and another wan, ah don't know his name. He took me out the Sheriff Court and he sat me down and wis speaking tae us, sayin' he can do me a good turn and, if ah get this Paul Ferris, he will help me out.

Ah says, oh yes, ah'll get 'im. So as 'ave got out 'ave told 'im whit they've said to me, whit they wanted off mé and he says jist keep playin' them along, it's the only way yer gonnae stay out. So ah wis telling 'em lies aboot things jist tae keep oot, but this man already knew and he made a couple o' meets with me, asking' fur information.

Don Lindsay: Ferris?

Russell Stirton: Yes, to ask aboot this boy Paul Ferris. Says they were gonnae get 'im. Ah says ah'll try, ah'll help ye's every way ah can (cough) and they knew ah wis seeing Paul Ferris, but, ah've explained to Paul Ferris whit is happenin' an' whit they're trying to do.

But ah says ah couldn't tell ye too much cause ah'm working on somethin' the noo. Ah wouldn't tell him exactly whit ah was doin'.

'Get this boy Paul Ferris fur us.'

So, by this time ah'm kidding on tae them that Paul Ferris is doin' this and doin' that and ah'll be able to get him fur ye. But in meantimes, Paul Ferris knew whit ah wis sayin' tae them. Ah wis tellin' Paul Ferris everythin' and he says it's okay by him.

It wis the only thing that's keeping me outta prison. Then the third meet wis today, suppose to be at three o'clock, but ah suppose tae phone him at half past one, but ah think ah got mixed up wi' the phone numbers. Ah'm not too sure, cos it's jist ringing out and we left and went out to Lenzie again and we (background singing) stayed there waitin' on him comin' in the car park. Had a mic on us, it's a back one and a wee bit round ma side (cough) and at this time, eh, ah didn't think he wis gonnae come, so then this brown Cavalier comes in quite fast, stopped and he's lookin' at me and ah'm jist lookin' at him and he got out the car. There was somebody walkin' across a footbridge an' he kept on starin' at him. Just lookin' at him ye know he jist kept lookin' and ah thought oh, somethin's wrong here. So the next, as he's walkin' up tae me, he's gave me some packages. Ah don't know what's in them and we walked down and were speakin.'

Don Lindsay: How did he give you the packages?

Russell Stirton: Give'm in ma hand. He took them out his pocket, in an inside, ah think it was his right-hand pocket he took them outae. The packages, he's handing m'them. Ah said ah need a phone number or similar tae that, tae get in contact wi' you when it's done.

Don Lindsay: Did he give you any indication what he expected you to do with the packages?

Russell Stirton: He wanted me tae, the first man explained that tae me, whit wanted tae say, ah don't know if he tolt his other man exactly the whole lot. Ah don't know, but the first man indicated to me this inspector that ah was to give Paul Ferris cos they wanted him off the street. Didn't want him walking about and ah says ah'm quite feart of that little man more or less. Ah says if ah dee anythin' tae him, ah says ah'm in trouble. But whit he says is he'll not be gettin' oot for a very very long time.

So's we were walkin' down, ah's discussing it wi' us. Ah wis a bit nervous and ah bit feart maybe because ah'd this mic on us, ye know and started talking away and ah says we'll get Paul Ferris and ah'm makin' out, yes we, ah'll get 'im, ah'll help ye: when is he gonnae go fur stuff, when is he gonnae do this?

Ah said, 'Oh he's goin' shortly, maybe the weekend. Ah'll get him fur ye. Ah'll gie ye ma hand on that and ah'll try tae get him in ma confidence and as ah was standin' there he says tae me, 'Yer no mic'd up, are ye? Ah says, 'Naw' and ah pull it down and ah went like that, ah showed 'im and he's lifted ma jersey up a bit. Ah've lifted it up cos the mic was down inside ma tracksuit, jist down a bit so he wouldn't see it, but what ah was worried about was the bulge in the back. Maybe if ah wisnae, jist maybe, y'know, self-conscious, knowin' it was there, he probably wouldn't see, but ah was worried about that, ye know, cos ah'm trying tae keep ma back away from, so that ah'm facin' him all the time and he started, sort of put, ah don't know, mair pressure on me like ye know, likes, 'You'll need tae get us a turn, you'll need to do this for us, right now and fast, or yer arse is oot the windae.'

He'd been puttin' a lot of pressure ontae me, y' know. Basically ah wis gonnae run because ah dinnae think, nobody would believe me. What they've done tae me y'know. How can ye go up tae court and say the police are liars, ye know, it jist doesn't happen.

Russell was bang on there. How else can you prove in court that the police are liars except when you have them by their own words *recorded for posterity*? It's a very hard call and even more so when police officers turn up to court as witnesses, wearing new uniforms with medals and other trinkets on show, along with the strands of silver on their hat and silver adorning their shoulders. Is it a stage prop to give them prominence and power; to make them totally believable, and give credence to every fucking lie they spin? Absolutely. Why would a decorated and senior police officer be lying? Some of them may well tell the truth, but my past experiences have taught me it's a charade. I know what they are doing – trying and failing to send me back to prison.

I listened to the rest of the STV interview and watched as Russell met with one of the Drug Squad who was later identified as DS Derek Ingram. I let the past few days' lack of sleep get to me and then jolted back to life, like an electric shock hit me. This part caught me by surprise:

Don Lindsay: Did they make it perfectly clear that they expected you to fit-up Paul Ferris?

251

Russell Stirton: Oh yes; yes. Paul Ferris wis number one.

Number one? I just wanted to leave the STV studios. I wasn't happy at all. It was the first time I'd seen and heard it all. It was as overwhelming as it was infuriating and I still hadn't heard it all. I still felt uneasy. *What the fuck are you watching this for*? I thought. *Go get them*!

I needed to do something and fast – thinking, watching – thinking and then... Fuck it – I'm going to visit Baird Street and sort this out once and for all. But then reality grabbed me and held me back. The days were gone where I'd react without thinking it through. I needed to fight with my mind, not with violence.

A quote from Eric Mitchell sprang to mind from Russell Stirton's secret recording. DS Mitchell said:

'Ye cannae fight the polis, Russell. It's a big outfit tay take on an' ye cannae win.'

Is that right? Aye, sure I couldn't win nor Russell – at that stage – but I was sick and tired of all the talking and threats.

And then Russell came on screen:

'Ah've done nothin' wrong. Ah've done nothin' wrong. Ah wouldn't be here askin' youse fur help if ah did it – if ah'd they drugs in ma car. They were put there. They were put there by the polis or by sumb'dy they made put them there.

Specifically aw ah want at the end of the day is tae find oot who put them there. That is all ah want, tae see who put them in ma car. Was it the polis? Was it somebody they got put up to it? It wisnae in ma car, know what ah mean?'

We were both in a dangerous position. From watching and listening to this at STV studios, I knew that I had to fight on my own – not that Russel was incapable, just that this was my fight. Several weeks later my parent's house was raided by DCI Charles Boulton from Lothian & Borders police, who were investigating corruption into the Strathclyde police force. I was detained and taken to London Road station; booked in and awaited court the next day.

That was my first experience of the new Sheriff Court in Glasgow. Brand new cell and much like an American design with bars on the front door so you could breathe, unlike the sardine tin cells from the old Sheriff Court – I found it all a bit surreal. As I sat in there waiting on my legal visit from Peter Forbes I heard someone crying. They were taken past my cell by the court police... it was none other than failed sergeant, Graeme Mitchell! I take no comfort in the fact that a grown man was crying.

When he saw me he burst into a verbal tirade: 'Look at what you've done to me.'

I looked.

'Well, now. I do hope you eventually tell the truth, Sherlock,' or words to that effect.

253

If things don't get this complicated in your life, then well done you – as for me, I had a co-defendant and both of us were charged on firearm offences. This came about after a police raid on STV studios where they seized all the audio and visuals that were to be broadcast to the nation. All the material content became impossible to make public cos it may have an impact on any forthcoming trial.

I eventually appeared in private at the new showcase Sheriff Court and was remanded in Barlinnie for trial. It was as familiar as ever, frozen in time, with the same prisoners, the same officers, the same look, feel and that unmistakable smell. I found it sad that there was a certain safety about it all. It was oddly reassuring. I felt able to fight from within prison without any risk to my family. I was there for a few months and then taken to court one day right out of the blue. I met with Peter Forbes at the court and told me the Crown was offering bail. WTF? It may seem strange, but I wanted to refuse bail. I wanted to go right to trial and then some. This offer of bail was nothing more than a stalling technique. I explained to Peter that I had no intention of taking bail. To be perfectly blunt, I felt safer in prison. I told him my rationale as best I could without sounding too scatty in the head. I knew the whole picture and he didn't. One thing about Peter was this – he never stood for any fanciful bollocks and had a way of calming me down. And that was fine, but it was still just me versus the might of Strathclyde police force.

'If the police are out to kill you, there's nothing any of us can do to stop them. If I was you, I'd make myself as public as I possibly could.'

It didn't fill me with confidence, but fight or flight kicked in again and I accepted bail then went to see Stevie Wilkie, a reporter for the *Scottish Sun* newspaper. I was aware that the Police Federation in Glasgow were covered by the Sun's lawyers Levy & McRae who were also legal advisors to the *Daily Record* newspaper. They were also reviewing the STV material for public broadcast. Coincidence? Paranoia? Of course!

I handed over all the relevant audio and visuals over to Stevie to prove my life and liberty were at risk. It was at this point I became aware of a judicial problem – it was called sub judice. In short, it prevents any information being made public before any trial. I felt like I'd shown my hand but not all the cards were dealt at that stage. The fight was still on.

I was living with Ann-Marie at her mum's house with Paul in the north of the city. I was gradually getting to know what being a father was all about. We were only weeks into our liberated bliss when the walls came tumbling down again. The police raided us and arrested me. Brace yourselves... it turned out that I was now a threat to the nation – kid you not. The next day, I was up in court in front of the Sheriff. The prosecution stood up and said that they would be unable to provide any further information about me to my lawyer and to the court.

The case was then elevated to the realms of national security. Peter Forbes looked at me for answers when none could be given – I was looking at him in the same way. It was a total sham. I couldn't negate anything that the Crown alleged and, in truth, I was well out my depth with it. I was carted off back to Barlinnie to await trial on the possession of the shotgun that I'd given to Graeme Mitchell.

I prepared myself for it. I plotted out my defence; I had several independent sources – the audio tapes and legal statements – that I'd copied and passed over to Peter Forbes. The trial at Glasgow High Court became another farce in the history of Scottish legal history. Graeme Mitchell was my co-accused and, on day one, I demanded that he was seated at the other end of the dock away from me. Much to my amusement the ashen-faced Mitchell was led away. He was eventually moved to my immediate left and I sat in the middle of the dock. It's the little things, eh?

As it got under way, I noticed large audio speakers in front of the judge as well as other smaller speakers in front of the jury and positioned for where I sat in the dock. It added to the surreal nature of these things. I mean, I discuss going to High Court like it's just a normal day, but the reality is far from it. For all I may sound confident and fearless as I emerge to talk to the press, it's a very nerve-wracking thing to go through. They can last days, weeks or months. You can't let your guard down once, you can't show aggression or get complacent and you can't ever assume to know which way it will go. It's just... *fucking unreal*. And those speakers – it looked like a rave was going to kick-off. I was half expecting Judge Jules, rather than the trial judge. It was almost a letdown.

In the end, it always comes down to the jury as masters of the facts. The trial judge in his summation was something special. He indicated that, because I had no defence, Scottish law suggested that the jury were to return a verdict of guilty – albeit they could ask for leniency on my behalf if they believed the evidence that I gave. I was well pissed off with the wig, but at the end of the day an instruction by a trial judge to tell the jury I was guilty seemed like it would only diminish my defence position.

I was convicted as directed and sentenced to three years imprisonment and Graeme Mitchell was set free. I'd gone a few rounds of fighting for my liberation and my sanity. It had been an impossible task. I just slipped back into prison mode and tried to work out where to go next. It was stressful alright, but I knew I'd never walk away from something that was just wasn't right. It's a huge case – it's one that requires a lot more reading cos there's just too much of it to go in here.

One day it will all come out and you can make up your own mind and become masters of the facts, just like a jury would do when evaluating all the evidence before them. It will serve as a future chapter of my unfinished business.

YOU'LL BE A MAN, MY SON

Paul was born on the 29th of April 1985, when I was held on remand in Barlinnie. I've already been through all the shit surrounding that. I'm always gonna regret not being there and it's something I've learnt to live with. My views on fatherhood only hit me when I was freed from prison in the latter part of 1985.

My son Paul and his mother Anne-Marie were invited to live in another part of the city away from all the corruption that was going on. I was probably a lousy father at that time. It's a tough thing to admit, but I'm not afraid to. I was fighting my own corner with threats to kill from police and the threat of planting drugs on me if I survived. It's probably understandable that self-preservation was the order of the day as well as maintaining a family life. I think that living in those kinds of pressures, something had to give and, in many cases, when parents do break up, it usually is for the best, as harsh as that sounds. I could still be a father and be there for him when I could.

When I was in prison and was told about the birth of my son, I did feel something special even in there and, in hindsight – it's a great word that, eh? Hindsight – makes it just as raw as it was at the time. No matter who we are or whoever we think we are – we all have to face whatever music that we should face. Rather than using hindsight to explain our way out of shit, we should just use foresight and there'd never be a problem.

Anne-Marie is well documented for saving my life in Rothesay in December, 1984. I'll always stand by that. The Thompsons put me in Rothesay and helped the police put me in prison. And it was because of Anne-Marie that I was actually there as in: I was alive and I was a father. That was better than being a dead one, whichever moral viewpoint you have. As a couple, we never really recovered from that episode. She didn't have much of an idea what I did for a living up until then. Bizarre as it sounds, I never wanted her to know about any of that. The less she knew the better. It protected her. If she wasn't involved, then she couldn't be questioned and couldn't give information away. But finding out in such a way – well, it goes without saying that it was a shock. *A big fucking shock.* I have never ever discussed my business or line of work to any of my kids or their mothers – it's just the way it'll always be.

My second son was only six weeks old when I was arrested in London by MI5. So with Dean, I was there and... well, I was *kind of* there:

The birth of Dean is something that I will never ever forget. Sandra was well past her due date of the 21st of April, 1997, and I had constant thoughts of delivering my son in bed. If you think my line of work was stressful, it's got nothing on the constant threat of childbirth. If it happened at home, it would all be down to me. Here I was in some sort of a déjà vu moment as Paul was born on the 29th of April. It looked like Dean could well be born on the very same day.

Karma, fate, even serendipity never prepared me for how to deal with a real life family issue of becoming a father again. The only different thing was that I was a free man and had to get my head sorted. That was easier said than done. I was in an environment that I had very little experience in. That's not a cop out – and no pun intended either – just the fact that all of this was new and by fuck I had to learn fast.

Did I panic? Well, internally and emotionally I was a total wreck – I had been up since the due date and never got any sleep. I had water constantly boiling and a stack of towels – that's what they always had on TV shows – so I was as prepared as I could be. I'm not kidding about the sleep: I used amphetamine – speed for those of us from the streets – and then ProPlus, coffee and anything else that would keep me awake. Now you'll understand about the emotional total wreck. You know the guilt and fear you have every Sunday morning after a big session? Imagine it a dozen times worse, but you can't block it all out under the comfort of your duvet. So, it probably wasn't the most rational thing to do, but it was a plan and it was *my* plan. Stay awake. Power through it. Be prepared. It's pressure... *it's a fuckload of pressure, but couples have been dealing with child birth for a couple of million years, we'll be fine*. I was frightened; I was well and truly in a zone that I knew nothing about, but had to show to Sandra a calm face. And all along, I felt very humbled by it all. Regardless of others coping in this situation, we're all different. To take a step back and look at the situation – we were preparing to bring a new life into the world. That's a special thing and it's not being over-dramatic to say it's a miracle.

Phone numbers... check. Names... check. Route to hospital... check. Time from A to B... double-checked. But even back then feels like a million miles away technology-wise. Your phone can sort all that out for you now; you don't need to think about traffic congestion. There's probably an app for giving birth. *Why was it not around then*?!

The lack of sleep: my whole body was screaming for some rest. I had no idea of time, day or night. It was just there. My heart was like a steam engine, running like a fuck-clock, full, and running at a steady pace. It wouldn't allow me to be still for more than two seconds. Boil some water. Tidy up. Check this. Do that. Is everything ready? Baby clothes. Clothes. Food. Sandra. Bottles. Food. Powders. Milk. Nappies... nappies? *Food-bottles-milk-tidy-Sandra-water-nappies-milk-powders...* baby clothes. Baby. Fuck! *Fucking baby*, man! It was time! Quick! Nobody panic. *Nobody paniiiic*!

Sandra's screaming was a form of comfort to me as I knew we had to get to the maternity ward. I was very calm in the knowledge that once I got her there, I'd be relieved of this pressure by properly trained medical staff. I had experience of driving in times of stress and pressure; I'd plotted and replotted the drive from home to hospital and even a plan B with fewer traffic lights. If ever there was a time to say, *I got this*, it was now.

Right. Plan B is just as important as A. This was a live situation – literally – and it was always open to change. The journey from home in the West End to the old Rottenrow Maternity Hospital was just a bit off the Charing Cross slip towards the M8 and then down. It sounded pretty straight forward, but everyone who has been there or even the thought of being there, will know exactly where I'm coming from.

This is the scenario: in a vehicle with my partner who is in obvious pain and about to give birth. Route A has many traffic lights, route B doesn't have so many but takes longer – what to do? You have nearly two seconds to decide. It took me less than the amber turning to red to decide and I floored it to 40mph, which felt like we were going at a walking pace. There's no way I could run a red or break the speed limit here – I couldn't afford the risk. Next stop: more traffic lights followed by a few swear words from Sandra who was in serious pain. We were still over 10 minutes away and then – *boom* – another flash-forward into my head: delivering a child on the backseat of the car while parked on the street. *Fuck that*! I kept going as fast as the traffic would allow and eventually arrived at the hospital. We were greeted by a guy in a high-vis jacket. He attempted to engage with me about removing my abandoned car, but I was already hallucinating. I looked back at it as I got Sandra inside. I was almost out-of-body by then, so fuck knows how she was feeling. There was the car, at an angle, the doors were open, the engine still running... it was surreal, almost like a getaway car from a job. There was no, *Shit, my car*! moment. All that was on my mind was getting Sandra into the hospital and with the professionals.

The next thing I know is that Sandra is on the bed and screened off. Her swearing? I've never heard the likes! Before I could even feel like a spare part, I was dragged back down to earth by a nurse. She gave me something to read about an epidural that could be administered to relieve the pain. She saw the look of relief on my face and reminded me it was for Sandra, not me. As if it couldn't get more surreal, I heard the voice of Sandra's sister, Debbie. As I was reading over the leaflet I noticed that there is a five per cent chance of paralysis cos it's administered into the spine. It suddenly didn't sound as good. I had a chat with Debbie and told her about the spinal jab and she told me to get home and have a sleep. It was music to my ears. Sleep for a bit, get back to hospital and see what the score is. Easy.

It was a very strange feeling walking to the car and then back to the house. I crashed out on the floor surrounded by a heap of duvets and the main landline. I was in another world by then. I vaguely remember a call from Debbie to say that

Sandra gave birth to a baby boy – I smiled and crashed out again. A baby boy. And the house phones were ringing like mad and I slept and I woke and I dozed and I-

Boom! *A fucking baby boy*! I had missed the birth of my second son, Dean. I was gutted. I drove to the hospital to see my mum, Sandra's mum, family and friends and, in particular, my mate James 'Jaimba' McLean who'd brought the biggest teddy bear I'd seen. I was politely asked to explain my absence at the birth and I looked them right in the eyes.

'It's very difficult to explain as where do I start? I've not slept for days in fear of a house birth. I've been taking stuff to stay awake.'

However I put it, it was never gonna win in comparison to actually *giving birth*, was it? What right-minded person does that? Fatherhood? You can't buy it and another chapter in my life was just around the corner.

THOMPSON & SONS

Things started to go down the shitter for the Thompsons. Arty was just there by name only. He was a fucking pantomime gangster, hanging onto his daddy's coat tails for a free ride. He set up a deal, only to get ripped off and had no idea what to do about it. How would he know? He wasn't a criminal or the 'gangster' he wanted to be. The only weight his name carried was 20 stone of flab. And that's where I was brought in; to recover the money that the fat, farting fuckwit managed to lose. I've heard different versions of how much loot they were actually taken for, ranging from £30k to £200k. The second figure is the closest, but I was told it was a lot less at the time. Again, it's all part of the gangland myth.

Arty got banged up and was on remand and speculation was rife as to who was behind the set-up. Old man Thompson jumped to the immediate conclusion that it was his associates, Blind Jonah and Tam Bagan. It wasn't so much a set-up than a self-inflicted fuck-up. Arty was playing the big *I am* and getting in well above his head with the 'expanding the empire'. The cops were onto him. And here's the thing: old man Thompson had been a police informant for so long that he thought no harm could ever come to his family. You'd be well within your rights to think that, given the situation. But it had been decided that Arty had to go and that was it. At their trial, Arty got 11 years, Jonah got seven and Bagan walked.

Knowing that Thompson thought he was in on it, Bagan stopped working for him.

Maybe Thompson could smell a few rats. Rats were common; there's always at least one in close proximity and he had been around long enough to attract the wrong attention. He suspected the coppers were after him, but in reality, they were just doing their job. They only took Arty down because the Thompsons had broken their word with regards to the business they were doing. They were taught a lesson – they weren't the only ones who could break their word. Bagan and Jonah were always going to be suspects: Bagan more so – even though he was done on some firearms offences, he essentially walked free. I don't think it was anything to do with him. At the time, they were all sloppy cos they thought they were untouchable. And Arty was that paranoid. It's common knowledge that, while he was in prison he couldn't shut up about being set up by Bagan. It seemed like, whatever they were doing, they were complacent about it. Whether Arty was up to things he shouldn't have been and the cops were clipping his wings, only they will know.

Being out meant that there'd be some sort of contact with Thompson. I was more than wary of the old man, as you know. If the cracks were beginning to show during the trial, then the walls of the Thompson-Ferris relationship would soon come tumbling down. I walked away from a job he offered me. Nothing too unusual there, but it

267

was significant as it was the first one I refused and it was after serving time from the set-up. It was at a boxing match and we were there to make sure Thompson and a few other boys were alright. But we also wanted fucking fed. We kept turning round and seeing all these plates of fish and pasta.

'Where's ours?' I said.

It was a fucking joke. We were picking off each other's plates, tight bastards! Another sign that there was no class from him. *Come and look after me on a night out, watch us eating, but you lot have to go hungry.* That night, Thompson asked if I could talk to the promoter. I went to his office and, for some reason, he thought I was fucking mercenary that would go and cut somebody's face for five hundred quid. *Fucking cheeky cunt.* I asked him what it was all about.

'Aye, he was meant to come with me and he went with this other bastard instead,' he replied.

And that was it. All the kid was trying to do was steer his own future. He was a rising star who wanted to get his career moving faster. I didn't see a problem with what he did and I didn't like the promoter – so, *fuck him.* And fuck Thompson. It turns out that the boxer was Gary Jacobs. He did alright for himself. I don't know if he knows about the shit that was going on in the background, but I'm so pleased he got away from that promoter. Good on him.

The upshot was that Thompson not only wanted some protection that night, but also wanted to make himself look good – and look important. He didn't give a fuck about us, or he would have shown us some gratitude in making sure we were looked after while on the job. And that whole *slice the young boxer up* shit didn't sit well with me either. I don't like being brought into something under false pretences. Fuck only knows what Thompson had been touting me around as. This was a prime example and it's no wonder people think I was his enforcer. And this is one of my points about misconceptions in the criminal underworld – exaggeration. I'm not saying I wasn't handy – I was at the fucking top of my game – but the thing here was that I was more for doing odd jobs here and there. Picking up bags was a usual job for me. As was going to see about money. There were times when things did get a bit messy, but my first rule would always be to go into a job with an open mind, rather than all blazing and angry. That's just stupidity. I've been known for years. If I knocked on your door to repay some money you owed, you'd know you were in deep shit and you'd do what you could to pay it. You'd know what would happen if I had to come back. That was always enough of a reason for people to pay up. Any job though:

'Paul, can you go and see what's-his-name and see about that thing?'

'Aye, no worries.'

That was it. I didn't want to know or need to know what it was. Why should I ask and why would Thompson tell me what it was all about, anyway? So, doing things like that was all well and good, but the ones he started trying to rope me into were not only impossible or too outrageous – they were just fucking bonkers. He wanted me to plant a bomb in the copper's car that he thought set his son up. Again: *Fuck you*. It was fucking insane. It was enough to make me wonder if he'd been sampling his own product. And speaking of which, with young Arty out the picture for a while, there wasn't anyone else for Thompson to replace him with. His other son, Billy, was seen pretty much as the black sheep of the family. And how fucking painfully ironic does that sound? I could have said the runt of the litter, but that's even worse when you've got Arty as a brother. In short, Billy was no street-player and was useless to Arthur in that respect. In fact, he was useless in many other respects – young Billy was a smackhead and an all-round embarrassment to the Godfather. He was incapable of running across the street, never mind running a criminal empire.

I stopped checking in on the old man after that last incident. So essentially, I stopped working for him, handed my notice in by not staying in touch. It was a lot easier to sever ties with people back then – it's not like he could have texted a sad face emoji or saw where I'd checked in on social media.

It wouldn't be the last we'd see or hear from each other though. Relationships built on violence that turn to distrust never seem to end well.

BLOOD ON THE STREETS

I teamed up with Tam Bagan and was living in the East End. Driving over for the first time with Bagan was when the name actually meant something to me. I'd heard him mentioned before and knew of him as a street-player, but our paths hadn't really crossed. He hadn't been so significant in my life. Yet.

'There's a character over here, Tam McGraw. Watch what you're fucking doing with him. If he ever comes across, asks you for anything, he's a snitch. He's a police tout and he's one for watching.'

As we drove past the area where he stayed, it was on my mind. A warning like that meant that the name and his MO were looming over the place and I didn't like the feeling that gave me. Tam McGraw's name cropped up again in a situation where somebody on a motorbike tried to assassinate Tam Bagan, but it didn't work out.

Round about that time, McGraw crawled out from under his rock and asked if I wanted him to sort Bagan out for me. I was a bit puzzled, cos I sorted my own shit out. McGraw made it clear that he only meant he could plant stuff on him – guns or drugs or whatever – and have him sent down and out of my hair. *What the fuck was happening to Glasgow*? I mean, seriously... *what the actual fuck*? A lad called Joe Hanlon was working for McGraw at the time. I knew his brother well, so when I was leaving, I muttered something to him about McGraw being a dick. Not long after that, me, Bobby Glover and Joe were tight as fuck – good pals as well as working together.

Things weren't looking so good for Thompson. His whole empire seemed to be on a downward spiral. He was a band with a shitty second album and no obvious hit singles. He was on his way out and should have done just that while the going had been good. One day, someone walked into his timber yard on London Road and tried to shoot him. The gun misfired and he got shot in the groin before the shooter made off. The Godfather was taken to hospital by his driver and said it was caused by a wonky drill while doing a bit of work at the yard. It was significant and he knew it. Never before would someone have had the balls to do such a thing in the past. But with his top boys flying the nest, there wasn't really anyone left to defend him. Arty would've ran a mile if he'd been there. And that's a big ask for Arty. The troubles didn't stop there; Thompson was easy pickings after that.

Bagan was a problem to both Thompson and McGraw. Thompson suspected it was Bagan who'd shot him in the groin and McGraw just wanted any threat eliminated from the streets. An altercation between the three of them occurred one day when the old man and McGraw had a sit-down in the Caravel where they were on their way to setting up an alliance. The Godfather was tooled-up and waving his gun all over the place.

After a scuffle, the old man was out cold and Bagan was poised to end him before McGraw begged him not to shoot. There was some distrust between the alliance after that, but they plotted to have men taken off the streets including me and Bagan. I heard of many threats at that time. Of course, you have to take them seriously, but you can also have a bit of a laugh about them. The thing is, I had loyalty on the streets and that was earned through friendship and mutual respect. Neither Thompson nor McGraw had any of that cos they had to buy friends and they associated with the law. I mean, even McGraw's son was round at my place one time telling me about his dad's ways, saying if anyone knew the extent of him working with the cops, they'd kill him.

In 1990, someone else had a pop at Thompson; he was walking home one day when a car mounted the pavement and drove straight into him. Different accounts say that the driver got out and started shooting at him and some accounts have put me in the frame for it. I could get all coy and enigmatic about it all and leave people guessing. I like to do that when I'm asked about these things. In this case, though: *would I have driven onto the footpath and knocked him over*? I suppose I could have, much the same as anyone could have. It wouldn't have been my style to do that, so the chances of it being me are very slim. *Would I*

have knocked him over and shot him while he was down? Again, I *could* have, but it still wasn't my style. And at that range when he's on the deck with a broken leg, I don't think I'd have missed. No one would believe it, but he seemed to think the coppers would when he shopped me, saying I was the driver. Those other hits he was trying to get me to do on his behalf – did he think I didn't know they were set-ups? He'd wanted rid of me for a while and, because it was now Open Season on the fucker, I know he was holding me responsible for the attempts on him and it left him with a convenient excuse to nail me.

A year later, Arthur 'Fatboy' Thompson Jnr, heir apparent to the plastic throne of the Ponde-fucking-rosa, was out on a two-day home visit pending his release from the bird he was doing for that heroin trafficking. It was the 18th of August, 1991. Did he just go straight home to his missus? No. Instead, he went to the Provanmill. He wasn't a drinker, but I've heard he was in a jovial mood that night. It was ridiculous. As the evening progressed, his actions became more and more outlandish, like a town crier reading from a scroll: *Hear yeeee, hear yeeee! Here is my list of everyone who's gonna get whacked...*

Silly twat. There was a team waiting for him before he'd even read to the bottom of the list. The cunt was a dead man walking before he'd even opened his pus. If ever there was a man who signed his own death certificate, it was Arty Thompson. I don't know if it was because of all the gangster films he'd watched, but surely that would make him more aware of what would happen to him. He knew how it worked. He was a street-player, albeit a very bad one. He was mouthing off about four men who he was going to kill. Those four men were no ordinary men; they were the kind you don't go making threats against in public – unless you do it to them immediately. One of those men was me. He had me at number four, which was an insult in itself.

According to the pathologist in court, Fatboy was given a Glasgow send-off: he was first shot in the face, glancing his cheek and spinning him round for the second shot to hit his lower back and the fatal wound was the last shot that hit the bottom of his anus while he was bent over. This was demonstrated in court as a shot-by-shot account. Hearing the commotion, his sister and mum ran to his side as he lay on the footpath. Old man Thompson apparently had a gun in his hand, but the shooter was long gone. They drove him to the hospital and he was dead within the hour.

Arthur Thompson was obviously upset. He shopped me for the murder of his son. There were other charges as well, such as me and Bobby Glover being done for the kneecapping of William Gillen. We were questioned and held on remand for a week in Bar-L, before being taken to Kilmarnock Sheriff Court. I was kept in Barlinnie for the murder and other charges until going to court and Bobby was bailed and free to go.

Bobby was quoted in the *Scottish Sun*. 'The police seem to think I am connected with the Thompson shooting and are determined to make the Gillen charges [the kneecapping] stick. If they do come up with something then it will have to be a fabrication.'

He said there would be no forensic evidence in his car to connect him to either crime. It had been impounded, but he used to get it valeted all the time cos his young son was always eating his chocolate in there.

'So I know there's nothing in the motor to connect it with that incident. There's no way I want to be killed in revenge for a shooting that's not down to me.'

ANOTHER GAME-CHANGER

On the 23rd of March, 1992 I was up in Glasgow High Court for the biggie. This trial went on to become the longest and most expensive in Scottish legal history, lasting 54 days. I was up for 12 charges in total: the main ones being Arty Thompson's murder and the attempted murder of old man Thompson as well. There was another attempted murder when someone got shot in the neck, a kneecapping and some other stuff... perverting the course of justice, conspiring to assault, possession of drugs and whatever else. Much has been written about me emerging from the courthouse in a shirt and tie, looking like an accountant (they always want to portray me as a wayward accountant), and 'smugly' giving a press conference on the steps of that famous North Courthouse. The trial involved the highest security they'd ever had. It was totally fucking bonkers: fuck knows how many polis were there, helicopters, machine gun guards, bomb squads, dog handlers. I thought they were taking me to the wrong court at first, but I suppose I was used to all that by now. And of course, there's all the media frenzy around it as well. Other than it being reportedly Scotland's longest ever trial, it's also supposed to be the most expensive in the country as well. I've heard it cost £4million.

It was a bitter-sweet victory. Ok, yes – amazing to walk free and it be proved that I was innocent of those crimes, but what a fucking loss in the long run. If this wasn't also the biggest eye-opener for me, I don't know what was.

What people fail to remember when reporting on stuff like this is the back-story to it. Firstly, it's no secret that I wasn't a fan of Arty Thompson. I've despised him and his dad on many occasions and yes, I didn't cry a single tear when I heard he'd been killed. But it's still someone being killed and that's never a good thing. In our line of work, when something like that happens, there are always accusations to follow, theories on the street, repercussions and revenge killings. That's pretty standard and to be expected in those circumstances. The killing of Arty led to Bobby and Joe being killed. That happened to them and it didn't happen to me cos I was locked up. So, to win my trial – I couldn't see it as a win, but a huge fucking relief to close that chapter of my life. I wish to fuck they'd been in court with me and we'd have had the biggest celebration ever, but it wasn't to be. They were still charged – their names still read out as being co-accused with me in the murder. Bobby was also up for the same kneecapping charge on Gillen. My two good friends were dead and I was up for murder with a load of other shit.

Further to the build-up, my dad came to visit me on remand. It was one of those visitor rooms you see in films set in American prisons, where they have glass between them. All because they think a visitor will come up and give me a gun on a visit. Well any notion of that is diminished

278

when you're on closed visits and speaking through a wire mesh on the table in front. Surreal as it was, that's the way my visits were for nearly eight fucking months. I have no doubt they were recorded by the prison security in conjunction with Strathclyde police.

'You shouldn't be behind that fucking glass. Not you. It isn't right.'

'I know,' I said.

'Well, I'm gonna go back and speak to them,' he said.

That was him; a man of principles. He'd been accidentally knocked over by that point and it was an accident, the truck driver didn't see him, clipped him, and crushed both femurs, so he was registered disabled. It's easy to jump to conclusions, but I know for certain that it wasn't a gang related thing. As a consequence, he got around on two sticks. It's heart-wrenching to see your dad have to go through something like that, for an active and fit man to have all that snatched away and have limited mobility makes you feel helpless as a son. Regardless, he was true to his word and went to Thompson's house. If Thompson had come out my dad would have shot him and that's a fact, so he decided to smash all the house windows he could reach. As he did so, bats, hammers and stuff came from behind. He was all but unconscious after that. They then dragged him out into the road. It was a pitiful attack on a frail man. They wouldn't have done it if they'd thought I was getting out, put it that way. They also trashed his car when it was parked – his pride and joy – and he was again beaten and had his face slashed. No prizes for guessing who was behind it. The guy who told me what had happened did me a favour.

'Go and deliver that for me, please.'

It was a letter to the Godfather. In it, I said, *Look if you're gonna go to trial – help me. If you're not going to help me, don't turn up.* In court when I heard his name called out I thought, *I'm out*! He was a prosecution witness and they were asking him questions and he didn't even look at me. It was obvious that although he got the letter, he didn't get the memo, so to speak. I instructed Donald Findlay to ask him a fucking direct question: *Mr Thompson, do you know who killed your son*? and he looked at me from head to toe:

'Yeah, I know who fucking did it,' he scowled.

And then the bell went for lunch. Downstairs I was stunned – totally numb. From everything that had happened in my life, I was shocked. I have no doubt that my face was drained of all its colour. My ruse here was – if Thompson thought it was me, there's no way he would say it in court. He wouldn't because of 'the rule'. Or so I thought.

'That man's a fucking loose cannon. Don't ask me to ask him any more questions,' said Donald.

That was one of the top QCs in Scotland... professionally embarrassed cos he was under the impression that I told him to ask him that question cos the reply was going to be something totally different. He couldn't have felt as bad as I did. That's when I lost all respect for Thompson. That's when I knew it had all been fucking nonsense – the big man, the man of honour, *the fucking Godfather*. And there he was, in the box in court, denying his involvement in crime as well. The fucking irony! He even said something along the lines of it was the press who'd created his gangster image.

At one point, he said: 'I am the first to admit that, in twenty or thirty years, I've picked up a reputation. I've been charged and accused of lots of things, including culpable homicide and robbery. But I've only been to prison once in the past twenty years.'

The other defence witnesses – some stood firm as friends and others made their excuses. I mean, you have to fucking well turn up as a law-abiding citizen, but a couple made sure they were debarred from their duties by sitting in on some of the trial. It's a common thing they do and pretend it was an innocent mistake. Even McGraw was called up as a defence witness. He was a no-show, but the fact that the police didn't take it any further spoke volumes. In fact, there were a few names who didn't show up and it was all a bit dubious. The only reason why the polis wouldn't go after someone and get their backs up is cos they could be damaging by what they know. Talk about this being a game-changer... it was like everything was being revealed at once. The whole of gangland Glasgow was unravelling before my eyes. With Thompson's revelations, he'd be putting himself in the firing line anyway. And, if I got out, which I obviously did, then there was the risk of execution for me as well. There were other stories surrounding the trial and witnesses – Thompson sending bullets in the post to people he knew would be acting as my defence and on the other side, the police leaning on people to come forward, using threats and hints to get them to act on their behalf. I can only say what I've heard. There were people like David Logue and Bernard Docherty who were totally fucked over by the police, with bully-boy tactics and threats as to what would happen if they didn't go in as prosecution witnesses. On the flip side, promises of immunity, money and witness protection were all lies and people like them were abandoned by the law as soon as their use was over.

The Thompson ranch got raided in September 1991. Apparently, to see if they were behind Bob and Joe's murders. The whole of Provanmill Road was closed off and there were sniffer dogs, armed polis and a helicopter there to show the public that they were doing their bit... all at the public's expense. They even cuffed the family and took them to the station, looked through their cars and spun the houses. The press were there almost before the police were! It was obvious to all why they were doing it. Apparently, all they found was a bulletproof vest.

Even Thompson started talking to the press: 'They wanted me to come out with my hands over my head like something out of *Starsky and Hutch*, but there was no way because I saw the photographer waiting on the other side of the street. Then they wanted to handcuff me but I refused. I want to make it clear that the CID behaved in a proper manner and I have no complaints about them. It is the gun-toting policemen I am unhappy about,' he said to the *Daily Record*.

The whole thing was a clusterfuck. The police were uninterested. They were playing their own PR game throughout and it seemed Thompson was now doing the same. He did a telephone interview with BBC Scotland and admitted for the first time that he'd been knocked over and shot. 'Now the police tell me my life is in danger – I think that's obvious.' He also denied that he knew or that he suspected who killed his son and asked for the violence to stop.

Sharon, Joe's wife, was interviewed for the *Herald*. She used it to put the record straight about things with Joe and it was good that she got the opportunity to clear some of the mud off his name. She mentioned that Joe used to tape practically every conversation he had – all undercover stuff – mainly in case he was ever fitted up by the police. She told the press about the recorder cos the police had gone dark and wouldn't comment on it. 'I don't know if there's anything on it. I want to see justice done here. If there's anything on it that could bring these people to justice, that's what I want to see done. I don't know why the police don't say they've got it instead of printing things about drugs. He has never, ever been involved,' she said.

In reality this is what it's all about though: street justice often works in my life and that's just the way things will work out. Justice as in *legal justice* was not for me. I was not the forgiving type back then or even now – it's just the way of the streets. It's what we were brought up to believe in and it's how we live.

When I heard *not guilty*, I wanted to hear Bobby and Joe were not guilty as well. There was too much confusion cos the court was in total chaos with people cheering and celebrating. It was only when I saw Donald Findlay and Peter Forbes's grins that I knew I was ok. I smiled back at them. As I say, it was bitter-sweet. There'd be all the media frenzy to follow and all the ubiquitous postulations that I was now gonna take over Glasgow and shoot the fuck out of everyone left standing. So, my version of me emerging from the courthouse in a collarless jacket (they always call it a cardigan – it fucking wasn't. Stylish back then, mind you), shirt and tie, looking like an accountant is one where I was so fucking relieved that the jury backed me. Not guilty on majority for every charge. I wanted an enquiry into Dennis Woodman being allowed to stand there on oath and talk shit. It was already known that he was a liar – a perjurer – and yet he was called up. It was fucking disgusting.

My recollection of emerging from the court was also that I could taste real proper freedom for the first time in ages. You can see by my whole being that there's a huge weight lifted. And I didn't want to hang around. There was a lot to digest and a lot of things to think about.

Stevie Wilkie from the *Scottish Sun* covered the trial after he gave evidence. I offered an exclusive interview for no fee as long as he took me from court to their offices and let the trail go cold. Stevie knew this and, more importantly, secured the exclusive from me.

COURTING CONTROVERSY

Remember right at the start when I said I was fucking infamous? Well I can safely say that was an understatement on my part. The whole trial was as controversial as anything you've ever seen in a film – and then some.

Day two and Donald Findlay halted proceedings. The previous day, there was some footage of me on BBC2 Scotland. In the clip, I was led into court from a police van in handcuffs. There was no denying it was me cos, well... cos it was me. Because the question of my identity was to be a major factor in the whole court case, the judge found the BBC in contempt of court. In his words, there was 'a potential risk to the administration of justice.' Fucking right on! There was also an article in *Scotland on Sunday* that didn't get past the eagle-eyed Findlay. It printed stuff about the trial as fact when it was clearly fiction. They too were fined for being in contempt of court. Arthur Thompson also went after them after they described him as someone within organised crime and criminal activity and all the rest of it. The world knew it was true, but he'd never been convicted of any of it. So, technically, he wasn't the head of an organised crime family. And he won – he got an out-of-courter and gave most of it away to a kid's charity.

Having Arthur Thompson in court was just a farce. He was asked if he is sometimes described as a gang leader: *I am 61 years of age, not 21 years of age. This is the witness box and over there is the dock – pointing at me.*

I mean, some of his one-liners were pretty good, but not when they're working against you. He also said that he didn't believe in the police and that they'd planted evidence to fit Arty up, saying it was them who were responsible for where he is today.

When asked about me, he said: 'I did not have much to do with him. He was an associate of my son, Arthur. He was a pal of my son.' The press would have a field day with that one, bearing in mind that they always made out he was my surrogate dad – now he's totally distancing himself from me.

Thompson wasn't even the worst thing about the trial. There were a couple of letters that surfaced. First, there was one that was circulated throughout Glasgow and other places where I knew people – all the big criminal types like Freddie Foreman and Frankie Fraser who were associates of the Kray twins. The letter has already appeared in a few places, including *The Ferris Conspiracy*. It was a fake and it was brought to court by me to show that my defence witness list was being somewhat intimidated by external forces and to highlight what was happening on the outside to those I needed to attend court. It was also sent to people who'd be brought in as defence witnesses – so, it was a ruse to turn people against me and discredit my name and my word both on the streets and in court.

Mr Paul Ferris
Reg No 7684/91
HM Prison
Barlinnie, Glasgow

12 February, 1992

Dear Sir,
I refer to the letter of January 1992 (sent on your behalf) which was passed to the Lord Advocate who acknowledge's [sic] the assistance given by you to Stathclyde [sic] Serious Crime Squad over several years.

However, inquiries [sic] have shown that your prior assistance was for 'Monetary Consideration' and not 'Public Spirited.' Accordingly the Lord Advocate feels unable to intervene in the matters outstanding against you.
Yours faithfully,
Mr A. Vannet, Deputy Crown Agent.

Basically, it was implying that I was a grass and had been working alongside the polis as a paid informant. It was on letter headed paper and seemed legit... apart from the fucking shit spelling. That was the first giveaway. What the man on the street wouldn't know is that Crown Office paper that size is light blue – not white.

I remember when I was first given this letter ahead of a meeting with Donald Findlay. 'Tell me who this is. Alfred Vannet. *Who is he*?!' I demanded.

In that situation, we couldn't have been more different. I had a calm but angry, demanding, taking-no-shit persona. And Donald was just Donald: a Victorian archetype – he had more tweed than Berwick! That, along with these big fuck-off sideburns, waistcoat, and chain fob, he was Holmes and Watson rolled into one. As my question hung in the air, you know what he did? He just laughed, but I was deadly fucking serious. I drew breath to say it again. Donald lit up and had a puff on his Sherlock Holmes pipe, exhaled and tucked a thumb into his waistcoat pocket... and burst out laughing again. I thought, *What the fuck is so funny about this? What the fuck's in that pipe?*

'Whoever composed this is an absolute buffoon, son! There are grammatical and spelling errors and, what you have to remember is that the people who supposedly wrote this do the charge sheets. If one single word or one single letter is wrong, it gets thrown out of court. The chances of them making this amount of errors in a two-paragraph letter are inconceivable,' he said.

At last! I wasn't sure how this scene was going to evolve, but it was starting to sound positive.

'The other part of it... The other part is that it's a 1992 letter and it doesn't have a DX number. Whoever wrote this letter took an old Crown Office header to make it look official, without knowing that Crown Office stationery was recalled in 2000 to encompass the DX number. This will probably be recalled again, to get your email address or your fax number on it. But the fact remains that this letter is a fake. It would simply be binned, so the date 1992 on a particular letter, without that on the top, gave it away immediately, regardless of the grammatical errors.'

Ele-fucking-mentary, my dear Findlay! He was calculated and deliberate. You'd think it was an act until you realised that's what he was like – I got the feeling that his Holmesesque image wasn't just for work either. And he was a young guy as well. I got the feeling that he'd never owned a pair of jeans in his life. And I kind of liked that about him – to me it was like he was keeping it real. He was living it from morning til night. We got Vannet in court and he testified that it wasn't his signature and that the Crown Office letter was an obvious bad forgery.

Next up was Dennis Woodman, a serial perjurer also known as Dennis Wilkinson. In my case, he is known as Dennis the Menace. He was known as a supergrass but he wasn't. A supergrass gives evidence against people that they have committed crimes with – this fucker sold people out and lied about them to get his own conviction reduced. There was a big difference. He claimed I'd confessed to murdering Arty while we were having a game of chess. Right, so I knew from the off that it was a load of bollocks, having never played him. I was serious about chess inside and he was known to be shit – it wouldn't be worth my time. The way we played in the seg unit at Bar-L, we had to shout moves from one cell to the next, so it was hardly an intimate setting where I whispered my confession to him – every fucker would have heard. The prosecution had put a lot of faith in Woodman as their star witness, so it was good news for me. The Crown already knew he was a total crank. A letter was read out from Woodman to his wife where he claimed he was in with Thompson and was going to fit me up. Thompson himself said that Woodman was a loon and it seemed very obvious that he was put in a cell near me in prison in order to manufacture evidence. He was spending time, lots of time, with a screw in there and it looked very suspicious. Then I found out he was going to give evidence against me and things started falling into place. Even his brother-in-law warned me about him. Woodman also said in court that Peter Forbes had offered him a lot of money a year – forever – if he dropped the evidence and didn't testify against me. That could have totally ruined Peter's career if it was believed.

'I am in a strange position here. I am in prison and at the moment I fear for my life because of Mr Ferris. I am just at the moment too frightened to say much because of what might happen to me. The Crown has to ensure the protection I need.'

He was grinning throughout and didn't appear to be worried in the slightest. He didn't even seem to be worried at how ridiculous his stories

291

were. He was asked how many times he'd changed his name and the reasoning behind each – it was all down to how many men he'd grassed on and made shit up about, the attempts on his life and the outstanding contracts on him. I've no idea why he'd keep lying about apparently dangerous criminals to reduce his own sentence – surely he'd be better off inside with the amount of people who'd be baying for his blood. He admitted to being paid for 'giving evidence', said that his wife had been kidnapped over the shit he'd pulled and told the court he'd been a supergrass in six high-profile trials. With Findlay on his back, Woodman ended up losing his rag and the judge didn't like it one bit. He said he'd allowed Woodman to shout and swear 'in order for the jury to assess what kind of person you are' but told him that he'd be held in contempt of court if he did it again.

Woodman said it was me, Bobby and Joe who killed Arty, with me being the one who pulled the trigger. He also said I'd confessed that I was going to take over the old man's criminal empire by blowing the Ponderosa up. He didn't stop there – he said that I'd confessed to kneecapping William Gillen, I'd told him I was a coke and heroin dealer and that I'd put a half a million pound price on his head for standing in the witness box.

He clashed with Donald Findlay throughout,

but Findlay kept his cool and was the clear winner. 'You may be the top dog in Scotland, but not down south,' he said.

'Don't flatter me, Mr Woodman,' came the retort.

Findlay had him on the ropes at every twist and turn of the farce. I think everyone in the entire court almost imploded when Woodman swore he was telling the truth... not only that, but he swore on the ashes of his dead children. It was later that his ex-wife was called up and confirmed that the kids were alive and well. What kind of fucking moron would do that? Going in for the kill, Findlay put it to Woodman that he'd got most of his information from what he'd read in newspapers and the rest was just regurgitated from hearsay conversations:

'In the many, many years that this witness box and its predecessors have stood in this High Court of Judiciary in Glasgow, aren't you the biggest liar ever to disgrace its existence?'

Woodman protested, but there was no one in that room that believed a word he said. Not even his name was the truth. I feel sorry for his kids.

When it was my turn to take the stand, I didn't hold back and gave it to the advocate depute with both barrels, so to speak. I knew the score – they try to get you to say what they want the jury to hear. I was accused of being a drug dealer and of paying someone as a hitman. The accusations were laughable and my one-liner replies outdid Thompson's. But it felt touch and go quite often. I wasn't entirely confident, even with Woodman's comedy routine. The main accusation was that I was a drug dealer. My motivation was to get Arty out the way because he was my competition. My 'lavish lifestyle with no apparent means of support' was a factor, because in 1991 I'd only earned around four grand. In Findlay's summing up, he defended that by saying I'd been in prison most of that year.

At the end of the trial, judge Lord McCluskey said: 'In this long trial, you have listened to an extraordinary catalogue of lies and deceit, cruelty and death.' I think that summed it up pretty well. Again, maybe an understatement. It was exhausting for everyone involved.

He added that 'even the worst of liars can tell the truth sometimes.'

RUNNING OUT OF TAM

The shit TC Campbell and Joe Steele went through inside was fucking harrowing. TC got beaten to fuck by the screws and went on hunger strike to the point of wanting to die. Steele – he escaped a few times and handcuffed himself to the gates of Buckingham Palace to raise awareness of their plight. That's without all the impact on their families. They never sat back and accepted their fate. Luckily, their convictions were quashed in March, 2004. As I mentioned in *Vendetta*, the bad blood between TC and McGraw never stopped. He lost 18 years of his life because of that cunt. Everyone and their dog knew that McGraw was behind the arson attack that killed the Doyles. Between him and Strathclyde police, the waters were muddied enough to ensure nothing would ever come of all the rumours. Around that time, John 'Blind Jonah' McKenzie left McGraw's mob and went to work with Arty Thompson and co.

McGraw invested a lot in 'legitimate' businesses and earned a fortune worth millions. He had bars, restaurants and property. There's speculation that he was also laundering a lot of his money through his taxi firm, Mac Cabs. There's speculation that he was able to do all that because he was under the protection of Strathclyde police. There's speculation that the speculation is not speculation – of course they were in each other's pocket. The corruption was so fucked up in Glasgow that – some would allege – Strathclyde police even supplied heroin to him that they'd confiscated from some other trafficker, for fuck's sake. So, rather than looking at him as just a dishonest and slippery streak of piss, make no mistake that he was good at violence and could hold his own in many a ropey situation. He'd done his time and worked his way up the ladder. As much as I despise him, he was as successful as he was a big stinking fucking rat.

McGraw and Billy McPhee walked free from major international drugs trafficking charges in 1988. McPhee was a close associate of his; a hitman and someone McGraw needed around him. In a list compiled in 2004 online, McGraw's up there in the top ten wealthiest drugs traffickers in the UK – makes you wonder how he walked from the accusation in court. It beggars belief, man. It really does.

The law caught up with him in 1998 when he was nabbed for and accused of drug smuggling.

McGraw had a nice little scam going where he'd take underprivileged kids from the East End schemes on holidays to Spain. The minibuses were slightly different in that they'd been modified to fill the floors and under the seats with cannabis. So, the police were eventually tipped off and they swooped in to find El McGringaw's stash. I'm surprised the kids didn't get in there first. There was a trial at the High Court in Edinburgh and, wait for it... McGraw walked. He got a majority not proven verdict. When the minibus had been pulled, it was his brother-in-law in the driving seat. That must have made for awkward Christmas dinners, eh? The smell of resin wasn't the only iffy thing about the whole incident. Needless to say, the brother-in-law was just another custodial casualty that surrounded McGraw. No idea why he didn't use one of his famous *get out of jail* cards on one of his own, though.

There were more serious casualties surrounding the fucker. When writing with Reg McKay this McGraw fucker may well have played a role in the stuff with Bobby and Joe, but Reg always used faction – he'd get a bit creative with word-on-the-street information and then sit back and see who spills the beans by pulling him up with their specific specialist knowledge. You may be as tired of hearing it as I am saying it, but the fact remains that it is unsolved. The police couldn't really give two fucks and they will never go out of their way to solve it. What am I saying? They already *know* who the culprit was. It was a very messy time on the streets and they must have taken a smug step back and watch everyone killing each other in gangland genocide. The police didn't have to do anything other than wait to see who might come out on top. At the same time though, they had Bobby and Joe's blood on their hands, so the less that happened the better it was for them.

Was McGraw behind it? Absolutely. I have to say I *think* so, but there's also that thing where you cannot libel the dead. In my mind, I *know* so. Everyone knew McGraw had a hand in it to put himself in favour with the old man. Why? To get closer to Thompson and in doing so, get closer to taking over. I was banged up awaiting trial, Bobby was on bail and being watched, Joe was with him and also being watched. It was known that the three of us worked together and we were all rumoured to be the ones behind Arty's murder. With that in mind, there was an eerie feeling on the streets as people braced themselves for further bloodshed.

On the night of their murder, Bobby and Joe were under 24-hour police surveillance and somehow, the police managed to lose them – during the exact window of time that they were murdered. We're expected to buy all this? Is that the most convenient thing you've ever heard? Two men being watched around the clock by the police and they get murdered? Fuck off!

It couldn't have been a one-man job; not against those two. When the police had no other choice but to act upon information, a forensic team was assembled to go to the Caravel to find evidence. It was a pretty hush-hush operation, and yet somehow McGraw got wind of it. The pub was flattened and disposed of the night before the forensics team arrived on the scene. Another random coincidence? *Fuck off*! Everyone on the street knew it was Trevor Lawson, one of

McGraw's men, who got the direct order to level the pub. He was in that tricky position. He couldn't really say no, but he was very well rewarded afterwards by getting a big payment and brought in on enough property deals that he was able to move into his own country fortress. He had to after what he did.

Following a lengthy enquiry that ended in 1996, Strathclyde police were cleared of any wrong-doing or involvement in granting McGraw's license to commit crime. I have no idea how. It's just one cover-up after another with them.

Once I'd been released for gun-running in January 2002 a lot of people were nervous. McGraw included. Yeah, that's a bit of an understatement. Without trivialising it, the number of people he traded in to the law or had a hand in their ruin was fucking staggering. If ever there was a dead man walking, look no further than McGraw. He was fucking despised. The perception was that I'd be baying for blood with a gun in each fist the second the prison gates closed. I would have loved to, but come on... that's exactly what everyone expected and it was the exact thing I couldn't do. It was probably a worse feeling having to keep my head down and stay out of trouble.

It was thought that people like Trevor Lawson would be on my would-be hit list. And rightly so. But the fact that he *thought* something would happen to him was a lot more interesting to me. Knowing he was walking the streets was bad, but he wasn't really walking the streets as a free man. He was fucking shiteing it; a paranoid wreck, always looking over his shoulder for the inevitable. That suited me. He'd made his own bed and someone would catch up with him one day, because there were a lot of people out to avenge Bobby and Joe. But everyone missed their chance. A scuffle kicked off in front of Trevor when he was in a pub. Because of his paranoia, he thought it was the beginning of a hit, a kind of red herring to draw him in, so he did a runner. He didn't just stop running when he got outside though. He did a full-on Forrest Gump and ran straight into the road and the oncoming traffic. It's a bit sad in that he was more or less forced into doing a job, but he was still a street-player all the same and was part of McGraw's team.

Not only was he a dangerous man, but he quickly became dangerous to even be around. His associates and bodyguards started dropping like flies, one after the other. If you were next in line to look after him, your days were numbered. You wouldn't want to be in the same room as him, such was the threat. He was getting so many attempts on his life that someone somewhere had to succeed. Mark Clinton seemed to be causing him some trouble because McGraw's men kept getting hit and Mark was known to be handy with a blade. If ever there was a time to cut your losses and get the fuck out of Dodge, it was now.

I found this in *The Guardian*:

In a rare interview, McGraw denied being the godfather of Glasgow and said: 'Glasgow's a town called malice. Everybody's jealous of everybody else. Nobody likes to see that you are getting on in Glasgow. I am not one of the controlling influences in the city. I don't think there's anyone capable of running this city. I'm not frightened of anybody but then they aren't frightened of me.'

Who the fuck did he think he was, using a song title from The Jam in an interview? I despised him even more for that.

McGraw was living on borrowed time and it was running out.

SPOOKED

REVEALED:
HOW MI5 SPOOKS BROUGHT DOWN SCOTS GANGSTER PAUL FERRIS

The spymasters of MI5 launched an astonishing surveillance operation to nail gun-running gangster Paul Ferris, it can be revealed today.

Frustrated Scots police asked the spooks for help after trying for years to bring the notorious hood to justice. MI5 spent six months on Ferris's trail, using all their skills in human and electronic surveillance to help police track his every move. And they got their reward in May 1997 after Ferris made a call to a London gun dealer – on a tapped mobile phone.

The offensive against Ferris, codenamed *Operation Shillelagh*, has been detailed for the first time in a new official history of MI5. The book, *The Defence of the Realm*, has been written to mark the centenary of the service. Ferris was the first gangster MI5 had ever gone after. The service usually focused on fighting threats to Britain's security. But Strathclyde Police knew they needed help to get him. He had repeatedly cheated justice, and had been cleared in 1991 of

302

murdering Arthur 'Fatboy' Thompson, son of his former boss Arthur Thompson Snr. The police were concerned that Ferris had spread his criminal connections outside Scotland and formed close ties in the London underworld.

Senior officers had even begun to fear that the Thompson clan's former enforcer had become 'untouchable'.

They asked MI5 to join the fight and the spooks first put Ferris under surveillance in December 1996.

The spies found out he had become involved with a London criminal network. He was running guns for the underworld, including terrifyingly powerful Mac 10 machine pistols that could fire 1,200 rounds a minute. Police and MI5 kept Ferris under surveillance. And by May 1997, they were ready to make their move. The spooks listened in as Ferris arranged to meet gun dealer John Ackerman. And on May 23, undercover officers watched him as he went alone into Ackerman's home, carrying an envelope full of cash.

When Ferris came out, he was holding a box tied up with string. It contained three high-velocity machine pistols, six 25-round magazines, three bags of ammunition, three silencers and a box containing four detonators. Ferris left the scene in a car driven by his accomplice, London crook Henry Suttie, then gave the guns to another gang member, Constance Howarth, who was driving a second car. Officers stopped Howarth and seized the guns. Ferris and Suttie were arrested later.

At the Old Bailey the following year, jurors found all three crooks guilty of gun-running. Ferris was jailed for 10 years and thanked the judge as he was led to the cells. Suttie and Howarth got five years each. MI5 surveillance reports were read out at the trial – the first time that had ever happened in a criminal case. Ferris's conviction was a cause for celebration for police – and satisfaction for MI5.

The author of the new history of the service, intelligence expert Professor Christopher Andrew, said: 'It was the first time MI5 stepped in to help police fight organised crime.

'In that first year, intelligence officers helped in the recovery of 50 kilos of heroin and in bringing 65 arrests. Chief among those arrests was Ferris.'

As Ferris sat in jail, MI5 Director Stephen Lander wrote to Home Office Permanent Under Secretary, Sir Richard Wilson, to tell him how well police and agents had worked

together on the case. Lander wrote:
'I have been encouraged by the
smooth running of this operation and
by its overall success. I understand
the police are delighted with our
contribution. More of the same to
come, I hope.'

Senior Strathclyde officers were in
no doubt about how important MI5's
help had been.

Graeme Pearson, former head of the
Scottish Crime and Drugs Enforcement
Agency, said: 'At that time, I was a
divisional commander with
Strathclyde and there certainly was
a feeling out there that Paul Ferris
was 'untouchable'. This book is an
object lesson in what happens to
organised crime figures when they
decide to operate out of their home
comfort zone, and suddenly find that
vulnerability is exploited very
professionally by organisations like
MI5.

'I believe this book will give the
public great comfort, knowing that
organisations such as MI5 are well
capable of working in close
partnership with various services to
put dangerous individuals and
terrorists behind bars, where they
belong.'

Belmarsh was all brand new; brand new cells and everything. But it was still prison. I was held there until I was convicted in 1998. The trial was at the Old Bailey and it felt surreal. I was thinking about the people I'd read about who'd sat where I was sitting in the dock in such an infamous court. So I was kind of dazed for a bit.

Within a minute being told to go back up, I was given 15 years. It was 15 and 10 concurrent and I thought, *Life, this is what I'm gonna get now*. Then I heard the arguments going and I heard the prosecution stand up saying it's my fault my Lord about the sentencing guidelines and I thought they can only give you 10, not 15. And I was listening to all that thinking I was gonna get five taken off, but there never should have been five added on cos he should know his sentencing guidelines. My head was fucking spinning. This is where it was reported that *the gangster thanked the judge for his sentence*. I'm sure a few have been sarcastic, but mine was genuine. You know... thanks *very much*. I ended up with 10 years – 10 and five concurrent. Fucking hell – what a reduction and what a result.

But the problem is, in England, this is the judicial system and it's very good. Whoever's number one on the indictment gets the biggest sentence. So this was an ongoing conspiracy. But that's down to multiple forces.

The trial was in court number one and was a unique opportunity that not a lot of people get. What the fuck were we doing in court number one? It was for security reasons. A friend of mine had tried to book a visit to come and see me in Belmarsh, but hadn't realised the system was very different to Scotland where you just turn up with your ID and you get in. Like when my sister Carol had come to visit me, you need the cops to go and visit you at home, take your photograph and all the rest of it. My mate James phoned up to arrange his visit, but wasn't prepared for the third degree.

'Listen, you fucking arseholes. Do you know we can get him out of there quicker than you got him in?'

So they were on high alert. If it was even a slight possibility that I'd get broken out, they had to take it seriously. Hence court one. It would be easy to get overwhelmed by the whole thing and lose your shit. It was very imposing. The first thing that struck me was how it was designed for somebody sitting there. You had the jury to the left, the judge facing you, the gallery upstairs to your right and you turn around and the stairs lead you down.

In the appeal, they agreed that Arthur Suttie's sentence (real name Henry Arthur Suttie) was wholly inappropriate because he was just a glorified taxi driver that I'd paid to take me on the run in London. I'd mentioned that in court. He just shouldn't have even been there. Constance shouldn't have been there and neither should her boyfriend, James. Another guy was involved who was just down to give me some baby clothes because my son Dean was just six weeks old.

So, Arthur's sentence was reduced from five to three, which meant he would walk out the door cos he'd served his time. He was a gambling man, liked the horses. I was delighted for him, really delighted for him. Then it was my turn. It was decided that 10 years was excessive, in light of the role that was played. I got reduced from 10 to seven. That was decent enough, I thought.

The judge said, 'You're getting out a lot quicker.'

'Aye, but not as quickly as you,' I said. Well, I couldn't help it.

I went back to prison to finish off my reduced sentence of seven years. My freedom date was now a fixed to the 21st of January, 2002. Just as well for me as it was Sandra's birthday the next day.

Outside the prison, Ferris said: 'I would like to thank my family and friends and supporters who stood by me. There have been quite a few significant events – most importantly the compilation of *The Ferris Conspiracy* with Reg McKay. There are other issues I will be willing to talk about but obviously I have to get back to Glasgow to see the probation officer and we will get a chance to speak some other time but today's not appropriate.'

As far as I was concerned, I just wanted to get my life back together. The stuff with Reg was going well and I was really enjoying it. I couldn't wait to get stuck into some ideas with him.

Before Ferris's release, Mr McKay said the pair had several books in draft form. The second, titled Deadly Divisions, is due out in March.

Mr McKay went on: 'Paul has said goodbye to being a criminal and wants to draw on his experiences and his knowledge of the underworld to write about crime instead.

At the time of writing this, I told Ray Burdis to get hold of the book, *The Defence of the Realm*, to pick up this story and see what he can use from it for the new Ferris film he's writing. The book, as the article says above, was to mark the centenary of MI5 and celebrate 100 years of its history. Ray was all excited and started reading. The book, as you may imagine, covers a lot and is around as thick as a fucking club sandwich. He phoned me up one day and said he was enjoying the book, but wondered when the part about me was.

'What bit are you up to?' I asked.

'The Cold War,' he said.

'Fuck me, Ray! That's just the 1980s – you've still got nearly 20 years to go. Just look in the index!'

THE FERRIS CONSPIRACY

I am a believer that things happen for a reason. I just got back from a couple of games of soft tennis and got back up into the cell to find some letters on the bed. Two were specific; a legal letter about the counsel's view with regards to a civil action case and a handwritten one. I didn't recognise who it was from. Although I had a lot going on and was waiting to hear back from people, the unexpected letters were the ones that always piqued your interest.

I opened it and saw that it was from Reg McKay. I'd had contact with him and even then it was so brief that I wouldn't have known without him reminding me in the letter. In it, he said that he wanted to write a book about the fatalities that he'd experienced when he was working in Blackhill and the history of Blackhill itself. There'd been a few fatalities amongst the Irish immigrants and a few locals through industrial alcohol. And a few of them went blind. I wasn't sure how to react. I couldn't work out why he wanted to write about Blackhill. Different minds, see? Blackhill was a place to forget, not to remember and immortalise in a book. At that time, I was dealing with a lot of stress based around the Crown Office letter, there were things I was just finding out about in my file and all the stuff I'd read about my 1992 case in the newspapers and all the rest of it. It wasn't a good time for me – my headspace was fucked; nonexistent. The things in my file that had been reported in the press weren't true and that was really weighing heavily on my mind. It was only while in that battered state and reading Reg's letter that I thought, *You know what? I've got nothing to lose here. I'm gonna give myself a chance, so let's fucking put the record straight.*

I made him a counter-offer to write a different book. Getting together with him meant that I could have my say. I was getting fucked over left, right and centre by the press. They could write lies about me and get away with it because their disclaimer was that they thought it was the truth. All I wanted to do was get the truth out – I wasn't arsed about money or anything else. So, to me it was: *You want to say somebody's a fucking grass, I've got no problem there – let's name and shame them, the Licensee – number one – we'll start with him.* The primary one was about the letter and if I could twist that enough, they'd take me to court – and taking me to court would save me £50k in legal fees because it would be action against me. Those were my motivations for writing my first book, sure. With the Data Protection Act being lifted in 1999 or 2000, just when I got to Frankland, that newspaper article in my file triggered me seeking legal advice on 'bad character'.

It felt like Reg coming back into my life at that point was significant. I can look back now and see what we did and when we did it and that took us both on such a mad adventure. When writing *The Ferris Conspiracy*, we had to play a game of cat 'n' mouse to get stuff through the prison security. I was banged up the whole time we wrote it, so that in itself was a bit of a triumph. I was getting documentation sent in and was picking it up at the gym, and talking to Reg on the phone. I say *talking* on the phone, but that was like a military operation. I had to say I was calling a mate called Gerry and that was our code when complaints from the prison security about writing a book set in. Gerry was Reg's wife's name – an abbreviation of Geraldine – so for me to talk with Gerry to tell Reg stuff was a way round being stopped from talking with Reg. Gerry passed messages on and our covert ploy worked. It was difficult cos someone would be listening in all the time. Talk about the fucking Ferris Conspiracy.

I'd never met him since I was 16 and the only time I got to meet him was when I'd go up to Bar-L for legal visits, to see the family, to talk to the lawyer about the content of books and things like that. Then I got a visit from Reg himself. So, let's see... would it have been around 1980 or '81 when I last saw him? Fuck me – near enough 20 years. It was a bit surreal. We wrote the book without actually meeting face-to-face. His only concern *was how do you want to put this?*

He was sending in copies of transcripts, you know, different versions and amendments and notes all the way to the final draft and I ended up with at least nine of them in my cell. I could've wallpapered your house for you with the amount of printouts I had in there. I'd said no to the first one – it changed, then another was sent in... no to the second, *bang*, another one appeared... so every time I'm getting one, the screws knew what I was up to.

'What do you fucking need all of them for?'

'I don't need them all. Why, like?' I said. I knew what was coming next: the question every writer gets, whether the asker even looks at it or not.

'Can I get one then, Paul?'

'I'll tell you what. That'll be worth a couple of quid in a few years time,' I said as I signed it and gave it to him. I told him to not go daft just yet cos I might ask for it back.

That's the first thing I learned about becoming a writer: everyone wants a free book. Whether or not they have any intention of reading it. And it's probably the only profession where people have no shame in asking that or how much money you make from it. I should start doing that with people I meet:

Oh, you're an electrician! Can I have some free wires and light fittings? How much do you earn a week?

You run your own garage? I need some new tyres. Giz four and I'll have a quick look through your accounts when you've fitted them. Cheers.

Actually, I shouldn't do that. I'd probably end up being accused of some Maltesers protection racket if I asked the wrong confectioner.

The reason why we called it *The Ferris Conspiracy* was exactly that – it was a total conspiracy against me. I was proving a conspiracy and that it wasn't just a figment of my imagination. I've gone on record about things with documentation to back it up. I've got the luxury to sit back and say, *Well, this is the position and this is why I did it.* For the authorities to actually back me when I was trying to prove corruption and members of a jury be on my side – well, that speaks for itself. The tapes I have of policemen issuing threats... they definitely speak for themselves too.

The Ferris Conspiracy was published in 2001 when I was still in prison. It sold around 20,000 copies in its first two weeks. Reg was just astounded. I didn't really know what was good from bad in terms of book sales, but had to conclude that 20,000 people wanting to read my story in the space of ten or so days is a bit fucking mental, eh? It goes without saying that it ruffled a few feathers. There was a big propaganda campaign in the *Daily Record* where they urged their readers:

DON'T BUY THIS BOOK, PARASITES INFEST OUR SOCIETY!

I mean, come on... you could substitute 'book' for 'newspaper' in that headline. In it, they said that I was making false claims of cops and corruption and who would believe a word that I say? This was an editorial in a Glasgow newspaper. It was a personal dig from the editor to me because the solicitors are also police federation sources, right? I thought, *If you want to attack me, fine. That's up to you. All I've done is harvested the negativity, used my website, and made my own comments with evidence to back up what I say.*

Writing the first book, for me, was all about the working relationship with Reg. When I was talking and writing to him he said, 'Paul, you need to lose the venom. We don't want to write a venomous book, we want it to be balanced so that the reader can read it as much as someone in the jury would sit and listen to the evidence.'

I was doing it for the enjoyment at first and, with a point to prove, I got issues off my chest. I probably did sound venomous and bitter. I *was* venomous and bitter. It was my right to reply to them all and it was me exorcising all the shit and the darkness I'd been stuck in. This was a totally new experience for me – a blank canvas – a way of replying to everything and to put my point of view across. Money-wise, I did get some from the second and third book. It was only a token gesture and any cheques that came in went to young Paul, my boy.

I liked us adding any black humour. It's what life is about. And we also had to cover the other side – the stuff you don't really want to get to, but you have to confront.

Reg asked me, 'Do you know what happened to Bobby Glover and Joe Hanlon?'

I don't know 100 per cent what happened to them. I was in prison, so I was relying on family and friends to tell me things. Reg and I had a heart to heart. He poured a glass of wine, that was just Reg being Reg, but I had one or two as well, and that was why I had to get a friend to pick me up.

I knew he was serious when he put his glass down on the table and asked, 'How far are we gonna go here, Paul?

'Reg, I don't know. All we can do is... I'll tell you the information from the streets and what I've been told by family and friends. And I'll tell you what I believe to be true and what I believe not to be true.'

So, when I told him about Bobby and Joe, I was just repeating what other people had told me: they were taken back to this pub and all the rest of it. So Reg sits for a bit, takes another sip of wine and goes,

'We're gonna use faction – a hybrid between fact and fiction. We'll throw it out, if you're happy with it. The people who've been involved in it will show their classic symptom. They've got to. They can't keep that [points to his mouth] shut. If they're reading it and going, *That's right, that happened...* or if they're going, *What a crock of shit, this is what happened...*'

Certain people did reveal themselves as knowing more than someone who was innocent by letting their lips flap. A lot came out at that time, by criticising what Reg said about it. So,

317

imagine what it's like to have two of your best mates executed? There was no closure for their families and their bodies were treated as crime scenes.

And then Reg got me to do a couple of reading sessions in Edinburgh, which was quite unusual, at the Mitchell Library in Glasgow and another big library in Edinburgh, at their book festival. These were big things for a true crime book. Firstly, it's true crime. Even if I had Shakespeare ghosting it, it's still widely regarded as bottom-of-the-barrel shite in the literary world. And then, of course, all us gangster types are thick as fuck, so how could I even read the book I wrote? And then the big issue – Edinburgh World City of Literature is a big deal for any writer, never mind me and Reg. He was as chuffed as I was; what a fucking accolade. And yeah, there was backlash. There were some very high horses around at the time, with saddles full of critics. How dare I infiltrate a book festival with a... with a... *with a book*? Fucking easy, mate. You can't complain when the publishers promoted the book by calling it:

A story of international gangsters, hit contracts, murders, bank scams, Essex-boy torturers, corrupt politics, crack-head hit-men, knife duels, securi-wars, drugs, guns, Yardies, terrorists and more.

If they were expecting *Wuthering Heights*, then these quivering shites needed to give themselves a good shake. I enjoyed doing it. The audience was kind of mixed. A lot of people wanted books signed; a lot were just there for the book session. I suppose it's the same as when any other author does a book event: sometimes they go well and you sell hundreds, sometimes hardly anyone turns up and you feel a right plumb. You never know – it's a popularity contest in a fickle world and there's always someone waiting to tell the world that it failed. There was obvious concern from the people hosting the event. This was a first, so they didn't want it to be their last. A senior Lothian Borders police officer gave an open statement:

If Paul Ferris wants to come to Edinburgh to promote his new book then Paul Ferris is entitled to come to Edinburgh to promote his new book. If Paul Ferris wants to come to Edinburgh and cause trouble, then we'll have to deal with it. If the guy says he's going straight, then who are we to say he's not?

Totally different in vibe in Glasgow compared to Edinburgh. They're worlds apart, man. If it had been the Glasgow Book Festival, I can guarantee that something would have happened to scupper my appearance. I just let them get on with it though. It's almost reassuring to know that I get under their skin even after going straight.

A lot of you will know that the book led to *The Wee Man* film. The film didn't necessarily follow the same tone and message as the book. It couldn't. It got word out further though. It created more of an awareness of me and led to more people picking up *The Ferris Conspiracy*.

And then Reg asked, 'Do you want to write another?'

UNLICENSED

On the 24th of September, 2002, Gordon Ross
was knifed to death outside the Sheiling Bar.
Another one of McGraw's boys, it was a
significant kill as it was slap bang in the middle
of his own turf in the East End and was surely
another message to The Licensee that his time
was nearly up. Next to go down was Billy
McPhee, who was also a close associate of
Gordon Ross. Fuck knows how, but he was lucky
enough to have survived a recent gunshot to the
face. Ironically, it was only a few days after
Gordon's funeral when he was seen off. He was
in a pub, his guard was down, and he was
watching the rugby on the big screen. The timing
was perfect. The assailant walked up to him and
stabbed him 27 times in front of a bar full of
people. No hesitation, no messing around. This is
the level of violence that was being committed. It
was a fucking family pub, the middle of the day.
He was stabbed all over – his bollocks, his arse,
his eyes – it was fucking brutal. The messages to
McGraw were stacking up. Mark Clinton was
dragged in and done for it. I think the main reason
being that with his particular set of skills, he was
the only man on earth capable of going in there,
confronting someone like McPhee and doing such
a job on him. Mark would be the last person
anyone would want coming after them. There was
no forensic evidence to link him to it and the
CCTV in the pub wasn't working that day. He

walked free from court in 2004 through lack of evidence and witnesses. Textbook.

As if the plot couldn't get any thicker, I got word from Mark that McGraw made an approach prior to the trial. A trade was offered. McGraw could give Clinton a get out of jail free card in return for him setting me up to be murdered when he got out. If he didn't do it, he was told that the whole case was watertight and he'd get sent down for McPhee's murder. An offer like that had McGraw's paw prints all over it. Rather than set me up, Mark told me about the plot. There were two men, Craig Devlin and John McCartney with McGraw at the time of the offer. They were both shot the next day. The gunman must have known they'd be wearing vests cos they were shot everywhere above and below the torso. The shooting happened in the Royal Oak bar. It was one of McGraw's crony's bars – or snitch's bitches, as we call them. In fact, he was with Devlin and McCartney when the shooting started and he managed to perform a 9.9 dive underneath the pool table and hide until the coast was clear. He then drove them to hospital with a police escort in tow. Aye that's right – a *police escort*. Who has that sort of a luxury when in a vehicle with two foot soldiers who were shot? Only one who has friends in blue uniforms. It was unheard of in the entire history of Glasgow gang culture and has never been seen since. It shows the level in which McGraw was connected for them to waste police time and tax-payer's money on

322

taking them to hospital. The nerve of it. Again, this all happened in the middle of the day in a busy pub and again there were no witnesses. You'd think that, even if you didn't see what was going on, you'd at least have heard a dozen gunshots in a bar. But no – *nothing*. The next day the pub got torched and that was the end of solving that one.

I met up with Mark Clinton on my travels through Barlinnie to Franklin. He's just plain crackers – a good crackers, though. Celtic through and through and was always causing mischief inside Barlinnie. I eventually met up with him when we got out, but he's a tricky customer. We were asked to take part in a documentary and I was a bit concerned that he wasn't gonna be shown in a good light because he wasn't really in a good place and was drinking at the time. He more or less admitted to three murders. Mark was loyal and reliable. Then he was battered unconscious one night in town. The mad bastard was just about to make off to escape some drugs charges, but couldn't resist going for a final night out. And it nearly was his final night out. He was in a coma in hospital a few days before making a full recovery. It goes to show that if things like that can happen to him, then they can happen to anyone. It also shows how tough he is. He's been in and out of prison ever since on various knife-related offences.

Mystery surrounded the whereabouts
of gangster Paul Ferris last night
after he was knifed in a street
fight with a sworn enemy.

Underworld sources claimed the
notorious criminal was the man who
left Tam 'The Licensee' McGraw
fighting for his life on Friday.

It is understood Ferris was also
stabbed twice during the vicious
battle. A gangland associate with
medical knowledge has been giving
Ferris treatment at a secret
location in Glasgow, according to
sources.

Ferris is said to have suffered one
wound to his left shoulder and
another to his left side. Both have
been patched up. Underworld figures
said he was staying at secret
address on the city's southside.

Don't believe everything that you read. This was
front-page news in Scotland and spawned
countless other articles. I read about it when I was
in Frankland and demanded a medical, cos I knew
I'd have to prove it didn't happen.

Tam McGraw died of a heart attack in July, 2007.
He was at home and taken to Glasgow Royal

Infirmary. At the time, Reg was asked by the press to comment on him:

'Even some of his enemies will take no joy in this,' he said. 'A death is a death. The man had a wife and family. On the other hand there are some folk who feel very embittered by Tam McGraw and his behaviour over many years and who will indeed rejoice. He became one of the most powerful gangsters in Britain, certainly in Glasgow, and he earned a great deal of that power by trading information with the police.'

I liked how balanced Reg was, yet still managed to get a dig in at the end. Fucking priceless. I mean, as he said, a death is a death and that's never a time to celebrate. A lot of people in our position, in Glasgow at the time, had everything to celebrate. There was a lot of blood on his hands and it was good riddance for a lot of street-players.

THE GODFATHER & SONS

To understand the origins of organised crime from an online starting point, you can only conclude whatever the research throws up; whatever is on the internet and available to you. There are many main players who are still alive and they are capable of casting doubt over the real goings on and, in most cases, dispel the myths surrounding two of the most notorious Glasgow gangsters of my era. Most of what you find online is the same content spread across every site and it's difficult to know what is fact and what is fiction.

The Godfather of Glasgow is quite a moniker, don't you think? I'm not sure what Arthur Thompson even made of it. I never once heard a single soul say it when he was still alive. To refer to him as that would just have been a bit... embarrassing, really. Actually, it was used a few times as a sort of incredulous comment – a bit of a piss-take and something to use against him. Never to his face. You'd only see it in print in the dozens of newspaper articles and front-page headlines. It was essentially a media label. It was a catchy title and it was used to sell newspapers. Every story needs a hero and a villain and *The Godfather of Glasgow* could be whichever one they wanted, depending on the angle and agenda of the story. To me, it carries connotations of power and wealth so the old man must have been chuffed with it, but there would be a lot of responsibility and caution to go with it. It was probably a burden more than anything but, as I say, I can't speak for him.

Along with the stories and myths we cannot ignore the media interest in Norval after the petrol bomb attack on the court or the Godfather for surviving a bomb blast that detonated under his car and killed his mother-in-law. Things like that were big news and enhanced their reputations on the street.

An urban legend, urban myth, urban tale, or contemporary legend is a form of modern folklore. It usually consists of fictional stories, often presented as true, with macabre or humorous elements, rooted in local popular culture. These legends can be used for entertainment purposes, as well as semi-serious explanations for random events such as disappearances and strange objects. Urban legends are spread by any media, including newspapers, e-mail and social media. Some urban legends have passed through the years with only minor changes to suit regional variations.

I was brought up on the myths of the men who had crossed The Godfather and ended up in the main concrete structures that propped up the Kingston Bridge via the M8. Thompson had literally cemented yet another myth into Glasgow folklore. And then we have the story about

327

unfortunate people who owed debts and were nailed to the floor as punishment for default in repaying a loan. Whatever the truth or local legend, it's probably better to advance with caution when researching The Godfather. I observed Reg writing one-liners about him with his tongue firmly in his cheek. There's also caution to be taken over Arthur's alleged connections to the Kray twins from London. Was he a gun for hire for the twins? Who knows? People will tell you he was, but how do they really know... because Arthur said so? None of the players of the time are around now, and that's what carries the legend on – no one to discredit it. Apart from me, I suppose. Did he go into their club armed with a shotgun on his tod and call them out, telling them he was *Arthur Thompson from Glasgow*? Who fucking knows? It's a great story, whether it's true or not. I think it was just as likely that the Krays came up to the Barrowland Ballroom, armed with sawn-offs and shouted that they were *Ron and Reg from London*. Putting it that way, how ridiculous does it sound? No one would be interested who the fuck they were and it would have been a total waste of time.

Stories like nailing people to a door, burying them in concrete and being a gun for hire for the Krays are all great stories to have on the streets when trying to extort money from a local bookie. But it's also well documented that he disposed of one of the Welsh brothers and his mate who were trying to lean on one of his extortion victims.

Whether he meant to take it that far or not is another question, but he proved he could react.

When he was questioned by Donald Findlay in court in Arty's murder trial, he denied ever owning pubs or clubs, denied earning over £100k a week from his loan-sharking and said it was *a load of nonsense* that he was a criminal overlord in Glasgow. Straight from the horse's mouth! Let's see... he denied that Fatboy was involved in the drugs trade, said he had no idea what a bulletproof vest was (the clue is in the name) or why there was one in his house, he had no idea why Arty would have guns or ammo.

The Thompsons, like any others of that time, were all about making a living. Arthur was doing it by any means that he could. He was into stuff. He had Fatboy with him and he was a good delegator. I think some things happened to go right and work to his advantage and others didn't. Not everything was planned. For example, running Patrick Welsh off the road and killing him may have been a show of strength, even if by accident. It was him acting alone and that was a mistake cos it put him in the firing line. Apart from would-be witnesses, there was the instant karma that came his way when he was nearly blown up. It showed he was vulnerable. It showed weakness. Would a gang of ragtag ruffians plant a revenge bomb under the car of The Godfather of Glasgow if he had such a fearsome reputation? Of course not. They planned on wiping him out and kept going after him. And – he didn't avenge his mother-in-law's murder either. That didn't look good. The car bomb was planted under the passenger side and not the driver's side – that's what saved him. The thing was, Arthur was so tight that he wouldn't even let his driver take the car home for the night. So, his driver had to get the bus along to the Ponderosa on a morning, knock on the door and then take Thompson round in the car. Arthur was always the passenger – that's why the bomb was on that side. It was more luck than being hard as nails that saved him. It's said that he started claiming Incapacity Benefit after that shooting when he went to the hospital claiming it was a DIY accident. Every cloud, eh? It seemed so typical to hear such a story about the old man even cashing in on that.

Was the Ponderosa an impressive Glaswegian mansion? No. It was a row of miner's houses. There were five of them: the old man had one and he got one for young Arty – each with stone cladding for consistency. It's usually said that a copper lived in the middle at one point, so there wouldn't have been so much activity and show of wealth going on. I really don't think that was the case at all. I certainly never heard of that, but it's one of those stories that gets told. A policeman wouldn't want to live there. Everyone knew it was where Arthur lived – you wouldn't just move next to him *by accident*. It's also said that there was a tunnel running under the houses in the middle to connect Arty's and the old man's. That could be true or it could be another story. It's certainly possible to do that... it would take many years and a decent team of builders and labourers though. And I just couldn't imagine Arty with a miner's hardhat working into the wee hours to do something like that. And anyway, I'd been in the basement of the Thompson house, and that's what it was – a basement. Just like many other houses of the time... no secret doors or walls and no escape tunnel.

Personality-wise, old Arthur was reserved and quiet; a typical *I knew your father* type. He wasn't a fair man at all. He had a scam going where all the timber being used by builders in the area would go missing, but would end up in Thompson's own timber yard. He had lads, including me, taking timber into his yard from wherever and he wouldn't pay us until we'd taken all the nails out – silly things like that, but always something to complain about or a reason to not pay or delay paying someone. Again, *tight*.

I think he outlived his myth. I think the myth was beneficial to him and, if anybody was going for The Godfather tag, then he was the last one. In any situation like that, anyone with that sort of prominence has got to be dealing with the authorities. It's just a fact. The media wouldn't label you as such and the polis wouldn't let them do it. Permissions were granted, stories were run and myths were created. That's how it worked. He made his way from working with the security services. He made money from the conflict in

Northern Ireland by selling guns and ammunition. It was all monitored; it was all with permission 'from above' and, at the same time, observing the need to cooperate with the Crown as that's where Loyalism is entrenched in Glasgow and always will be.

Irrespective of his media name and all the rest of it, anybody who wanted to be The Godfather after that knew that he had to work with the coppers and the authorities and there was only one candidate left who fit the bill. I never thought Thompson would have done that, but he did. Godfathers don't do such things. If he was as big as they said he was, you wouldn't be reading this book cos it wouldn't exist. This book wouldn't exist because I wouldn't exist. A lot of people say I was lucky I was in prison when my two mates were killed. Ok, fair enough. When you're in prison, you're a lot easier to find though. When I got out in 1992, I never left Glasgow. I was still there if anyone wanted to settle a score.

As for Arty... he was just living off his dad's reputation. And the longer that went on, the more that reputation began to wane. Like many others at that time, he'd play people off against each other and he'd offer anyone up for his own advantage. He'd fuck anyone over without a second thought and was barely even loyal to his own. He was selfish. Even a blind man could see that his time was running out. When he was killed, there were so many that wanted to do it and so many that could have done it I doubt the truth will ever come out. I've kept the myths alive in the past by adding fuel to the rumours and I've offered up my own stories. For me, that's something to enjoy. If they can live off myths to enhance their own reputation and elevate their criminal standing, let them live off myths about their demise as well. So, we must suspend all our beliefs about gangland. It seems Arty was so important that an actual hitman was brought in to execute him. It couldn't have been anyone on Arty's fucking list – that would just be boring and obvious. The hitman would have been a professional – you can't expect a mere apprentice to do such a job on an underworld fucking kingpin, can you? And how difficult would it have been tracking Arty down, with him being so low key and readying himself for his return to the streets? The night he was done – every man and his dog knew where Arty was. He had a lot of enemies and he'd made even more when he was inside throwing his weight and his dad's name around. In fact, we know that Arthur had to pay a gang to look after his son while in prison cos he was so out of control with his threats and son-of-the-godfather talk. The old man was even quoted at the time as saying, 'Maybe it was a case of mistaken identity. Or maybe someone had it in for me.' Strange that he forgot to repeat it when he was my defence witness, eh?

What do I think happened? Well, I've said my piece in print already. I think with all the attempts that were made on both Thompsons, it was just a matter of time before they were successfully disposed of. Although I'm putting to rest my unfinished business, things like Arty's murder are best unsolved. It's best to keep guessing cos there's always gonna be a smoke screen here and a red herring there.

There were far more powerful folk in Glasgow than the Thompsons – it's just that they preferred to remain unknown and remain in the shadows. I know the families and all have moved on with fantastic personal achievements – some of them have grandchildren who are academics or known sports people. They gave up a past life to invest in their grandchildren; got out when the going was good and while they could – without being greedy.

Arthur Thompson died of a heart attack on 13th March, 1993. It's a fucking miracle that the old man made it to die of natural causes, but it came as no surprise that it was a heart attack that finished him off. He died after giving evidence against me as a prosecution witness and that's what he'll be remembered for. Thompson was fucking lucky to have died when he did. I'm glad he died and I hope it was painful to his last breath.

REG

EXCLUSIVE: CRIME WRITER REG MCKAY BATTLING CANCER

10 March 2009

The bestselling author and regular contributor to the Daily Record has two brain tumours and one at the top of his lung.

He is having chemotherapy at the Beatson centre in Glasgow. McKay, 55, had shown no symptoms until losing power in his right arm six weeks ago.

He said: 'One minute I felt fine, the next a doctor told me I would be dead in six months, probably less. But that has changed to possibly longer since. They think I may have germ cell cancer - very treatable if it's caught early enough.'

McKay added: 'If I have three months, three years or three decades, I'm living life to the full. Cancer doesn't kill you - it's giving up that's deadly. That's not for me. An occasional gangster has taken unkindly to what I've written about them and made serious threats. I didn't let those get to me, so why should I let cancer bother me?'

McKay is the top-selling writer of true crime in Scotland. He has published 16 books in 10 years.

His wife Gerry, 42, was diagnosed with breast cancer two years ago.

STU: A WRITER'S TRIBUTE

I phoned Paul yesterday to talk a few things over ahead of meeting up with him and Steve. He mentioned he was writing the second line of an email to me at the time. One of those bizarre coincidences – even more so that he was writing it about the same stuff I was phoning up about. That felt a bit eerie. Paul mentioned the word *serendipity* that Reg used to describe such things. It was a nice touch.

'You're a writer. Reg was a writer. Academics. I can only use that word on special occasions and this is one of them,' he said.

I felt quite moved by it. Regardless of Paul's tribute to Reg, I've found this whole process very different to my other books. I felt a connection to Paul and Reg that I wasn't expecting. I think I was expecting to be reporting on Paul's life and saying something about Reg at some point. During this time, I've read as much of Reg's work as possible: Ferris, McGraw, Thompson. I was also reading other stuff about Glasgow and loads of Paul's court transcripts and undercover audio recording transcripts. I made notes on the pages of the books as well – something I usually call vandalism, but I felt sure Reg wouldn't mind. It's not easy playing catch-up on someone's life, as well as finding out about someone else who I'd only get to know through reading their books.

Importantly, I read Reg's *Cancer Diaries*. Not all. I got in touch with a journalist from the *Daily*

337

Record and she said I was welcome to visit their place and hunt for them (I could only see the odd one or two online), but then she found as much as she could and emailed them over. I didn't mention I was working with Paul. I thought that may be more of a door-closer than an opener. Each one of the *Cancer Diaries* was a little anecdote, a parable even, an observation... all the while, they were Reg's subtext. He was telling us something about himself each time, but in a way a good writer would. I felt each one of them very poignant and I could only imagine his struggle in putting the words on the page. As a ghost-writer, he was one of those unsung heroes; always in the background, but he was prolific and gained recognition from it – and that's a pretty rare thing in this game. Reg was able to tell people who he was and what he was about; to step out from the background because people were just as interested in him: Reg the person, not just the writer. I liked how he used the diaries to show his character through it all; to show what it was like living through something as horrific. He knew it would be his legacy.

I'm glad that the Record gave him that award. It would have meant everything to him to get something for his writing. I know writing true crime is looked down upon by those 'real writers' and I don't mind. I'm sure Reg was the same and I'm sure he shrugged it off as well. It's a niche; a compulsion to investigate and tell a story – I can tell he loved it as much as I do.

It's a big step to pay tribute and it's also a big step for Paul. He's only ever worked with Reg and this process is a new and different one for him, but it's a familiar journey. No two writers will ever work or write the same and I knew Paul would have Reg in mind with anything associated with this project. I sent Paul bits of the Little Green Bag chapter to start with. It's my favourite element of the story because it opened up so much in terms of Paul's bigger story. The reality of it is a lot different than in *The Wee Man* film. Sending that over got Paul onside – he mentioned it was Reg's favourite too.

I've felt both honoured and daunted writing this. It's not like I'm the replacement guitarist in a band and there's going to be instant comparisons. I don't mind that and I certainly don't mind being second to him. That's not what it's about to me – it's about discovering a writer and finding respect and admiration for them. One thing that made me smile when reading about Reg: he said his books were the most shoplifted books in Borders (now gone) bookshop. I've been told by Waterstones staff that mine are the most shoplifted books in their Newcastle store – that's why they have to keep them behind the counter most of the time. I like that – it means they count as a firm sale!

Many don't see what we go through as writers. If you're lucky enough to be with someone who brings you snacks and refreshments, then it's your other half who sees the daily struggle. That's an important thing to bring in here... *your other half.*

I'm lucky enough to be with Jen; she's my voice of reason. She understands my work and we have breaks together when she's at home. She supplies me with energy drinks. I drink lattes by the pint. She listens to me moaning about timelines, jigsawing information together, and hears me shouting at my computer and puts up with the hundreds of post-it notes I'm always scribbling on and leaving round the house. That's just me 'being all writery', or *stroppy* as it's also known as. Gerry was Reg's other half and, when we talk about paying tribute to Reg, we cannot do it without also paying tribute to Gerry. They were a team. I've never met Gerry and I don't want to cause upset or accidental insult by bringing her in. I just know how much Reg would have valued her in his own journey as a writer and having that support is one of the biggest parts of writing. Knowing they shared a mad sense of humour reminded me of my relationship with Jen. You need a balance and, from what I've heard about her and the quotes I've read, I know she'd have given him that and I'm now smiling as I type. She'd have been his sounding board and his voice of reason. She'd have brought his snacks and a nice glass of wine on a night – maybe a Chilean Sauvignon Blanc or a nice Chardonnay. As Reg's health deteriorated, she helped him write. She was his rock.

A DARK DAY

FAREWELL TO RECORD COLUMNIST REG MCKAY: THE KING OF THE CRIMEWRITERS

20 October, 2009

Tributes poured in yesterday for crime writer Reg McKay, who lost his battle against cancer. Reg, one of Scotland's most popular writers, moved many through the publication of his brutally honest *Cancer Diaries* – a weekly feature in the Record since March this year.

His account of how he dealt with the illness was uncompromising but it generated a huge amount of positive feedback from readers. In recent weeks, Reg, 56, was too weak to type his column but wife Gerry took dictation to keep the account running until the end.

Despite his taste for Armani suits and fine white wine, Reg is best remembered as a champion of the underdog in society.

His first career was as a social worker but his writing meant he would later become close friends with notorious gangsters, notably gun runner Paul Ferris.

Reg stood firm beside wife Gerry, 42, when she was diagnosed with breast cancer two years ago. She won her battle only for Reg to be struck with the disease in January this year.

Gerry said: 'Reg is the love of my life and we lived through so much together. He made it very clear to me that he loved me right to the end and he worried more for how I might be affected by his illness than he did about himself.

He was generous throughout his life and the most honest person you could meet, which is why he made such a strong bond with Paul Ferris. He was often referred to as a former social worker but not many people knew he was a director of social work.

When he decided to write about crime, he did so with a rounded approach. He was aware of the reasons behind social problems and the way people could be pushed towards crime. He was always compassionate.'

Gerry told how she was touched to read his columns in the Record, which revealed how deeply he felt about her.

She said: 'He dictated his columns to me but he would miss out the end, which normally meant he would later add a reference to me. We talked about everything and we could laugh about stuff, even when times were dark.

After I was diagnosed with cancer, he was a rock and he lived through that crisis with me. It seems very wrong that he would then have to face a cancer battle himself but that's the way it happened.

He said he would live his life right to the end and that's exactly what he did.'

Reg was born in Keith in Banffshire in 1953 and his family later moved to Glasgow. As a teenager, Reg was slashed twice, attracting trouble because of his north-east accent while living in Govan.

After school, he gained a master's degree in psychology and sociology from Glasgow University. He worked with the homeless in Edinburgh and had ambitions to become a journalist in his early 20s, however, he stuck with social work for 20 years, mainly in Glasgow. As well as becoming a council social work chief, he was Scottish director for children's charity NCH before starting his second career as a writer.

As well as scores of tributes from readers, Reg was praised yesterday by public figures:

Socialist politician Tommy Sheridan said Reg gave him support in times of huge stress as he fought his recent famous libel action.

He said: 'The world really is a poorer place without Reg McKay. He was a beautiful human being who would make a three or four-hour conversation feel like 10 minutes. He was the most successful crime writer in Scotland and he understood the social reasons for crime.'

Sheridan said Reg was discriminated against by the writing establishment.

'Some looked down their spectacles at Reg but he deserved great credit for his achievement in his bestselling books.

His columns in the *Daily Record* were powerful because he chose to deal with a subject that affects a quarter of our society in some way or other.

He was brave enough to confront life, warts and all. I was at his house last week and he spoke about the number of people going through the same experience.'

BBC Scotland's former crime reporter Bob Wylie said he often sought Reg's help. On one occasion, he asked for Reg's assistance in trying to buy a gun to show how easily available weapons were in Glasgow.

Bob recalled: 'Reg said it would be no problem. He asked if I wanted it for lunchtime or tea-time.'

Former cop and fellow crime writer Harry Morris, known as Harry The Polis, spoke of lunching with Reg at Glasgow's posh Rogano.

Harry said: 'Reg said, 'Do you realise that after I go, there'll be no more good crime books?'

I replied, 'You're right. I picked up your latest book the other day – couldn't put it down'. And before I could add the punchline, he reacted first, 'Don't tell me, they're still putting superglue on the book covers!''

Reg published 16 books in 10 years, including *The Ferris Conspiracy*.

He kicked off his column in the Record on March 14 this year by declaring he had two brain tumours and one at the top of his lung. He had shown no symptoms until losing power in his right arm six weeks earlier.

He wrote: 'Dead man walking? Me? Maybe, but as long as I'm walking I'm living. And kicking. Watch this space.

Cancer doesn't kill you – it's giving up that's deadly. That's not for me.'

Borders bookshop once told Reg he was their most stolen author because so many of his books were nicked from their stores.

Reg said in an interview: 'Sure, I'd love to be accepted in literary circles but it's never going to happen. I get letters from people saying my books are the first they've read since school. That can only be a good thing.'

He admitted to having received scores of death threats from crooks, aggrieved at the way he portrayed them in his books.

Reg's funeral will be at Craigton Crematorium in Cardonald, Glasgow, on Saturday at 9.45am. Mourners are asked to wear black with a splash of red.

MY MATE REG

Reg's health seemed to deteriorate right out of the blue. His wife Gerry had already suffered from breast cancer. It wasn't until Gerry came back with results from some tests that there was some improvement, but her cancer had been severe. I could see that when I'd go to visit. Throughout, Reg had been the strong one in the relationship. And they were a brilliant couple; great to visit. Reg was an epileptic and Gerry has a great sense of humour. She got him a brand new Lexus and bought him a private plate EPI... on the count of him having epilepsy – that's just how they were – the cliché of laughing in the face of adversity is true because people like them were doing it.

Reg was apparently sitting at his computer one day and his right arm started fitting and he had to hold it steady. That's when he shouted to Gerry for help cos he didn't know what was happening. He said, *I'm going to sit in the passage* then he just went down. He had an aneurysm on the brain that was affecting his spinal cord and his movement and different things. I've met a lot of brave people in my time, but Reg was a different breed. I know how difficult it was for them both, but they muddled through it day by day. And because of Reg's writing and journalism, it became news. So there was a public side of it to deal with as well. As if dealing with terminal illness isn't traumatic enough, imagine having to give a statement about it to the newspaper you write for. In typical Reg form, he faced up to it and wrote about it. To do something like that, really did show the measure of the man. You know my relationship with the *Daily Record* by now, but here's where I can say something good about them: Reg got a trophy from them for his *Cancer Diaries* feature. It was all he ever got from the literature world and I reckon he should have got more recognition for what he did. He was a force of nature – totally uncompromising. The award was well deserved.

The success of his books has made Reg immortal. I fucking love that. What I don't love is when I see newspapers saying that he wore Armani suits and making some wise-crack about that being a contrast to his roots. He never wore Armani suits; they were black, tailor-made suits. It's just lazy journalism.

Even now, you go into the library, you'll get Reg McKay, go online, you get Reg McKay. That's Reg's testament. It's who he is. The *unfinished business* part of it is that nobody really knows how we did the book, what our relationship was and what our integrity was. What were our reasons for doing it? There are snippets here and there – me with my wanting to get some truth out there and Reg's obvious reasons were that he'd become an author and he wanted to tell a story.

'Paul, what do you think of this?'

'Too near the mark, Reg. Or if that's what you thought, that's what you thought, and it's not for me to interfere with your work.'

But he had enough confidence and trust in me to ask my opinion. And likewise, I'd take stuff to him. That's how the partnership worked. I liked getting his opinion on anything, really. He was an intelligent bloke and one whose opinion mattered. When he analysed my writing style, he looked at it, read it and went, *That's very pictorial*. The reason why it was very pictorial was because it was a memory recall – it's the rest of the work that nails it; the stuff that Reg would bring to it, the words to tell the story of the picture. And it worked. We worked so well together because he *got* me – that makes all the difference.

So the second and third books: we wrote them via a combination of emails. I still found it difficult to type. I lose my train of thought because of the lack of speed that I'm typing. That's just how I am. I'll be thinking way ahead of how fast I can type and end up wondering what the fuck I was doing. And the handwritten stuff; sometimes you write so fast that it's illegible or could be misconstrued. I say you but we all know I mean me. It was all just trial and error. Reg would interview me in a similar way to how I'm working with Steve and Stu on this. Reg would crack away, ask the questions, record it all, type it up and go through it. The good thing there is that we both had something to refer to, where Reg could ask more detail or get me to clarify something. I think it protects the integrity of both parties.

I got a flavour for writing. I really enjoyed the process and I wasn't sure that I would. The thing is, storytelling is the oldest art form in the world. We've been doing it since we were painting on the inside of caves and writing inside pyramids. For all I liked doing it, I wasn't going to get carried away with it all. As the great philosopher Dirty Harry Callahan said, 'A man's got to know his limitations.' I think that's true of everything. He also said, 'Nothing wrong with shooting as long as the right people get shot,' so, you know... I reckon he'd make a good defence QC. Anyway, on the strength of our sales, the publisher pushed Reg to get another three-book deal.

'Reg, I can't commit to another three books. You're a writer, an author; you're doing what you're doing. I don't want to feel as though I'm saturating the market with fucking nonsense. You know, I'll do it if I feel there's a need for it.'

I didn't want to tie him down.

We had a very professional relationship, right up to the very end and full credit to him for doing his diaries. He knew he was dying and he took a stance on it and said, *If I'm going to die, I'm going to die on my own fucking terms* and that was totally surreal to me. It was bravery that I'd never seen before. Of course, through working together, we became friends. You're always going to have a connection from producing work together and it was an added bonus that I got a mate out of it. The last time I saw him was probably about a week before he died. I can't really put into words what it was like seeing him like that. We're all old enough to know what it's like to lose someone, and some of you may have been in this position too... being close to someone who is terminally ill is... well, impossible to cover with words. It changes how conversations go, it changes what you talk about and even the slightest trivial thing you might say – *I'm going to the football next week* or *I can't wait for the next episode of Coronation Street* – is a poignant reminder of how precious time is. Shit doesn't matter when you don't have much time. We talked about *Unfinished Business; the Gangster Chronicles* – the next book we were planning. As a matter of fact, *Unfinished Business* was an original subtitle of *The Gangster Chronicles*. I knew there was never gonna be another book. He knew. We both knew he was dying and it was fucking heart-wrenching. We came to a specific chapter and we were thinking about words to capture what it was about and Reg said, *I've got it – Fuck It!* To name a chapter *Fuck It* was saying he'd had enough and he was going to get all this out and I knew deep down that it wasn't going to happen. He didn't have enough time for it to happen. Not even Reg could get the words out in time. I think he was shafted by one of his publishers over that three-book deal they got him into, though. They gave him an advance and they knew he was dying. If he didn't uphold his contractual obligations, then the advance he got had to be paid back – meaning Gerry would then be liable for it. He was at the level where his advance was maybe £30,000. That's a lot to have hanging over you and he made sure he was debt-free before he died.

Gerry told me that Reg arranged his own funeral, his own black coffin, sermon... everything. He even double-booked the crematorium in advance.

'What did he do that for? I asked.

'He knows half of his mates might turn up late,' she said.

That was classic Reg – thinking of others, but seeing some fun in it as well. If ever there was an opportunity to quote *My Way* by Frank Sinatra, this would be it. He had his friends there, just as he wanted. He had one that was a sports commentator and he was so fucking funny, talking about when he and Reg used to have a laugh and a joke and all the rest of it and I'm standing there kind of bewildered thinking, *This is great*. Then this guy Raymond Mead just strolled up the aisle like fucking Antonio Banderas and started playing the guitar and sung a tribute to Reg. I thought, *I'm gonna start crying here, I can't do it, I can't do it*. Gerry asked me to sit next to her. If I was thinking I couldn't cope – how the fuck was she feeling? How could other people do it? She got up, totally professional, said what she had to say, but I couldn't say a word. I wanted to. I could imagine Reg shaking his head at me, having a smile. I've just never been able to function in that situation and this was no different. *And that's fine*, I thought. We're all different and we all handle stuff differently. There were a lot of business and entertainment people there and it was a proud moment to see so many there for him. I was Reg's co-author; best friend. It was a tribute to a life rather than a service. He picked a black coffin cos he wore black clothes: the cool one at the party; the one you're drawn to before he even speaks – the one you're drawn to and want to know what he's got to say.

Reg's work is still selling. That's the legacy he created – Scotland's best-selling crime writer. That's when I realised we should be moving towards producing a docu-drama. The dialogue's already there. Reg kept all of it and there's still loads of stuff that needs to be aired. It's just a matter of deciding what we want to do and how we want to progress. That's my reward – the loose strands. And it's all further to his legacy. I mean, we wrote a fucking book together without actually meeting. That takes a lot of faith. He wrote that letter to me, reaching out, without a clue of who I really was.

This is my tribute to Reg. *The Ferris Conspiracy* was a tribute to Bob and Joe and *Villains* was a tribute to my dad. There's a famous word, especially in Glasgow: gallus. It means someone is a bit cheeky, confident... they've got swagger. Reg had gallus alright.

I'll always miss him. You don't meet someone like him and forget him in a hurry. I hope we've done him proud with this book. We always knew we had a bit of unfinished business to settle. It's never fully over, but this is a big part of it put to rest.

THE WEE MAN

Arthur Suttie was my co-defendant in 1997 when we got arrested in London by the security services. Arthur was very friendly with Joey Pyle Snr and Arthur had given him a copy of *The Ferris Conspiracy*. Joey liked and passed it on to Wilf Pine who dug out his contact list and made a few calls. Wilf passed away in 2018 and was well known for being only the second Englishman to be accepted by the mob in America. He became friendly with the Genovese family in New York when he was managing Ozzy Osbourne. One thing always leads to another when you've got people like this around you, and the name Ray Burdis came up in conversation. He'd already shot *The Krays* (no pun) and had over 30 years in the industry. He was in semi-retirement in France, but wanted to come back to the UK. Perfect! So he toyed about with the idea of a movie, then all of a sudden there's a script, and a rewrite, and another. I'll not say it was 'easy' cos no film is just easy to bring together.

Most other towns and cities in the world welcome the film industry for a number of reasons: it brings money in; it gives their councils something to shout about and the tourist board love all that stuff as well. But thanks to Strathclyde Police and the authorities, none of that happened. They just didn't want *The Wee Man* to go ahead. They thought blocking Glasgow would have done the job. Usually, sending an advance script for scrutiny is the point where you go tell someone to go fuck themselves, but sometimes you have to jump through a few hoops to get to your end goal. And in film world, you want to keep everyone on side and have good relations and all that bollocks. If only someone told the coppers that. They still refused permission to shoot in Glasgow, refusing everything that was based on *The Ferris Conspiracy*. The production company had everything all geared up to head up north and had to drop their schedule at the last minute. They took Glasgow away from the big visuals and had to drop a lot of people from the cast. We know it got made, but it wasn't without its difficulties. Authorities are usually proud to have their city featured in a film. Even if not, it makes them some money. So – *Hello, Strathclyde police force. I know you're reading this. If you want to prove I am lying, take me to court.*

Do I need to go into the criticism of the film itself, do I need to defend it? If you like it, you like it, and if you don't... well, you don't. I mean, it's not a fly-on-the-wall documentary. Stuff happens in it that's accurate and some of it is artistic license to follow the conventions of telling a story in a film. Every book adaptation uses the same method. No, I didn't cast it. No, I didn't write it. Yes, I did discuss it with Martin Compston. I think he played a fucking blinder in it. More criticism of it has been directed at me and that I come across as a sympathetic character who is (in parts) likeable. Well, fuck me. That's the main reason for keeping a movie-goer entertained and stops them switching the thing off, isn't it? If I was portrayed as a complete cunt, then it would be called *The Cunt Man*. Henry Hill would have turned *Goodfellas* into *Cuntfellas* and *The Krays* would have been *The Cunts* (although that would have been fucking funny).

Asking for the advanced script before giving a decision, that was unheard of in the industry anyway. They already knew or surmised that the unfinished business I had with them was gonna drop into the movie and it scared them. And rightly so. But the movie was a different thing altogether. They were probably too dumb to make the leap that it is a film to entertain people, but were just bricking it in case the corruption was exposed. Once they knew they were in the clear, it was a way of getting one over me by refusing permission. The only thing there was that the film was fuck all to do with me – I got paid by the company for optioning the film rights. It was only the people of Glasgow who missed out on any money that would've been paid to the authorities for permission to film, as well as the jobs it would've created while employing local people. Still though – well done, eh?

I've never been known as the wee man – just so you know. It's, I suppose, a term of endearment in Scotland. Every area has it: *How's it going, wee man*? Just like calling someone mate or darling or even bruv. Once the film rights of a

357

book sells and it goes into adaptation, there's not a lot of control you have over it. With films, the writers are using your words as a basis to tell another story; one that works on screen. The book is the idea and the script becomes the blueprint. I read somewhere that film is a metaphor, and that's completely true. The opener of young me hearing the screams and seeing the police brutality is taken from *Conspiracy* and used as a storytelling technique. I had brilliant parents. The discipline they used was just like every other household of the time: you know a kick up the arse here, a clip around the ear there... time for bed, turn the light off, and the classic – *do you think we're made of money*? You'll probably remember one of them, if not all. For me, one of the biggest and best things was being allowed to stay up on a Friday night to watch the black and white horror movies. There was always something like Frankenstein or Dracula on. And the reason why I'd never switch my bedroom light off was that I didn't want to jump out of bed and have somebody grab my legs! They wouldn't if the light was on, see? But as a kid I remember the screams; the fucking horrible screams. You wouldn't hear animals screaming like that – it's something I've never heard since. Although I associated one with the other – the screams going on outside validated my fear of monsters existing. And, if they could be outside in a van, then the fuckers could be under my bed. It's not such an out there way of thinking, really. We lived on the brow of the hill and it was a quiet, secluded area. If you were gonna smash somebody about in the back of a van then up our way was the place to do it. The police would do it anywhere though; I doubt it was just next to my house. They operated at night, but there wasn't really anything to hide. It's just what happened. That's what the police were, that's who they were and what they did and that's why nobody liked them. That's why anything got sorted out our own way and that's why they were never fucking welcome. They also knew the shit you'd get if they talked to you and made out you were on friendly terms. I guarantee I'd know who'd been in the van the next day – everyone knew. It was more bullies. They were the monsters.

They drafted coppers in to form what they called the Northern Constabulary. It was the big fucking rugby players and farmers; the ones that, if you wanted to have a fight, these guys were up for it. In their defence, they wanted to have peace on the streets and their way of achieving it was to get in there first and create peace by... well, by kicking the piss out of anyone. It was bad enough that the streets were riddled with kids stabbing each other without having to worry about these hard as fuck blokes wanting to batter you to a pulp. Although, that was the point. Kids on the street were no match for beasts like them. They had no markings on the vans (Group Disorder Vehicles) and wore overalls. They were pretty much like the Secret Service. They didn't discriminate – anyone was fair game: a guy coming back from the pub and singing, someone returning from night shift, someone going out to night shift... and as a happy coincidence, there's always the chance they'd grab someone who was actually up to no good and it all become real police work. Blackhill was predominantly Irish Catholic, you know, so it was like a Celtic versus Rangers thing.

We got to the point where keeping the light on and the fear that the screaming induced was becoming quite a problem for me. The film could never do something like that justice – I don't think the most psychological of horror films could ever get it across on screen. I couldn't get back to sleep once I'd heard that shit; I was a right state. I've since heard cats fighting at night, you know when it sounds like a wailing baby and puts the shits up you? That's nothing. Anyway, my dad came in one night and I naively said, 'Can the police not stop it, Da?' And my dad just looked at me. It was like his heart melted. And then walked away. It was like he'd cry if he tried to speak. He couldn't tell me it was the police who were doing it. I'd find out, but he couldn't tell me there and then. They were just snatch squads; that's what we called them. It was only when I was in prison as a young offender that I heard the term snatch squad again. People getting dragged into cells and smashed up by the screws. It brought it all back to me. So, that side of the film was real, just told in a different way – more cinematic.

The film won two BAFTAs. It won one for Daniel Kerr who played the young me. He was a 10 year old boy – what a way to start an acting career. It also won the audience award and that kind of shut everybody up, because it's the people that buy the books who buy the tickets to put the bums on the seats – and they were the ones who decided. We were up against *Les Misérables* as well. It was a phenomenal achievement, so full credit to Ray Burdis for his hard work and dedication to the project. He got criticism, but you have to learn to take it on the chin. He's been around long enough to know the score on that front. Interestingly, the interview that Ray and I did for STV vanished off their site, but someone managed to rip a copy in time. Ray got 90 per cent bang on. It was as close as it could have been. And then I always feel I have to add 'given the restraints he had', but I shouldn't. It works as a film. Comments like, *it doesn't look like Glasgow* and *Arthur Thompson sounds Irish* are all well and good, but it's easy to have a pop at any creative output. Martin Compston's fucking brilliant, but I'm sure someone has said something about him as well. I was sat down the front in the VIP bit for the premiere screening. At that point, it was pretty early in the film and I just needed to get out. It was nothing to do with the film, but it had just covered my childhood and we were into me growing up... the childhood stuff had triggered my mechanisms and I was having a whitey. I didn't want to get up and leave cos all eyes would be on me to gauge my opinion. Walking out would be a headline-grabber. But I got out for fresh air and all was fine. And then later when I was back out for more fresh air, people were outside having a smoke and whatever and were asking me questions, saying how much they liked the film. After all the shootings and beatings in it, the one they always ask about is the dog. I laugh at that, it makes me smile each time, but it's not a laughing matter. When people kept asking me about the dog, I looked over at Ray each time. When we caught each other's eye, he looked back with a *Whaaaaat*? expression. I was sure it was a wind-up and he was just sending people over to keep asking me the same thing. Ray had said a couple of things about the violence and I could understand his position as director, but he said we cannot show any violence against that kid. I mean, it would be another eight years before Daniel could legally watch it anyway. I gave Ray a variety of different incidents that he could work into the film, if he wanted. So, in real life, the Welshes did kill my dog, but not in the way it's portrayed in the film. To see a dog get kicked on screen (it wasn't actually shown) is worse than seeing it happen to a human. It's how we are. The truth here was that they killed my dog by whacking it with a stick. The snowdropping lowlifes were stealing off the washing line and it went barking at them. There's more around it, but let's not dwell. It was distressing as a youngster and shows what that family were like.

The film itself was a standalone thing and it was something that I didn't want to get involved with for personal reasons. I was invited down to London several times. I went on set and noticed straight away that there was a ceramic mug in a prison scene.

'You don't get that in prison in case somebody cracks it and then...you know,' I said.

It doesn't matter how fucking horrible tea is; it always tastes nicer out of a china cup and not a plastic one. But you don't get such luxuries in prison. So, just wee quirky things like that. And then if I kept going on set, I'd see a million other things and I'd already said that's not what I wanted to do. Asking me what should be in a scene or how something could be said is like asking Brian Coult a simple question about interaction design – you just don't do it. There was the usual stuff where I had a scheduled visit to talk to Martin while he was in character and advise him on being me. You've got to do that for the press – pretend you don't know you're being watched and look as though you're discussing Stanislavski method over a cuppa while they take photos. It's all a game. We were discussing football, but who's to know? That was all my involvement, really. The production side of it was all handled brilliantly. As I say, the rights were bought and it was out of my hands. I wasn't going to force my opinion onto a creative process – they knew what they were doing. The Record had a few digs at some point. It stands to reason that they'd have to write negative stories. One was found at the bottom of the *Scottish barrel of shit journalism* about how pirate DVDs did the rounds and impacted on box office sales. It was probably a tenuous slant to say that Paul Ferris wouldn't make as much money as he'd like and people were essentially thieving off him. The truth is nothing like that. Another headline was *Portraying this wee man as a big man is criminal.* I see what they did there – nice bit of clever journalistic word-play. The piece said I was *swanning around TV studios, puffed up and promoting and profiting* from the film. Another headline was *BAFTA Scotland 2013: Paul Ferris absent as The Wee Man wins audience award.* This one said I was banned from the red carpet. I wasn't. I stayed away because it was based on my story – it wasn't my film to go and take credit for. Ray picked the award up because... wait for it... because it was *his film* and I'm pleased for him. And, if you watch *Love, Honour and Obey*, you'll know for certain how talented he really is. Of course he was asked about me not being there – ask him about winning his fucking award instead and stop trying to dampen the success of it by creating a negative Ferris slant. *Paul Ferris should not benefit financially from new film*, *Film makers charge £2k to appear in film about life of notorious Glasgow gangster Paul Ferris*... the list goes on. I laugh at their negativity, though. They think they're damaging me or the film by talking about it – but they're talking about it! And when a newspaper is talking about a film, people are reading about it. And, when it's in Glasgow's newspaper, it's the film's target audience. It was all nice free publicity. They are always going to cause outcry by bringing money into it. In their eyes, I'm not allowed to earn a living because of my past. I could have waited for Martin Scorsese or Christopher Nolan to offer me millions, or I could have given it to someone I knew for a nominal fee to get the story out there. The press don't know what I made from the movie. I could have sold the rights for a single pound coin – just to see it on the big screen.

It comes in right at the end:

In remembrance of Reg McKay
The inspiration for the film

The film, everything I've worked on, would not have been possible without such a driving force like Reg. He'd never be forgotten in something like the film – for me, it was a great opportunity to pay tribute.

STEVE: FINISHING BUSINESS

Meeting Paul Ferris was no easy feat. Our first face-to-face meeting was in November, 2016, arranged through our mutual friend, Brian. I'd spoken to Stu loads about the project and he was as excited as I was about getting together with Paul. The seed had grown considerably and, as Brian picked me up in Glasgow to take me to a hotel on the outskirts, he told me that Paul had a proposition. The hotel was in a lovely country setting and Paul was already there to greet us. I browsed the menu and Paul urged me to try the haggis. When in Scotland and all that! After our Scottish feast and a bit of football banter we got down to business. Paul explained that he would like to write another book and pay tribute to Reg McKay. He already had the idea of the title in his mind... *Unfinished Business*. We briefly discussed his ideas and what he wanted to include.

We arranged to meet in January 2017 to begin the interviews; Paul said that he was happy to travel to Newcastle and stay overnight. I booked him into a hotel close to our Mojo Risin' offices in the city centre and we got started. The first interview was at my house in Gateshead. I wanted to extend the hand of friendship and invite him into my home (I was once told that Mafioso would only ever consider somebody a friend if they were invited to another home, but this is not the reason I invited Paul!). The next interview took place a couple of weeks later at the office and we hooked up with his good friends, Stephen and Albert Sayers. This was the day I also introduced Stu Wheatman to Paul. We shared a few glasses of red and, as we all left with smiles on our faces, we knew we were on to something.

Despite hitting it off with Paul on the phone and now face to face I still felt that I needed to build up a rapport with him. I was also unsure of how he would respond to questioning, despite committing to the project. I knew his life story well but I didn't want the book to be a copy of those that had gone before. I therefore decided to mix up life events during interviews. I would take Paul back to his childhood and the days of being bullied and how he eventually fought back and punished his persecutors. I would then fast-forward to now and his time spent with his kids and how he had turned his life around. Paul went with the flow and would give informative answers each time. When the tape recorder was off Paul would continue to talk about things and, at times, I would find myself putting the recorder back on so that we didn't miss anything vital.

I found Paul had a tendency to move onto other subject matters as we were talking, so I mentioned this to him. He thanked me and told me to keep him on track. He'll not mind me saying so! That was a real key moment in our working relationship for me because he was happy with me taking the lead. It also meant that he was comfortable with me and I could push the boundaries as time went on.

For each interview I would take my scribbled notes from watching TV documentaries or reading one of his books and I would make notes as we talked – just in case another question sprang to mind. I was quite concerned that we may have too much material and Paul began discussing the possibility of a follow-up to this one. Time will tell!

My other worry was that the interviews may not make sense to Stu when they were completed. Paul worked with his son, Dean, after I typed up the interviews and added anything we missed or anything lost in translation. They were then passed on to Stu to digest. Once that was done he started firing off more questions to me and Paul where necessary, and started to piece Paul's story together.

The final interviews took time to arrange due to family commitments. I travelled to his home outside Glasgow to see him in his own environment. The SAS would struggle to get where Paul lives, but I travelled up with Brian to his remote farm. Once we'd navigated the mile and a half of dirt track in Paul's 4x4 we were soon inside having a well-earned cuppa, watching his hens prowl the farmyard from the window. I wanted to interview him there because I felt I may see a different side to him. I didn't. It was testament to how far our friendship had progressed. Me, Paul and Stu met up a few more times in Newcastle to go over some more details. I think no matter how many times we met up, we'd never find a point to close the story. There are so many other bits that we weren't even able to go into within these pages; probably too much information – it's all a balancing act. There will always be parts of the story that are going to intrigue us more than others, and that's a whole new line of questioning to gather more material.

The whole story of Glasgow's gangland is still ongoing. And it always will. It has been raging for a hundred years now and shows no signs of slowing down. I'm proud that we've been able to tell a part of it.

FUCK IT

Don't worry, we aren't at the point where I start saying crime doesn't pay and stick in at school. You're old enough to make your own decisions, just like I was. And, like many other 'gangster' books, my life has been full of all the clichés you can imagine: the coincidences, the good times, bad times, trials, tribulations and a fair few murders thrown in for good measure. I'm not gonna list all my regrets either. In fact, the only regret I have is bringing so much trouble to my mum's front door when she didn't deserve it. She'd had enough of all that with my dad and Billy.

With a lot of my story, there are many misconceptions. One that a lot of people have latched onto is that I was more or less brought up by the Thompson family. Within the story of Glasgow's underworld, we're kind of synonymous with each other, but me and the old man weren't just some double act. I like to keep up to date with the media and, most of the time, I read stuff that didn't exist and never happened. It's all somebody else's stuff and I'll be sat thinking, *Is this me? Where did this come from?* I hate the myths as much as I love them. I think. I mean, I like that they are around but it's the untruths that have clouded the whole story. Call it what you will; Chinese Whispers, urban myths or whatever. It's a double-edged sword.

There's a word Reg used to use to describe stuff: *serendipity* – the occurrence and development of events by chance in a happy or beneficial way. It was only after hearing him say that, that I recognised it. For example, I saw Davie Moran aka Davie McAuley at a bus stop one day. It seemed odd as in, *what the fuck's Davie doing at a fucking bus stop*? Bearing in mind that me and him go way back, to the point that I asked him to be Paul Junior's godfather and he accepted. Time had passed since those days. He was older, so I suppose him being at a bus stop was just out of context for me. I was driving past slowly, and stopped to have a chat. He was on the passenger side and leaned in when I wound the window down.

'Davie, what the fuck you doing?'

He got in and said he had something to talk to me about. I could tell it was serious; he was already wearing a frown before he'd clocked me. We made a bit of small talk until there was a safe place to pull up and talk properly. He had a photo in his wallet of him and a pal and said he wanted some assurances from me if he told me something. I've heard a few people lead into conversations like this, but I wasn't expecting it of Davie. It was like he'd been building up to this for some time – and he probably had, it's just that he'd never had the opportunity. He was a bit shaky-handed with the photo and he'd put it away before any of the relevance became apparent. He wanted me to guarantee his safety, in exchange for some information. That was putting me on the spot, to say the least.

'Davie, I've known you for a long time. You're Paul's godfather. If you've got something you want to tell me, that's up to you. Go ahead and do it,' I said.

Once he started telling me stuff, I knew it was as close to the truth as possible. There were details in it that I'd already heard about, but these details were things that only someone close to it would know for certain. He told me that Billy Manson and another were directly involved in the murders of Bobby and Joe. The other was Davie's brother-in-law.

I think Davie wanted out after the death of Thompson and cut a deal to tell all about Bobby and Joe. It had been weighing heavily on his mind and he'd been too scared to say anything while Thompson was alive. He was carrying too much around with him and offloaded it onto me. He told me that Manson had a silver Renault and could be found driving it, with the brother-in-law usually in the passenger seat, should anyone need to know such information. The condition of telling me was that, if anything should happen to Manson, like an accident while they were driving, then it was his only hope that the brother-in-law would come out unscathed. I understood. I told him I had no idea if either of them would be safe if they were in an accident. Who could predict such things, after all?

372

It turned out that a hit squad followed the silver Renault and subsequently ambushed the driver. Billy Manson was stabbed repeatedly in the head, neck, face and body and was left for dead. The brother-in-law then jumped out of the passenger side, pulled Manson from the driver's seat into the passenger seat and drove to Glasgow Royal Infirmary where medics saved Manson's life. The brother-in-law did a noble thing in saving his friend, but karma always finds a way when it comes to street justice. And it did. Karma somehow found out Manson's address. Apparently, there was a CCTV issue at his flat to begin with. Manson must have been a paranoid wreck. As he was recovering from the attack, he was on some pretty hardcore painkillers. And that's where the rumour mill comes into play. There are a couple of street theories as to what actually did happen to Manson: one is that he committed suicide and the other is that he was force-fed the strong painkillers which led to his overdose. I've heard these stories as well as one that he was force-fed Fentanyl; a painkilling drug that's said to be up to 50 times stronger than heroin. Whichever theory you believe, there are probably a few more as well. It must have spooked his brother-in-law though – he went to the police and is now in the witness protection programme.

There's another theory I've heard about Bobby and Joe's murder. This one starts with them killing Arty Thompson. Manson was a good friend of the old man and was indebted to him after a stint in prison when he was looked after. Billy Lobban is Manson's nephew. On that night, Lobban phoned Bobby at home to meet up with the pair later that night to sort some business out. They all got into Joe's Ford Orion and that was the last time they were seen alive. It's then said that they drove to a nearby place where they were shot. There's also talk that someone from London who was up for Arty's funeral drove the car and parked it near the Cottage bar where it was found the next day.

We've also got a man called Paul Hamilton to add to the mix. Lobban has gone on record to say that he was visited by Billy Manson in prison who told him that he'd shot Hamilton and killed him. Paul Hamilton had been one of my defence witnesses in Arty's murder cos he saw me out that night and proved that I was nowhere near the scene of the crime. Manson told Lobban that Arthur Thompson wanted Hamilton killed for 'giving' me the alibi. In this story, Manson is still pals and indebted to Thompson, so he carries out the killing. Thompson also thought that Hamilton was passing top secret information about his business to me – another reason to have him taken out.

This is the same Paul Hamilton who had been boasting about driving the blue transit van that had carried Bobby and Joe's bodies. He liked a drink and would often be heard telling his tale. He never said that he was the gunman, just the driver.

When you go around saying things like that, you need to be good at dodging bullets yourself. He wasn't that picky about who he told the story to after a couple of beers, so it was a given that Arthur got wind of it.

Whichever story is true, one that remains as a constant fact is that McGraw went round to tell Eileen Glover that Bobby was dead before the police knew about it. He seemed to be the constant fucking snake in everyone's story.

After all this had been and gone, Davie Moran also told me about a conspiracy plot on my life. I'd heard a few similar threats, but when it was from someone like him, who was both trusted as well as keen to tell the truth to help himself out of a situation, it was something to take seriously. He was offered a vast amount of money to set me up to be killed in his garage in Shettleston. I was then to be removed to an industrial unit across the road. The plan never got any further than that. It seemed that karma was on my side that time as well. For all Davie had been a bit of a rogue and into stolen car and bike parts and whatever else, he managed to get stuff off his chest before his time was up. I'm not sure how old he was, but he had looked a bit dishevelled when I saw him at the bus stop that time. I'm not sure when, but Davie Moran died of a heart attack after all that.

I became aware of the Thompsons when I used to climb over the yard to take a shortcut through the graveyard to my gran's. I'd see young Arty, ironically at his bedroom window with a telescope rifle taking pot-shots at people as they walked past, oblivious as to where the assailant was positioned. As if standing well back, out the way, doing something half-arsed and hiding wasn't metaphor enough. But that was him and he never seemed to be out the house – not running with any gangs or even just playing out as a kid.

Arthur was known in our part of Glasgow. You just *knew* who the Thompson mob were without even knowing why. They were omniscient. But there was never any need for me to know who they were, even right up to when I was in my teens. You'd be in touch with them or approach them or whatever it was people do if you needed something, I suppose. So, if you needed a quick loan – they'd help you out. They'd end up owning your soul and having someone like me come for you when you couldn't keep up repayments. Think Wonga, but with a worse consequence than an arsey letter and a CCJ. Arty Thompson was in the nick at some point for firearms offences and was out at the same time that I was in that bar to meet up with Blink. Arthur wasn't a flamboyant larger-than-life character. He didn't flaunt his wealth, other than get driven round in a nice car. I think it was his reputation that I was more aware of than him as a person. So, for example, if he goes in somewhere and has a drink, there'd be a whisper that he owns the licence for the pub and if he's seen in a different flash expensive-looking car, he owns the car, he walks along the pavement... he owns the fucking street. That's the aura and myth that was puffed up and belched out for fucking years and years and years. So I think it's important to not over-glamorise it, to tell it how it is and, if it's gonna hurt somebody, then so be it. I only really came to know them over a short period of time. I didn't like or dislike them – I was just... indifferent. It's not like we socialised and I've always had enough friends. If anything, we were using each other to make money.

So, Fatboy's portrayal in the film – it didn't happen quite like that, but that's artistic licence for you. I thought Stephen McCole gave a brilliant performance. For all Arty was a bit of a tit, I think he had his moments. I mean, I've *heard* he was pretty fearless. That might have been true up against someone he knew he had an advantage over and knowing he had the threat of his dad behind him. And that's fine. Bullies operate in such a way. When it was up against someone like the Welshes, well, he knew his dad's name wasn't enough to scare them off. That's a situation I saw him in and that's how I know he bricked it. There was a time when I was with him in my Volvo and I saw a pack of Welshes outside their house. It's almost like I had a switch somewhere in my head – immediately I drove towards them. Looking round in the car, I knew there had to be some form of weapon lying around.

'*Fucking find something*!' I shouted, but as I pulled up, a few of them just turned, whipped sawn-offs out and started blasting fuck out of the car. Arty shit a brick. It was far too front line for him – this only happened in his gangster films and all he'd ever be was a plastic one. So he was screaming for me to get us out of there and that's what I did. But for a different reason: I needed a gun. I dropped him off – safely – picked a shotgun up and was straight back after them. Arty? He went home to tell his daddy all about it. The cops were there when I returned. They gave hot pursuit and I had enough time to ditch my shooter before getting pulled over. They searched the car and impounded it and that's when I got done for carrying offensive weapons.

Arty would never risk anything where he knew there was a chance of not coming out on top. Remember what I said early on in the *Fight Club* quote? '*How much can you know about yourself if you've never been in a fight*?' I think it probably scared young Arty that he didn't have his own reputation or the means of earning one. He was supposed to be the Godfather's son and, well...

One of the Thompson cousins was driving a stolen car when he knocked somebody down who was crossing the road. My younger sister, Maureen, saw what happened and gave the police a statement. What can you say, she was young and naïve – thought she was doing the right thing. In fairness, she *was* doing the right thing, but not in Blackhill. When my dad heard about it, he wanted to go down to the Ponderosa and see Thompson and put him straight, but I said I'd do it. I went round and was invited in. This was probably before Fatboy even got out from his guns thing.

'Listen. My dad's asked me to come round and have a wee chat with you to tell you that my sister's given a statement against so and so [I think it was John Thompson]. She won't go to court. She'll retract her statement, so there's nothing for anyone to worry about.'

And Arthur was fine. It was probably a bit intimidating. *Probably*. It was just a different situation and the first time I'd really clocked the old man. Up until then, he was the fucking bogey man. After that, he was just a man. He seemed a bit wary, a bit cold, a bit off even. I just assumed that's how his type were. I got a couple of packs of cigarettes off him. My mum never smoked, my dad never smoked, but what the hell... and a half bottle of whisky. It was a token gift to give my dad for sorting it out. My name cropped up in later conversations in the Ponderosa when I became someone worth talking about – when I started picking the Welshes off – that's when the old man knew it was me who'd been at his door that time.

It doesn't feel right that the Ponderosa has been romanticised as some sort of orphanage, as though my mum and dad weren't capable of looking after me and I was taken in by the Thompsons. The timescale from me being around

16 up to 21 years of age, I'd met Thompson senior and junior probably a dozen, maybe 20 times. And that's the history. Remember, the old man said in court that he never really knew who I was. I spent more time in detention centres and prison than I spent at home. I was a teenage delinquent. It was like I had a bungee rope on my back – as soon as I was out the front door of a detention centre I got hauled back in. That was probably the case 99 per cent of the time: the revolving door syndrome. So for those five years, the only people looking after me were either my mum or the prison staff or people when I was in hospital. Some were good, some were bad, some were really good and some were really fucking terrible! I wasn't a child crime prodigy that Arthur brought up as his own and I seriously doubt that he thought more about me than his son. He didn't fucking know enough about me. He wouldn't have even known my name if it wasn't for all the shite we got dragged through by association. I've even read that old man Thompson had a photo of me on his mantelpiece – a fucking framed photo. To quote a journalist: *It was even said that Arthur had a picture of the enforcer he recruited at 19 on his mantelpiece, until it all went wrong.*

Yes – that quote is a thing. It exists. And I wonder how many people believe it. I mean... are you fucking serious? I don't know where to start. I can only imagine Reg laughing away at it cos it's one of the lines he used to put out to people to see if they took the bait.

The rumblings about me taking over his business were always going to happen. That's a logical thing to assume – if it was all a tangible thing... it's not like handing me the keys to a pokey flat or something. I know people muscle in; they wait til one pops his clogs or they sort them out and take it over by force. It's always been about territory and control. I know Thompson was raking the money in with one hand and getting it ripped out of the other. There were always sharks around and the most astute businessman or criminal is always vulnerable to attack.

But it's almost a laughable thing looking back now. A fucking Godfather living in a gaudy ex-mining house? I'm not just trying to rip the man apart, especially as he isn't around to defend his name. It's just – no, I don't buy it. I don't buy it at all. I never heard him getting called that. I know Arty referred to him as such, but he was constantly watching *The Godfather* movie anyway and probably thought he was Michael. I think, like many things of this nature, it was a name given to him by the media. It was newspaper stuff to elevate his position and then when he died, it was Tam McGraw... he was gonna be the next Godfather. And why not? It would be more plausible because they both dealt with the cops and it was only right that one informant should be replaced by another. That would be the right way to go about things. But that didn't happen either.

To be The Godfather of Glasgow, Thompson would have had to rule over the types of criminal I mentioned earlier – the ones you'd never hear about. There were people operating in Glasgow that he didn't know existed and they were the type who'd go through the likes of Thompson before he knew what time of the day it was. Add to that the fact that you've got so many firms, so many families all battling for different areas of Glasgow, then you can see how impossible it all was. Can you control all the radgies and schemies on one side of the scale and all the serious organised crime multi-millionaires at the same time from Ponderosa HQ? Can you fuck. He was big in his own backyard. That's commendable enough.

We made a name for ourselves; some lived, some died, but we were there. And we were just one part of Glasgow – one part of a city and it was happening everywhere. You've got Celtic, you've got Rangers and, as mad as it sounds – just because of that, it's always gonna be divided and you'll never get true loyalty. No one could ever rule as a godfather over the whole of Glasgow.

A WORD FROM REG

He'd always send stuff on to me to read over. I'd send him stuff. We'd discuss ideas for anything. I haven't read all of his *Cancer Diaries*. I know Stu got hold of them as some research material, but I couldn't bring myself to read them and I don't think he could either. There's something about Reg' bravery that chokes me up, the thing I have with death from way back when my granddad died, it just gets me.

When we were looking for stuff to go in this book, I found an email from Reg. It was a draft of one of his diary features for the *Daily Record*.

Dead man walking? Who me? It's not that I'm unused to the threat. There have been enough grumpy gangsters, tormented torturers, murderers and paedos all muttering those words at me. Never mind gruff-voiced anonymous phone calls.

I pay no heed to them, but this was different. This was more than personal. This was real. It started with my arm that morning. My right hand had been bothering me for weeks. It had gone weak, limp, useless. A trapped nerve the doc said and put me on the waiting list for a hand surgeon. A bit of a disability for a full-time scribbler no longer able to type, it was getting on my wick. That was all.

Then that morning it went mental on me. A judder in my fingers moved up my forearm to my shoulder until it was thrashing about like it was demented. The same useless arm had taken on a life of its own.

Gerry, my wife, somehow got me in her car and rushed me to the A&E at the local Royal Alexandria Hospital in Paisley. In the motor I couldn't hold my arm down and it was smashing against the dashboard, slapping Gerry on the side - hard. If you can recall Peter Sellers films, think crazy Dr Strangelove on speed. This was some trapped nerve. As quickly as it had started its shenanigans, my arm quit them 30 seconds from A&E. But no way was I turning back. Demented arms need exorcising.

Even early on Friday morning, A&E in Paisley is busy with casualties littering the cubicles and corridors. A busy triage nurse didn't look me in the eye once. Maybe my black leather jacket hurriedly slung over the black vest led her to make assumptions? 'I'll just book you in under minor injuries,' she declared. Injury?

Minor? My arm's mad dance had left me too knackered to argue.

A sweet-mannered doctor saw me in minutes. Within half an hour I was being X-rayed and scanned. The NHS failing? Not on my shift.

Four hours after we'd entered the hospital we were shown to a room and I knew there was trouble coming. Not a booth but a quiet, private space. A bad news bubble and one with two cops hovering at the door. I hoped they were loitering there for someone else. How bad could this news be?

'I'm sorry,' said the poor doctor. 'I have terrible news. You have a tumour at the top of your lung.'

As Gerry quietly wept, he added: 'Then there's the tumour in your brain.' Looking me straight in the eye, he repeated: 'A tumour in your brain.'

That's when I asked: 'How long do I have to live?'

'Six months,' he replied, 'if that.'

He could have said six days or six weeks, it made no difference to me. No fear or dread over came me. The truth is I felt nothing. I just heard and consumed.

I wondered if it was the same for other people when told they're about to die? I suspected not, but I was about to learn a great deal from others in similar situations in the next few weeks.

'You've known for a while there's been something seriously wrong, haven't you?' the doctor said. He was a kindly man so I just looked at him and didn't scream: 'No, I bloody didn't.'

I could have added: 'One duff hand equals two tumours?' It seemed so unreal.

Only three months before, I had had a full medical check, including a brain scan.

Everything had been clear. Now I have tumours? But he was a good man, so I kept my thoughts to myself.

With Gerry composed, I thanked the doc for being candid and caring and we took our leave. The corridor was empty of uniformed polis. They must have heard the conversation - those walls were paper thin.

Outside, the car park was busy with visitors. As soon as we started driving, I realised I'd been thinking too much and feeling too little, but not the way you might think.

To be blunt, I needed to pee. What would I do? Walk back up that steep hill?

Go back into that place? Would I hell. Gerry pulled the car in close to the edge, where there were bushes, and I stood and relieved myself as citizens milled around behind me.

Not my kind of behaviour but as I stood there I prayed that some busybody would pull me up. I was just about angry enough for them. What would they do? Kill me?

On the way home we made a stop. I needed a heavy dose of steroids and the strongest painkiller they could prescribe - the one junkies use when their smack supply dries up.

It was near closing time but we found a chemist and Gerry went in to collect the goods. As I sat in the car thinking and smoking, she was taking too long. In the shop, she had burst into distraught tears.

She's my woman and strong and she still went through hell. What if she had been a frail, elderly, lonely or poor person? Could she even have afforded the prescriptions, never mind got to a chemist on time?

Then there's the grief.

Minutes after being told I was about to die, it was clear to me that those with the least suffer the most.

The next two days were a haze of thinking, talking, cuddling and planning. I was overwhelmed by the need to organise things - my will, funeral, gifts to friends, letters to my loved ones.

Is this a man thing where we want everything to be neat and tidy? The second day in I looked at Gerry. Two years before she had developed breast cancer. That month, she was due her second annual check. It had been the most important thing in our lives until my diagnosis. I'd forgotten about her. I sat alone in my study, where for 10 years I had written books about the horrors of humanity, and thought about my wife. I sat there and wept for her.

From that minute, self-pity went out the door. What a waste of a life. I was going to spend every second living my life to the full with the people I love. It is the only way to be. The only way to live.

Then there are the books I'm writing, including the one that will wipe the smiles off the smug faces of those pleased to hear of my doom. The real deal, warts and all.

Too much to feel and do to mope.

Thank God it only took me two days to buck up. Telling a close friend you are about to die is much harder than being told you are about to die. Making sure loved ones knew became top of the list for Gerry and I.

All were different. My singer-
songwriter pal, young Raymond Meade,
cried gentle tears then asked for a
fag. Youngest brother Tich headed
back from his home in Australia, Gav
and Kat from Canada. Big Tony
Higgins made me laugh.

Then there were Catholic candles,
Protestant prayers, even a Mormon
service and a Japanese woman cutting
a ball of string. None of which I
believe in. All of which I am
grateful for.

Gerry's family arrived with pots of
food - all cut small. When you lose
the use of your good hand there's
stacks you can't do - write, sign
your name, brush your teeth, do your
buttons or cut up food.

Within hours of being diagnosed I'd
made it clear - no one was going to
do anything for me, especially cut
up my food.

COURT DOCUMENTS

These are all in relation to the Rothesay arrest, discussed in the Little Green Bag chapter:

POLICE WARRANT: 12 DECEMBER, 1984

CHARGE SHEET
What I was up for in court regarding the Little Green Bag.

TRANSCRIPT OF PROCEEDINGS FROM THE SHERIFF COURT OF GLASGOW
Some of this is quoted in the book, but we reproduced it here so you can read it at your leisure.

PRECOGNITION OF GEORGE DICKSON
He says they had information that I was at Thompson's flat. Two people knew I was there.

ANNE-MARIE'S STATEMENT
It's been a long while since I looked over any of these documents. Her age is noted as 18. I was 21. We were just kids.

REPORT FROM THE DEPARTMENT OF FORENSIC MEDICINE AND SCIENCE
This was crucial evidence for my case.

POLICE WARRANT

INFORMATION AND WARRANT TO SEARCH FOR DRUGS

At Rothesay this 12th day of December 1984, appeared before me JOHN
McILNAIRNIE one of Her Majesties Justices of the Peace for the County
of Bute, SIMON McLEAN a Detective Constable in the Stratholyde Police
Force, who being solemnly sworn and examined by oath, depones that he
has reasonable grounds for believing that there are drugs or substances
specified in parts I, II or Part III of the second Schedule to the
Misuse of Drugs Act 1971, within the premises at 24 Argyle Street,
Rothesay, and occupied by ARTHUR THOMSON or in possession of a person
or persons therein.

Deponent _Simon McLean DC_

Justice of the Peace _McIlnairnie_

Argyll and Bute

In respect of the above information, I hereby grant Warrant to Constables
of Stratholyde Police Force, at any time within one month of the date
thereof to enter if need be by force, the said premises at 24 Argyle
Street, Rothesay, and search said premises and any person found therein,
and if there are reasonable grounds for suspecting that offences under
the Misuse of Drugs Act, 1971, h ve been committed in relation to any
drug or substance specified in Part I, Part II or Part III of the second
Schedule thereto seize and detain any of the said drugs or substance.

Dated this 12th day of December 1984

Justice of the Peace, Argyll & Bute

CHARGE SHEET

GLASGOW,

20 December   19 84

X COPY FOR PAUL JOHN FERRIS X

62051/84
C11362/84

UNTO THE HONOURABLE THE

SHERIFF PRINCIPAL of GLASGOW and STRATHKELVIN or his SHERIFFS.

THE PETITION of J. M. TUDHOPE,

Procurator-Fiscal of Court for the Public Interest;

HUMBLY SHEWETH,

That from information received by the Petitioner, it appears, and accordingly
be charges, that

PAUL JOHN FERRIS, born 10.11.63, NOW IN CUSTODY, (1) on 2 August 1984,
without lawful authority or reasonable excuse had with him in a public
place, viz, in Robroyston Avenue, Glasgow at a part thereof near Robroyston
Road, offensive weapons, viz, a pick-axe handle, a wooden stave and
2 knives; Contrary to the Prevention of Crime Act 1953, Section 1(1);
(2) did on 10 December 1984 in King Street, Glasgow at Trongate, assault
Raymond Bonnar, c/o Central Police Office, Glasgow who was sitting in a
parked motor vehicle registered number CHS 746Y and did stab him repeatedly
on the arm and shoulder with a knife or other similar instrument to his
severe injury and did attempt to murder him; (3) did on 12 December 1984
in the house occupied by Arthur Thomson at 24 Argyle Street, Rothesay,
unlawfully have in his possession a controlled drug, namely Dimorphine,
a Class A drug specified in Part I of Schedule 2 to the Misuse of Drugs
Act 1971 with intent to supply it to another in contravention of Section 4(1)
of the said Act; Contrary to the Misuse of Drugs Act 1971, Sections 5(3) and
25; and (4) having on 24 October 1984 been granted bail at Glasgow Sheriff
Court in terms of the Bail etc (Scotland) Act 1980, Section 1, and being
subject to the terms and conditions therein, did on dates and places above
libelled/without reasonable excuse fail to comply with a condition of said
bail, namely that he would not commit an offence while on bail in respect
that he did commit the offences libelled in charges (2) and (3) hereof,
whereby he is guilty of an offence; Contrary to the Bail etc (Scotland) Act
1980, Section 3(1)(b).

in charges (2) and (3) hereof

                                                    Procurator Fiscal Depute

In/

TRANSCRIPT OF PROCEEDINGS

CASE No. 62051/C11362/84

UNDER THE CRIMINAL PROCEDURE (SCOTLAND) ACT 1975,

as amended by the

CRIMINAL JUSTICE (SCOTLAND) ACT 1980,

and relative Act of Adjournal

TRANSCRIPT OF PROCEEDINGS AT JUDICIAL EXAMINATION
WITHIN THE SHERIFF COURT OF GLASGOW AND STRATHKELVIN AT GLASGOW

RELATING TO

the questions asked and answers given, including
declining to answer, under Section 20A

in the Petition of

Procurator Fiscal,
Glasgow and Strathkelvin   against   PAUL JOHN FERRIS

DATE: 21 December 1984

SHERIFF: W G Stevenson, QC

NAME OF ACCUSED APPEARING: PAUL JOHN FERRIS

FOR THE PETITIONER: Mr I Johnston, Procurator Fiscal Depute

FOR THE ACCUSED: Mr Forbes, Solicitor, J C Muir & Barr
                                     121 St Vincent Street, Glasgow

SHERIFF CLERK: Miss F Clyne, Sheriff Clerk Depute

---oOo---

Sheriff: Now Mr Ferris have you read the 4 charges against you?

Accused: Yes.

Sheriff: And you understand them?

Accused: Yes.

Sheriff: And have you also read another piece of paper which is attached to the
          charges which contains statements that you are alleged to have made on
          the 2nd of August 1984 at various places in a police van and at a
          police station. Do you understand what these bear to be?

Accused: Yes.

Sheriff:/

Sheriff: Now you have been brought here today for the sake of being judicially examined with regard to these charges, that is to say asked certain preliminary questions regarding these charges and regarding the alleged statements. You are not bound to answer any question which may be put to you. You are entitled to consult your solicitor before deciding whether you wish to answer or not. If you do decide to answer, any answer which you make will be recorded and may be used in evidence at any subsequent trial. If on the other hand you decide not to answer and that's entirely a matter for you, your failure to do so may be commented on at any subsequent trial. Do you understand?

Accused: Yes very clearly.

Sheriff: Would you put your questions please?

Fiscal: I'm obliged M'Lord.

---oOo---

Fiscal: Are you Paul John Ferris?

Accused: Yes.

Fiscal: Were you born on the 10th of November 1963?

Accused: Yes.

Fiscal: You have received a copy of the Petition dated 20th of December 1984 containing 4 charges alleged against you?

Accused: Yes.

Fiscal: Have you had the opportunity of discussing those charges with a solicitor?

Accused: Yes I have.

Fiscal: Alright. The first charge Mr Ferris alleges that on the 2nd of August 1984 without lawful authority nor reasonable excuse you had with you in a public place, that is to say Robroyston Avenue, Glasgow, offensive weapons, that's to say a pick axe handle, a wooden stave and 2 knives in contravention of the Prevention of Crime Act 1953. Do you understand that charge?

Accused: Yes I do.

Fiscal: Do you deny that charge?

Accused: No.

Fiscal: Now the third charge relates that on the 12th of December in the house occupied by Arthur Thomson at 24 Argyle Street, Rothesay, you unlawfully had in your possession a controlled drug namely Diamorphine in contravention of the Misuse of Drugs Act 1971 with intent to supply it to another. Do you understand that charge?

Accused: Yes.

Fiscal: Do you deny that charge?

Accused:/

394

Accused: Yes.

Fiscal: Is there any comment or explanation you would wish to give regarding that charge today?

Accused: Yes there is.

Fiscal: What would you like to say about that Mr Ferris?

Accused: I would like to state from the beginning to when the police came to the house in question. The police came to the door while I was watching TV with my girlfriend, a football match was on the TV, that's when I heard the banging at the door. There were several bangs and I quite distinctly heard a voice from inside the house stating that they were the police and that they were armed. My girlfriend got up off the couch and walked toward the door leading to the hallway. She looked along and saw police officers standing there, there was 3 of them, each one had a gun. My girlfriend told me that there was men at the door and they were all armed. I then went out into the hallway myself and seen them standing there in a position with their armes outstretched and the guns were pointing at my head. They then said to me "Get on the floor and put your hands behind your back". There was one officer in particular the tall one with grey hair I believe his name is Mr Dickson, he put the gun at the back of my head and said to me "You know what this is" and "don't attempt to move". I was then handcuffe taken into the adjoining bedroom across from the livingroom where I was searched. All the officers in question came into the room while another officer sent down for a police woman to come up to look after my girlfriend They were searching around the room and I asked them what they were looking for, they said it was in connection with an attempted murder in Glasgow and that they believed that they were looking for either a knife or a gun. Whi searching the house it was Mr Dickson who seemed to be in charge. He pulle out a package from somewhere, I didn't see what it was, he had his back to me and within seconds of each other all the CID officers asked him what it was he had. He then searched me, put the stuff out of my pockets on to the ground next to the wall unit and I asked him again what it was he found he says "Its just powder", he then took the sachet of powder and put it inside my wallet, it wasn't in any folder it was just put inside the outer covers. He then took me from that room and asked me where Mr Thomson was, I replied that Mr Thomson wasn't down, he says, he then said to me "Whose stuff is this?" I says "What stuff?" he says "The brown powder" I says "Its not mine I don't know nothing about it", "Well it must be Mr Thomson's then, where is Arthur?" I replied to them that Arthur wasn't down, they then said to me "His car's round the back" I says "I am using the car, its me that's driving the car" when I replied that all the officers looked at each other and then took me into the other room. While I was in the other room I was strip searched and they seemed to be searching inside my pockets for anything else that I had, they then left me, went into the livingroom to see if my girlfriend had been dressed yet. They took a statement off he I believe and while one of the uniformed officers was watching over me in the room, the CID came back in and explained to me that I was being held in Rothesay/be taken up to Glasgow the next day as there wasn't a ferry. I was taken to Rothesay Police Station and I was cautioned and charged with attempted murder which I replied I didn't know nothing about it. While I got took to Glasgow they took the tracksuit that I had on from me and gave me a change of clothing, they never gave me any explanation why they were taking/

Accused:	taking the tracksuit. I was then taken to Court and that's all I have to say about the drugs charge.
Fiscal:	You have a typewritten copy of statements which you are alleged to have made. Do you have that before you?
Accused:	Yes.
Fiscal:	It is alleged that on the 2nd of August 1984 in Robroyston Avenue, Glasgow, to or in the hearing of Sergeant David Christie and Constable Donald Fraser, both officers of Strathclyde police, you said "Self defence" Now did you say that to those officers?
Accused:	Yes I did say that and I've got an explanation for saying that as well.
Fiscal:	Could we just carry on to the next part Mr Ferris at the moment. Its also alleged that you said in a police vehicle in Robroyston Avenue on the same date, the 2nd of August, again to those same police officers, after being cautioned and charged there you replied "They're tools of the trade". Did you say that?
Accused:	Yes I did say that.
Fiscal:	And thirdly its alleged on the same date at Baird Street Police Office, again when you were cautioned and charged by those same police officers, again said "They're tools of the trade". Did you say that?
Accused:	Yes I did say that.
Fiscal:	Alright. Do you want to explain why you said these things?
Accused:	Yes. While I was asked if I admitted the charge I said yes that was to the Procurator Fiscal, the reason for the first explanation of self defence I was referring to one of the offensive weapons mentioned namely a wooden stave. The wooden stave is in fact a martial arts stick and its used for the purpose of self defence, that was why I had mentioned self defence, it was nothing to do with any other offensive weapons that was in the car, that's why that statement was made, self defence. On the second reply that I made "They're tools of the trade" which is true, I work for a garage which is Triangle Garage its in Birkenshaw Street, Dennistoun, I use the pick axe handle and the both knives that were mentioned on the charge are in fact 2 Stanley knives which I use in due course of my work along with the pick axe. I have witnesses to say that I do and have been seen using them in my work. There was also a number of other offensive weapons in the car which they could have taken there was also items like hammers, screw drivers, iron bars, jack levers that they could have taken as well and classed them as offensive weapons but they didn't. The only ones that they took from the car were the ones that were at the back seat of the driver's seat. The second reply that I made "They're the tools of the trade" was because that I do use the items in question in work.
Fiscal:	Is that all you wish to say?
Accused:	Yes.
Fiscal:/	

GEORGE DICKSON

PRECOGNITION OF GEORGE DICKSON
(Witness No.12) Det. Sergeant,
Strathclyde Police,'A' Division
stationed at Stewart Street
Police Office, Glasgow

22 yrs

I am forty four years of age and have twenty two years police service.

The background to my involvement in this case was that I was the office in charge at Stewart Street Police Office regarding an attempted murder on 10th December 1984 in King Street, Glasgow.

The person assaulted had noted the registration number of a vehicle involved which was YSF 666W. The police wished to investigate the now accused, Paul Ferris in connection with this matter.

Detective Superintendent Young of the Serious Crime Squad obtained information to the effect that Paul Ferris could be found in the house of Thomson at 24 Argyll Street, Rothesay. There was a meeting between Mr. Young, my boss and myself on 12th December when it was arranged that I would accompany the officers of the Serious Crime Squad to Rothesay with a view to attempting to apprehend the now accused, Paul Ferris.

There was not a Petition Warrant for the apprehension of Ferris but a Search Warrant was obtained by local Rothesay Officers.

We arrived in Rothesay in the afternoon and met officers from Rothesay and thereafter observations were taken on the house at 24 Argyll Street, Rothesay. The observation started at approximately 8 p.m. and continued until about 11.30 p.m. but I was not present on observation duty the whole time.

Mehta/...

397

Fiscal: Is there any other comment you would want to make regarding those
            charges 1, 3 and 4 on the Petition?

Accused: No.

Fiscal: Thank you. That completes the judicial examination M'Lord.

Sheriff: I declare this judicial examination to be closed.

I hereby certify that the foregoing transcript is a complete and accurate record, as
provided for in paragraphs 2(7) and 2(8) of the Act of Adjournal (Procedures under
Criminal Justice (Scotland) Act 1980, No 4) 1981, of all questions to and answers by
the said PAUL JOHN FERRIS in examination.

                                Signed ..... *Elaine McMillen* .....
                                        (Shorthand Typist)

ANNE-MARIE

I have known Paul John Ferris since around the end of 1983.
On Monday, 10th December, 1984 at approximately 2.00 p.m. Paul telephoned me
to my home saying that he was taking me on holiday to Rothesay. We had planned
to go away together. I was to meet him in Central Station on midday, Tuesday,
11th December and we were to go across to Rothesay together.

On 11th December I did not turn up for the meeting. I had a doctors appointment
in the morning and I was baby sitting for my Sister in the afternoon. Paul went
ahead to Rothesay and telephoned me at approximately 5.00p.m. on 11th December. I
said that I would come to Rothesay on Wednesday, 13th December. I went down and
Paul met me in Wemyss Bay. We went over to Rothesay. We walked to the flat
where he was staying. This is owned by the Thompson family. We went straight
to the flat. We did not do any shopping. We got there around 2.30 p.m. At
around 4.00 p.m. we went out to Templetons Super Market. We drove there in
the Daimler/Jaguar Car parked at the back of the house. I understand that this
belongs to Arthur Thompson. We bought a lot of food in Templetons Super Market.
We planned to stay for a week or so. We then went to a video shop. We hired
two videos then went back to the flat. We had something to eat and watched both
videos. By then it was 10.45 p.m and we were just going to go to bed.

I then suddenly heard a loud banging noise. I was in the sittingroom. The
television was still on. There were three bangs. Six people barged into the
house. One shouted words to the effect "I'm Police, Ferris come out" Paul
was in the sitting room also. I looked out of the sitting room into the hall.
I saw a gun pointing at me. Paul was behind me at the door. The Police got
Paul/...

Lights were seen to go on and off in the flat and accordingly we were of the opinion that there were occupants and at 11.30 entry was obtained to the house.

Detective Sergeant Trimmer and McIntyre were armed, and they were first into the flat. They were followed by myself and D.C. Godall of the Serious Crime Squad. D.S. McIntyre shouted a warning to the occupants to show themselves and first of all Annmarie McCafferty appeared and just after her the now accused Paul John Ferris appeared.

this was when Dixon put the gun to the back of my head, in full view of my girlfriend.

D.C. Goodall and myself put Ferris on the floor and put his hands behind his back and he was handcuffed. Other officers carried out a quick search of the house to ensure that there was nobody else present and that the house was safe.

Thereafter Ferris was lifted onto his feet and was taken into the front bedroom from the hall1 In the bedroom D.S. McIntyre advised him that he was in possession of a search warrant and thereafter a search of Ferris was carried out by Mr. McIntyre. During the course of the search various items were found including a wallet. It was really a small wallet normally used for bank cards and similar to the wallet used by police for warrant cards. I saw Mr. McIntyre take this from the track trouser pocket of Ferris and put it on the nearby bed. When it was on the bed it opened and I could see that there was a bank change bag in between the wallet and when it opened this could easily be seen. It was one of these change bags that I think is kept for silver and the top folds over so that it is secure. There was no other form of securing the bag such as cellotape.

I did not open the bag but I saw immediately that it contained a powder and there was a possibility that this powder might be a controlled drug. The rest of the wallet was searched and in the

400

Paul and took him into the hall and put him face down on the floor with his
hands behind his back. One of the Police Officers put a gun to his head and
told him not to move. I was terrified. The Police Officers took Paul into
the end room. he was in there for approximately an hour. A Police Woman
took me into another room, to try and calm me down. I was in there for
approximately half an hour, and then taken into the sitting room where the
Police took a statement from me. They brought Paul's blue wallet in which he
keeps his bank cards and they showed it to me. It was closed. They opened
it and showed me a plastic bag and asked me if I had seen it before. Ittwas
just about the size of the wallet and it was folded. It was very thin. I had
not seen the plastic bag before. I had seen Paul's bank card wallet several times
that day. In particular I had seen him with his wallet in the super market
and in the video shop. Paul keeps cash and his bank cards in this wallet. He
paid for the purchases in the super market and the video shop in cash. In my
statement to the Police I did not mention having Paul use his wallet in the
course of the day. I was to upset to think. It was not until I got home and
had a chance to think that I realised that I had seen Paul using the wallet
earlier that day.

After about an hour Paul was brought out of the bedroom. He was handcuffed.
Both the Police and Paul told me I should stay in the house that night but I
was too frightened. I went to the Police Station and spent the night in a
cell voluntarily.

Before we had gone to Rothesay Paul and I had planned to go away together so
I had packed cases for Paul and I. Paul clothes were in my house. All his
clothes are in my house.

In Rothesay Paul was wearing a track-suit. His keeps his bank card wallet in
track-suit trousers. The last I saw of the wallet was Paul putting it into
his track-suit trousers when we were out shopping . I did not see the wallet

clothes which I had brought for Paul and I were still in a suitcase. The clothes which I had been wearing were on my bed. Around 10.00 p.m. I had changed into my dressing gown. Paul tracksuit top was on the bedroom. There were just jackets in the wardrobe. The last time I was in the bedroom was when I changed into my dressing gown at 10.00 p.m. I did not notice Paul's bank card wallet on the floor.

When I got home to 82 Wallacewall Quadrant I found that the Police had been searching my room also. This was apparently for weapons. They found none.

DEPARTMENT OF FORENSIC MEDICINE AND SCIENCE REPORT

DEFENCE WITNESS

DEPARTMENT OF FORENSIC
MEDICINE AND SCIENCE

TEL: 041-339.8855 EXT. 574
041-339 9596

Reference 0027e/17/85/RD

THE UNIVERSITY
GLASGOW G12 8QQ

21st March 1985

H M A -v- PAUL JOHN FERRIS

Examination of Two Productions and Track Suit Trousers

Acting on the instructions of P D R Forbes, Esq. of Messrs J C Muir & Barr, Solicitors, 121 St Vincent Street, Glasgow G2 5EN, I the undersigned examined the following items at the times and locations noted below —

(a) Plastic Wallet containing Cashline Card (Crown Label No 7)
(b) Plastic Bag containing powder material (Crown Label No 8)

both examined on 18th March 1985 in the Procurator Fiscal's Office at Glasgow High Court, in the presence of Mr Speirs, Depute Fiscal, and two officers from Strathclyde Police Headquarters, Pitt Street, Glasgow.

(c) 1 Pair Blue Trousers.

The latter was uplifted from the Production Keeper, Custom House, Clyde Street, Glasgow and was examined in the Forensic Medicine Department, Glasgow University.

The results of my examinations were as follows —

(i) Plastic Wallet containing Cashline Card (Crown Label No 7)

This was a blue plastic wallet of the normal type issued by the Royal bank of Scotland and it contained a "Cashline" Card. There were a few white particles in the interior of one of the plastic pockets of the wallet but no evidence of any grey or white dust-like powder as described in (ii) below.

(ii) Plastic Bag containing powder material (Crown Label No 8)

This was a green transparent plastic bag labelled "£10 in 20p". The original contents of the production were contained in a small glass screw-capped bottle and consisted of a fine grey powder. The interior of the plastic bag and the exterior were both covered with a film of dust similar to the material contained in the bottle. The bag was intact and no holes were observed in it other than the normal opening.

(iii) Pair of Blue Trousers

This consisted of a pair of blue track-suit trousers with a single side pocket made of a fine net-like white material and a close-woven blue material. The pocket was removed from the trousers by cutting. The pocket was turned inside-out over a sheet of aluminium foil and emptied of any particulate material. Only a very small amount of loose particulate material was recovered and this consisted mostly of blue fibres. The particulates and the pocket itself were washed with water and the water washings were examined for the presence of diamorphine with NEGATIVE results. The estimated limit of detection of this method was 5 microgrammes.

Robert C Anderson

OPINION

(1)   The bank bag which held the powder was not designed for transporting
        substances of this type and it is therefore possible that some of the
        powder might have spilled from the bag. Indeed, there were traces of dust
        on the exterior of the bag although, without chemical analysis, it is not
        possible to confirm that this dust was diamorphine. It is possible that
        the dust on the outside of the bag resulted from the transfer of the powder
        from the bag to a screw-capped bottle during the police examination of the
        production. This is supported by the absence of dust or powder in the
        interior of the plastic wallet which was used to carry the bag.

(2)   There was no diamorphine present in the track suit trouser pocket. The
        test used was both sensitive and specific.

Robert c Anderson

R. A. Anderson,
B.Sc., Ph.D., C.Chem., M.R.S.C.,
Lecturer in Forensic Medicine (Toxicology),
The University of Glasgow.

ABOUT THE AUTHORS

STUART WHEATMAN

Stuart is a writer whose books include: *The Machine* and *Cage Fighter* with Ian 'The Machine' Freeman; *The Krays: The Geordie Connection, NME: From the Bender Squad to the Gremlins, The Krays Behind Bars* and *The Sayers* with Steve Wraith; *King of Clubs* with Terry Turbo; *The Jam Unseen* with Twink, *Slimmer Charlie* with Charlie Walduck. He's currently writing his first novel and more true crime non-fiction.

❀

STEVE WRAITH

Steve Wraith is an actor and writer who lives on Tyneside. His previous books include: *The Krays: The Geordie Connection*, Race *for the Premiership, The Krays from the Cradle To The Grave, NME: From the Bender Squad to the Gremlins, The Krays Behind Bars, The Sayers* and *The Milk Thief.*